The Royal General Farms

in

Eighteenth-Century France

The

Royal General Farms

in Eighteenth-Century France

By GEORGE T. MATTHEWS

COLUMBIA UNIVERSITY PRESS
New York 1958

To Mildred

Preface

This study is an examination of an old-regime French tax-collecting agency, the General Farms, and of that agency's leadership, the Company of General Farmers. It seeks to describe the taxes collected by the General Farms and to analyze the organization's bureaucratic structure and procedures. It seeks, further, to define the administrative relation of the Company to the General Farms, on the one hand, and the financial relation of the Company to the royal government, on the other. It is a study in fiscal administration; it is also a study in the financial history of the late Bourbon monarchy in France.

A mass of information hitherto scattered among many sources is brought together in this book. The object has been to give as clear a picture of the General Farms as possible and to estimate the efficiency of its operations. Here lack of any firm quantitative data has been a stumbling block. The central accounts were either destroyed in the Revolution or burned in the great fire of the Tuileries of 1871, when so much of the financial record of the old regime went up in smoke. In this connection, statistics drawn from the published writings of Antoine Lavoisier have been of utmost importance.

Attention should be called to certain matters of form. The term General Farms requires a word of explanation. The French phrase *fermes-générales du roi* was purely conventional. It was merely an abbreviation employed in common usage. But the official title of the General Farms varied from time to time. The standard lease of September 16, 1738, refers to the General Farms as *fermes-royales-unies.* In other documents it was often called *fermes-royales,* or again, *fermes-unies.* The original seventeenth-century form was *fermes-unies et générales des domaines et droits du roi.* In the eighteenth century this was shortened to *fermes-royales et générales-unies.* For all of these uses the brief English title General Farms has been favored. A further point should be made. Eighteenth-century usage considered "General Farms" plural and singular by turns. For convenience, the phrase will be treated here as a singular collective noun. The term *fermiers-généraux* was also a conventional form. It has usually been rendered as Farmers-General. For consistency it will be translated here as General Farmers.

At best the subject of antiquated taxes and fiscal mechanisms is crabbed and unlovely. This is even more true of the present part of the subject, the chief sources for which have been encyclopedias, dictionaries, and manuals written by tax collectors in the prose of bureaucrats. Their language had none of the grace and wit, and little of the clarity, for which eighteenth-century French is noted. It is to be feared that the style of this study may reflect that of its authorities. Moreover, no more than passing reference has been made to the private careers of those famous and opulent General Farmers whose scandalous conduct shocked and amused Paris and Versailles. The personalities of the General Farmers are obviously incidental to the main concern of this book, that of depicting and analyzing their collective role as financial agents of the Bourbon monarchy.

I wish to take this opportunity publicly to express my gratitude to the Department of History of Columbia University, which made available, from the Dunning Fund, the substantial subsidy which made publication of this book possible. Thanks are also due to Professor Shepard

B. Clough for his sponsorship of the study, for his most helpful scholarly criticism of the manuscript at each of its many stages of development, and for his friendly assistance in the publication of the book. Dean Jacques Barzun, more than he perhaps realizes, also encouraged my labors with timely and perceptive advice and criticism. Professor John Wolf, of the University of Minnesota kindly read the manuscript and offered me encouragement at an extremely crucial moment in the work's progress. Finally, I must acknowledge my debt to Professor Walter L. Dorn, who early stimulated my interest in eighteenth-century France, and to Professor Peter J. Gay, who gave me timely aid in the task of proof-reading. I need hardly add that whatever errors in fact or generalization may be found here are entirely my own.

G. T. M.

New York
July, 1957

Contents

MAPS

The Royal General Farms

in

Eighteenth-Century France

1. The General Farms and the Fiscal System

On March 20, 1791, the National Constituent Assembly completed the dismantlement of the fiscal machinery of the old regime: the last lease on the General Farms was re-scinded.[1] Tax-farming, coeval in development with the money taxes with which the Valois-Bourbon kings had built their realm and as characteristic of their financial habits as the venality of offices, was abolished. Thus ended the "greatest, most difficult, most complicated financial administration"[2] of the late French monarchy, an administration which just prior to the Revolution annually collected and remitted to the government more than one half of its revenues from taxation and supplied it with millions of livres in credits.

The General Farms was a comparative newcomer among the various agencies and institutions which had sustained the authority of the kings of France. In 1791 the General Farms was only one hundred and ten years old. But tax-farming, that method of administering the collection of public taxation of which the General Farms was the most notable example in modern history, was very ancient in France. Although the General Farms was not founded until the time of Colbert in the reign of Louis XIV, it was

---

[1] *Collection complète des lois*, II, 322-324.
[2] Lavoisier, *Oeuvres*, VI, 570.

the direct descendant of a series of royal tax-farms the prototypes of which were the medieval revenue-farms. In the eighteenth century royal tax-farming was conducted on the basis of legal principles, and employed technical procedures and terms, which had originated in the practice of seignorial revenue-farming in the thirteenth century. A brief examination of this medieval form of fiscal administration will serve as an introduction to the eighteenth-century General Farms.

THE PRINCIPLES OF REVENUE AND TAX-FARMING

Revenue-farming was a method of fiscal administration by means of which a holder or proprietor of a legal right to an income or source of revenue assigned that right for a limited time to an individual, known as the revenue-farmer, in return for a lump-sum payment or the guarantee of a steady income in installments. The difference between the amount paid to the proprietor and the amount of revenue actually collected (less the costs of that collection) constituted the profit of the revenue-farmer.

In France revenue-farming appeared before the advent of public taxation at a time when the proprietorship of landed estates and the exercise of civil authority were almost synonymous terms. As a technique of fiscal management, revenue-farming developed when the income of the land-holding French lords was being converted from customary goods and services paid largely in kind into money payments in the form of rents, dues, fees, fines, and tolls. By the close of the Middle Ages revenue-farming was the established practice of nearly all great holders of landed estates or large-scale proprietors of sources of money revenue, including the king.

The principal features of revenue-farming were as follows: The holder or proprietor of rights to a source of money revenue placed those rights "out on lease." He created thereby a revenue-farm. Such a farm had a dual aspect. On the one hand, the farm was the legal act of

leasing the rights in question; it was the "lease or the
renting of a fund, an inheritance, or any kind of right." [3]
On the other hand, the farm was also the rights so leased:
legal rights to the exploitation of the source of revenue, to
the ownership of the yield of that exploitation, rights
which explicitly included the authority to enforce payment
of the rents, fees, and tolls included in the farm. So
constituted, the revenue-farm was placed at auction and
leased to the highest bidder. The revenue-farmer taking
the farm signed a rental contract or lease with the proprietor of the farm. The lease was always for a definite
length of time. According to its terms, the farmer paid
the proprietor a stated amount of rent, known as the lease
price, in monthly or annual installments for the duration
of the lease. In addition, the farmer posted with the proprietor, upon signature of the lease, a surety bond in the
form of a cash sum. This bondsmoney served the dual
purpose of guaranteeing the farmer's financial responsibility and good faith and of providing the proprietor with
an immediate advance against future installments of the
lease price. Such bondsmoney generally carried interest
and often was in reality a loan secured by the yield of the
revenue in question.

The proprietor, in thus temporarily alienating his rights
over the revenue, made no guarantee as to the quantity of
the yield and bore none of the costs of the exploitation or
collection. The farmer organized and paid for the exploitation privately, assuming all the risks of the enterprise and sustaining all the loss. By like token, he enjoyed all of the profits. From the proprietor's point of
view, the long-term cost of revenue-farming, represented
by the profit of the farmer, was offset by the immediate
down payment of the bondsmoney and the guarantee of a
steady income from the lease price of the farm. "The
proprietor . . . in order to avoid the danger of receiving
much less, abandons the hope of gaining more; preferring

[3] *Encyclopédie méthodique: Finances*, II, 117.

. . . a fixed and limited sum, but free of all embarrassment, to more considerable sums bought by the cares of management and the uncertainty of events." [4]

A revenue-farm could comprise a variety of kinds of income and sources of revenue. It might be a landed estate, producing a marketable surplus. In this case the farmer was in effect a tenant agriculturalist. More frequently, however, the farm consisted of both the estate and the seignorial rights pertaining to it; rights to rents, dues, and fees commuted into money payments. In this case the farmer was a true revenue-farmer. The farm might also include a legal monopoly over the sale or transportation in a given locality of some economic good, such as salt. It might encompass the right to collect tolls for the use of bridges and roads or permission to transport goods upon rivers running through the lands of the proprietor. If constituted on certain of the rights of a sovereign prince, the revenue-farm might become a tax-farm and the revenue-farmer a tax-farmer. The farm often was limited to the exploitation rights to one source of revenue from one estate of the proprietor. It might, however, engross all the rights to money income from all the estates of a single great holding. In this case the farm was known as a general farm and the farmer as a general farmer.[5]

Revenue-farming was practiced by most great lay and ecclesiastical landholders in the thirteenth and fourteenth centuries. Indeed, confined to real property income and to simple seignorial rights, revenue-farming continued to be a method of administering the fiscal affairs of large holdings until the end of the old regime. The agricultural and seignorial general revenue-farms of the eighteenth century were the analogues of the fiscal General Farms of the royal taxes.

[4] *Encyclopédie, ou dictionnaire raisonné,* VI, 513.
[5] Rambaud, *La Question des fermiers généraux,* pp. 14-40.

THE ORIGINS AND MECHANICS OF ROYAL TAX-FARMING [6]

Royal tax-farming was the application of the principles of revenue-farming to money taxes as a source of public revenue. In juridical form and in basic technique, the tax-farm did not differ from the revenue-farm. The legal relation between a tax-farmer and the king was the same as the relation between a revenue-farmer and the proprietor of an estate. Confusion between the proprietorship of the feudal king over his personal income and the right of the sovereign monarch to public taxation persisted to the end of the old regime. The coexistence and common parentage of the royal General Farms of public taxation and the general farms of private or seignorial revenue served to perpetuate that confusion. [7]

The medieval king was a patrimonial landholder and a feudal suzerain before he effectively exercised the attributes of modern sovereignty. His income derived from his family domain and from casual fees and fines due him from his position as feudal overlord. As holder of great landed estates, he reacted to the penetration of money and market exchanges into the economy in the same manner as other large proprietors. The king commuted the goods and services traditionally owed him in kind into money payments. He then farmed the rights over these personal domainal revenues. He created revenue-farms. From

---

[6] This study confines itself to royal tax-farming. It should be pointed out that, in addition to agricultural and seignorial revenue-farming, tax-farming was practiced by the many authorities in eighteenth-century France which retained vestiges of the right to levy and collect taxes. Princes in possession of *apanages,* such as the duc d'Orléans, generally farmed the rights and taxes pertaining to those jurisdictions. The church commonly farmed its tithes. Tax-farming was the preferred method of the *pays d'état* for the collection of taxes in their names. Brittany farmed its *devoirs,* Languedoc its *équivalent.* See Necker, *De l'administration,* I, 81-82; Marion, *Histoire financière,* I, 49-60; Stroum, *Les Finances,* I, 324.

[7] *Encycloyédie méthodique: Finances,* II, 117-126. See also Montesquieu, *The spirit of the laws,* Book XIII, Chaps. 18-19 and Mirabeau, *Théorie de l'impôt,* pp. 110-114.

at least the thirteenth century the *finances ordinaires*—the feudal king's personal and domainal, ordinary and permanent sources of revenue—were managed in large part through the agency of revenue-farms.[8]

In the course of the thirteenth and fourteenth centuries the French kings gradually asserted their latent claims to sovereignty.   One aspect of sovereignty was the ability to levy money taxes upon subjects outside of the royal domain.   By the fifteenth century the kings had established a practical monopoly of the right to levy or to sanction the levying of public taxation; the *finances extraordinaires* were clearly instituted.   At first these royal taxations were emergency subsidies, the right to collect them being granted by various authorities representing the three legally recognized estates, either national or provincial, for the period of a crisis.   They were regarded initially as extraordinary supplements to the ordinary domainal revenues of the king.   But the chief emergency was war, and war was an almost permanent condition of royal political life.   Taxes originally levied and collected by the king with the consent of the estates gradually were levied under Charles VII (1422-1461) and Louis XI (1461-1483) by royal fiat without consent.   Royal taxation, at first transitory, became next a periodic and finally a permanent feature of the kingdom.[9]

When the king first levied public taxation, he usually committed the collection rights to royal tax-farms.   The techniques of revenue-farming, already applied to the royal domainal *finances ordinaires*, were easily adapted to the new *finances extraordinaires*.   Revenue-farming thus became tax-farming.   The permanence of royal taxation entailed the permanence of tax-farming.   By the

---

[8] Dupont-Ferrier, *Les Officiers royaux,* pp. 546-549; Roux, *Les Fermes d'impôts,* pp. 3-7.

[9] Perrot, *Les Institutions publiques,* pp. 388-396; Clamageran, *Histoire de l'impôt,* I, 483-498, II, 47-48; Dupont-Ferrier, *Les Institutions financières,* II, 2-3, 22.

mid-fourteenth century tax-farming was firmly entrenched in the fiscal habits and practices of the French monarchy.[10]

To the rudimentary government of the fourteenth and fifteenth centuries tax-farming offered two advantages: it relieved the king from the necessity of developing (in a direct sense) his own system of tax collection, and it satisfied an urgent need for cash. Royal taxation originated in times of emergency; it also preceded in large part the creation of a professional, salaried corps of state officials. The monarchy, in haste to draw a quick return from a tax levy, created a local tax-farm for each new tax and leased the farm to a tax-farmer. The tax-farmer financed his tax-farm by means of private capital, recruited and paid the staff of tax collectors, and bore the costs of the operation. Moreover, the tax-farmer, through the instrumentality of the bondsmoney paid into the royal treasury upon signature of the lease, made available a part of the revenue from the tax in advance of its collection. By resorting to tax-farming, the late medieval government shifted the burden of those public, fiscal functions it was incapable of assuming onto the shoulders of private individuals who were prepared not only to assume them but to profit from them. The government need only levy a tax and auction the rights to its collection to the highest bidder in order to receive, at no capital outlay, an immediate cash return and a guarantee of a steady income for the duration of the lease. So long as the lease price was paid into the royal treasury, the monarchy was free of responsibility save for the necessity for general surveillance in the interest of preventing flagrant abuse.

When the tax-farmer leased a new farm, he undertook to organize its administration. Many types of taxes required for their management a considerable capital investment; weights and measures had to be purchased, toll gates had to be constructed, other sorts of buildings

[10] Roux, *Les Fermes d'impôts,* pp. 22-23; Dupont-Ferrier, *Les Institutions financières,* II, 71-72.

had to be bought or rented. All taxes required skilled agents for their collection: excise men, customs officials, guards, bookkeepers, accountable receivers, and directors. It was necessary to train this personnel, to coordinate and discipline their activities, to draw up effective rules and regulations. Once the tax-farm was in operation, it became, in consequence, more than a mere body of tax rights, more than the simple act of leasing those rights. The tax-farm became also an establishment of physical, human, and procedural parts and skills. It became a bureaucracy.

These bureaucratic elements of the tax-farm were not abandoned or dismissed upon expiration of the lease. The king, by a variety of methods, reimbursed the tax-farmer for his capital investment and assumed ownership of the new physical appurtenances and administrative organization of the tax-farm. The bureaucracy of the tax-farm became a permanent property of the king, an inseparable adjunct of the tax rights upon which it was founded. From the sixteenth century, when the king leased an established tax-farm, he rented out not only the right to collect certain specified taxes, but the fully developed instruments of collection as well. Thus the tax-farm became a continually functioning agency which could pass from tax-farmer to tax-farmer under a series of leases without disorganization, loss of identity, or interruption of service.

With the establishment of such bureaucratic and continuous tax-farms as fixed features of royal civil administration, the mechanics of tax-farming could be more intensively exploited. Certain fiscal and financial tax-farming techniques which in the Middle Ages had been regarded as accessories to the main business of tax collection became of crucial importance in the sixteenth, seventeenth, and eighteenth centuries. These techniques offered the chronically impecunious monarchy several advantages which outweighed all considerations as to the long-term cost of the system. Under the Bourbon dynasty (1589-1792) tax-farming became as indispensable to the financial existence of the regime as the venality of offices.

Primary among the advantages which the government derived from the establishment of continually functioning tax-farms was the assurance of a stabilized income calculable for years in advance. In late medieval times leases generally ran for but one year. This term was gradually extended until in the seventeenth century most tax-farms were leased for six consecutive years. The annual lease price (the amount of rent which was due from the tax-farmer each year) was written into the terms of the contract and was receivable by the royal treasury in regularly remitted installments due on a definite schedule. Thus, although the yield of the taxes included in the tax-farm might fluctuate on the short term, the return to government was fixed by the conditions of the lease. The government was guaranteed a steady income not subject to the hazards of war, pestilence, famine, business fluctuations, or political disturbance, all of which had a direct and adverse effect upon the yield of the taxes. The monarchy never had at its command more than a rudimentary credit and banking system. It possessed little financial reserve. Consequently, the tax-farmer was a crucial figure in its financial life. He personally assumed the risk of loss due to low tax yields. He cushioned rapid and unexpected declines in the yield of a tax by continuing to pay into the royal treasury the installments on the annual lease price agreed upon, hoping to recoup when conditions improved or to make up his loss by increased vigilance and efficiency in the actual collection of the levies. Should the tax-farmer fail to fulfill his obligations, his bonds-money was forfeited and the government was free to negotiate a new lease with a more dependable financier. Of course, the opposite might as likely occur. The yield might be unexpectedly favorable; the amount collected over the term of a lease might be considerably above the amount of the lease price. In this case the farmer profited, or, to put it in another way, the government paid a high discount rate for a stabilized income.

The assurance of a fixed receipt for a tax-farm over the course of a lease provided the means for an organized system of governmental expenditures based on the mechanics of the tax-farming system. New functions were added to the tax-farm; it became a disbursement agency of the central treasury. The tax-farm founded upon a locally levied tax afforded a means for the discharge of locally incurred governmental obligations. An expenditure by the government payable in a locality in which the farm was operating could be managed by ordering the tax-farmer to pay the sum directly out of current receipt before he remitted to the royal treasury. When certain of the tax-farms grew great in size and engrossed taxes levied on whole provinces or finally on the whole kingdom, permanent orders assigning definite types of expenditures for payment against specific receipts from particular taxes were written into the terms of the lease. Such orders became part of the tax-farm and were continued from lease to lease. Thus, for example, from their inception (1522) the *rentes sur l'Hôtel de Ville* were secured by the receipt of the *ferme des aides*.[11]

The disbursement of government funds by a tax-farm was effected by advance deduction of the sum involved from the annual lease price due at the royal treasury from the tax-farmer. A governmental expenditure managed in this manner was known as a charge. The difference between the total number of charges and the annual lease price was called the *parti du roi*, which represented the only net revenue available to the royal treasury from the receipt of the farm. The heavier the burden of charges laid upon the receipt of a tax-farm, the less actual cash was remitted by the tax-farmer to the government, the less specie needed to be carted from the provinces to the

[11] Vührer, *Histoire de la dette publique,* I, 13-15.

royal treasury only to be carted back to its place of origin. In this way also the necessity of treasury officials to negotiate with private merchant-bankers for commercial bills of exchange with which to effect the transfer of money was avoided. By the time of Louis XIV the governmental use of the facilities of the bankers was almost exclusively confined to those transactions involving payments abroad for which the channels of international commercial credit were required. Thus the tax-farms in the seventeenth and eighteenth centuries functioned as treasury clearing houses for the transfer of government funds by means of bookkeeping balances while the tax-farmers tended to assume the functions of financial agents. It was but a step from the assignment of payments against specific tax receipts to a full exploitation of tax-farming as a source of short-term credit.

Through the mechanism of the charges, the government found the way to borrow extensively from its own tax-collecting agencies. In times of financial stress the direct charges, or orders of government directing the tax-farmers to pay government expenditures, could be increased until they exceeded the lease price. By continuing to honor the excess charges, the tax-farmer sustained the government on his private credit; he honored the overdraft of the treasury. The farmer paid the charges and deducted their amount, plus an interest charge, from future lease prices. In effect, the government borrowed the receipt of future leases from the tax-farmer. By this means the government could anticipate or spend its tax revenues a year or more before their actual collection.[12] Thus the tax-farm had added a financial function to its basic functions of tax collection and remittance, transfer and disbursement of government funds. It had become a rudimentary state bank.

By the mid-seventeenth century the practice of using

[12] Martin, *L'Histoire du crédit*, pp. 8-9; *Encyclopédie méthodique: Finances*, I, 91.

the tax-farm as a source of short-term credit had been formalized around two sorts of credit instruments, known as the *assignations* and the *billets des fermes*.[13] An *assignation* was a direct evidence of government indebtedness. When the government contracted a debt with an individual, the discharge of that debt was assigned, in principal and interest, against the lease price of a certain tax-farm for a certain year in the future. The tax-farmer, upon being presented with the *assignation*, could accept it at discount before its due date, pay its face value and accrued interest upon its maturity, or renew the debt for another short term. In any case, the amount of the *assignation*, plus interest to the tax-farmer for his services, was ultimately deducted as a charge from the lease price due the royal treasury.

The *billets des fermes* were credit instruments by means of which the tax-farmer could borrow from the investing or speculating public. They were short-term notes usually running for nine months to a year and paying a moderate rate of interest. Often, within a short-term period, the tax-farmer's obligations to pay wages, to buy stocks of salt or tobacco (for sale in government monopolies which he might be farming), and to finance government *assignations* and other direct charges as well as to meet installments on the annual lease price, exceeded the immediate revenues due from the tax-farm. In such a case, the tax-farmer sold *billets des fermes* on the money market, buying them back or refinancing them when presented for payment. The *billets des fermes* were issued initially and directly by the tax-farmer on his own personal credit. But, ultimately and indirectly, the *billets des fermes* were as much instruments of government indebtedness as the *assignations*, because the amount of outstanding *billets des fermes*, plus interest, was always deducted as a charge from some future lease price due at the trea-

[13] Marion, *Dictionnaire des institutions*, p. 50; Hennet, *Théorie du crédit public*, pp. 40-41.

sury.[14] In effect, the *billets des fermes* were old-regime counterparts of modern treasury notes. But even more, since the *billets des fermes* were negotiable, it might be suggested that they were a form of fiduciary money. In issuing them, the tax-farmer, acting as a financial agent of the royal treasury, expanded the money supply for the purpose of paying government debts.

The foregoing analysis reveals that tax-farming was inherently a method of tax anticipation. Every element in the tax-farming technique—the advance remittance of receipt in the form of the bondsmoney, the assumption on the farmer's part of the obligation to finance the current operations of the farm, the acceptance of the responsibility to maintain a stable receipt and to manage governmental expenditures, the honoring of government overdrafts in the form of excessive charges and *assignations,* and finally the issuance of the *billets des fermes*—enabled the government to borrow the equivalent of its own tax revenues in advance of their actual collection or receipt.[15]

In the late Middle Ages the chief attraction of tax-farming was that the king could obtain, in lump sums, money ultimately to be derived from public taxes but for the collection of which his government was not yet equipped to construct the necessary administrative machinery. The practice of tax-farming persisted in the sixteenth century because of its ready adaptability to a policy of constant inflation of the floating debt. By the late seventeenth and eighteenth centuries the tax-farm's basic fiscal function was often buried beneath its assumed functions of a financial institution or primitive state bank. By like token, the tax-farmer acquired a new role in this development. In the late Middle Ages he was an entrepreneur making a managerial profit from the operation of the tax-farm. But in the seventeenth and eighteenth cen-

---

[14] Harbulot, "Etudes sur les finances de l'ancienne France," *Révue des sciences politiques,* LVIII (1935), 207.

[15] Capéfique, *Histoire des grandes opérations financières,* I, 109.

turies he was, in addition, a financier making a banker's profit from handling a large element of the state debt.

THE GENERAL FARMS AND THE COMPANY
OF GENERAL FARMERS

At this stage in the discussion, it is necessary to draw a distinction of cardinal importance to an understanding of eighteenth-century tax-farming in France. It is necessary clearly to distinguish the General Farms from the Company of General Farmers.

The General Farms was a piece of royal property comprising a series of tax rights and the administrative machinery necessary to their enforcement. As such, the General Farms was a segment of civil administration. It was a royal bureaucracy consisting of a considerable capital investment, a corpus of standing rules and regulations sanctioned by the king, and a huge body of personnel, the most important members of which were permanently employed royal officers, directly commissioned by the king. The function of the General Farms was to collect taxes and to remit, disburse, and transfer royal funds on government order. As a bureaucracy, the General Farms possessed the equipment, the personnel, and the procedural routines to perform this function without regard to the purely tax-farming relation that existed between the government and the Company of General Farmers. When, as happened on certain occasions, the government could find no financiers willing to accept the General Farms on lease, this bureaucracy did not cease its activities. The machine subsisted, persistently going about its appointed tax-collecting business.

The Company of General Farmers was a syndicate of financiers which periodically acquired tax-farming rights over the General Farms by virtue of the lease it signed with the king. Those rights entailed two responsibilities, two functions. In leasing the General Farms, the Company guaranteed to render a *service à la régie de ferme.* It also guaranteed to render a *service du trésor royal.*

The Company's *service à la régie* concerned its role as managerial head of the General Farms bureaucracy. Whenever the Company had the General Farms on lease, it directed that organization in its current operations. It hired, trained, advanced, or fired the employees; it bought stocks of salt and tobacco and sold them in the name of the king; it maintained equipment and buildings. The Company established policies for the many facets of the activities of the General Farms and provided the leadership for the execution of those policies. The conduct by the Company of its *service à la régie* was important. But it was not in itself sufficient reason for the continued practice of leasing the General Farms to the Company.

The *raison d'être* of the eighteenth-century Company of General Farmers was its skill in manipulating the credit possibilities of a tax-farming lease. This constituted its *service du trésor*. From the point of view of the government, the Company's primary function was the facilitation of a policy of tax anticipation. All the various ways in which tax-farming was used to supply the treasury with a steady stream of long- and short-term credits were dependent upon the financial strength of the Company of General Farmers. The whole credit superstructure which the government had erected upon the basis of the tax-farming leases was contingent upon the ability of the Company to advance the sums demanded before their actual collection from the tax payers by the General Farms. This required capital. That capital was accumulated by the Company of General Farmers from the partnership contributions of its members or through its borrowings on the public money market. Thus the Company functioned as a financial middleman in the service of the monarchy. On its own credit backed by the profits derived from an exploitation of the General Farms, the Company borrowed from those who, for good reason, were reluctant to lend directly to the king. In turn, it advanced this money through the mechanisms of the bondsmoney, the charges, the *assignations*, the *billets des fermes*, to the royal treasury. To the endemically bankrupt monarchy, this *service du trésor* was indispensable. It was the ultimate determinant not of the existence of the General Farms, but of the fixed policy of leasing that organization to the Company of General Farmers.

From a purely administrative point of view, at any time during the eighteenth century the government could have ceased the practice of tax-farming the General Farms. An alternative method of managing the tax-collecting machine was not just a possibility: during the first quarter of the eighteenth century it was often an actuality. In the event that the government could not persuade the Company of General Farmers to accept the General Farms on a tax-farming lease, the General Farms was invariably committed to the care of tax commission or *régie*. The commissioners were government officials who managed the General Farms for a salary, not for profit. They signed no lease, nor did they guarantee the government a fixed receipt. The government assumed all costs of collection. It also retained that share of the yield which normally constituted the profits of the tax-farmer. When the General Farms was placed in *régie*, its structure, personnel, equipment, even its name, continued in existence and continued in its regular course of fiscal procedure. The bureaucracy now took its orders from the commissioners rather than from the Company of General Farmers.[16]

---

[16] Necker, *De l'administration,* I, 76-77; *Encyclopédie méthodique: Finances,* II, 126. Considerable variety was possible in the detailed composition of any given *régie*. Often the commissioners received bonuses or percentages of the yield. Frequently the percentage increased in the event a certain minimum of yield was surpassed. In this case, the *régie* was called a *régie intéressée*. The commissioners often were organized into a financial company which posted a collective surety-bond with the government; the bond paid interest. Contracts between the company of commissioners and the government arranging remittance of receipt were common. Thus a *régie* might resemble a tax-farm. By like token, a tax-farming lease often approached the terms of a *régie* contract. From the middle of the eighteenth century no lease on the General Farms embodied pure tax-

Thus in the eighteenth century a method of fiscal administration alternative to tax-farming was known and frequently practiced. Yet the government consistently regarded a commission for the General Farms as a temporary measure, a means of keeping the tax-farm in operation while it persuaded the tax-farmers to resume their activities. The reason for this preference for tax-farming was that the commissioners could not readily assume the *service du trésor* of the tax-farmers. With a commission the opportunities for tax anticipation were limited. In the first place, the government paid the costs of collection. This meant that instead of receiving an immediate advance of cash, the government was constrained to provide the money necessary to operate the tax-collecting machine. In the second place, because the commissioners enjoyed no opportunity to make a profit, their credit standing with the investing public was negligible. It was impossible to finance operations through *billets des fermes*. In the third place, the use of *assignations* was crippled. The floating debt could be carried from year to year only with great difficulty. Thus, when the General Farms was placed in *régie*, the policy of tax anticipation was hampered.

The General Farms could have collected the taxes without the Company of General Farmers. But without the Company the government lost one of its chief sources of credit. Therefore, throughout the eighteenth century it was always anxious to lease the General Farms.

DIRECT AND INDIRECT TAXATION IN THE OLD REGIME

Up to this point, attention has been centered upon the general principles and mechanics of tax-farming. It is necessary now to specify that area of taxation which was customarily reserved to the tax-farming system.

---

farming principles, that is, a situation in which no costs were borne by the government and all the profits were enjoyed privately by the tax-farmers.

It has been observed that between the middle of the fourteenth and the end of the fifteenth centuries the *finances extraordinaires* became permanently established in France. To the landed patrimony and feudal rights of the king had been added the public taxes of the kingdom. Initially such taxation comprised a great variety of taxes and other sources of money income, which in character and in name were ill-defined and hardly distinguishable one from the other. Gradually, however, distinctions were drawn. Personal taxes which were assessed upon a particular subject, such as the *tailles*, were separated from those which were levied upon the market economy, such as the *traites* (customs duties) or *aides* (sales taxes). Those taxes which clustered around the *tailles* developed into what may be called direct taxation, while those which were grouped around the *traites* and the *aides* may be called indirect taxation.

The terms "direct" and "indirect," however, had no place in the vocabulary of the old-regime government. Fiscal officials used the terms *impositions* when speaking of direct taxes and *perceptions* when speaking of indirect taxes. An *imposition* was understood to be a tax which the king imposed specifically upon an individual. It was regarded as an explicit expression of sovereign will and hence as a personal obligation owed by the subject to the monarch. The individual had to pay the *imposition* without recourse, appeal, or legitimate evasion. A *perception* was a tax levied upon the impersonal activity of the economy, upon the production, exchange, or consumption of economic goods and services. It was not directly imposed upon any specified subject. Rather it was a duty paid by the subject only in so far as he might also be a merchant, a producer, or a consumer. It could be legitimately evaded by decision of the individual not to indulge those tastes or practices which made his actions taxable. Whereas an *imposition* tended to be borne only by the nonnoble, nonecclesiastical classes, the *perception* theoretically was collected without regard to social status from anyone engaged in the economic activity which it taxed.[17]

In the thirteenth century both *impositions* and *perceptions* were indiscriminately farmed. But by the end of the fourteenth century tax-farming had already been restricted to the as yet fiscally inconsequential *perceptions,* while the *impositions* had come to be regarded as the direct, indeed the central, responsibility of the maturing royal government. For the *impositions* were not only the most important source of revenue available to the king; they were the very sign of his sovereignty, of his right to tax his subjects outside the royal domain. Moreover, bearing almost exclusively upon the peasantry, whose persons and lands were fixed, tangible, and familiar, it was possible to assess and collect the *impositions* within the framework of existing village, parochial, and provincial institutions. The civil organization which the late-medieval kings wove to govern the disjointed realm of France was, initially, largely a fiscal network designed to administer the *impositions.*

With the *perceptions* the case was different. Not only were they of least financial and political importance, but they were intrinsically more difficult to manage than the *impositions.* The late-medieval monarchy was not equipped to deal with individuals in their guise as producers, wholesalers, retailers, merchants, and consumers. The complicated activity of an economy of buying and selling was too diffuse yet too localized, too subject to unforeseen changes, for a rudimentary government to cope with on a centralized basis. Taxes levied upon such an economy of daily exchange transactions throughout the kingdom could not be organized around existing civil and political forms,

---

[17] Moreau de Beaumont, *Mémoires concernant les impositions,* II, xiii-xiv; *Encyclopédie méthodique: Finances,* II, 528-529. Professional fiscal officials, such as Moreau de Beaumont or Rousselot de Surgy, editor of the *Encyclopédie,* never used physiocratic or "modern" terminology to describe taxes. To them direct taxes were *impositions* and indirect taxes were *perceptions.* See also Brunot, *Histoire de la langue française,* VI, Part I, 484.

most of which had been shaped in the relatively stable, agrarian world of the Middle Ages. Consequently, as taxes (such as excises and customs duties) which required intensive bureaucratic management were levied, they were farmed. As commercial and industrial monopolies were created, they were leased to concessionaires who were in reality tax-farmers. At the same time, the exploitation of the old domain was continued in the hands of the revenue-farmers.[18]

This administrative distinction between the indirect and direct taxations endured to the Revolution of 1789. In the eighteenth century the General Farms embraced the principal *perceptions*, indirect taxes. But the *impositions*, direct taxes, were managed directly in the king's name by an agency known as the General Receipts.[19] A brief examination of the direct taxes and of the General Receipts will serve to set the General Farms and the indirect taxes in their proper relation to the fiscal service of the monarchy as a whole.

THE DIRECT TAXES AND THE GENERAL RECEIPTS

In the eighteenth century there were three taxes commonly classified as *impositions*, or direct taxes: the royal *taille*, the *capitation*, and the *dixièmes-vingtièmes*.[20]

---

[18] Dupont-Ferrier, *Les Institutions financières*, II, 5-21, 44; Perrot, *Les Institutions publiques*, p. 391.

[19] Noël, *Etude historique sur l'organization financière*, p. 32.

[20] The *capitation* was first promulgated as a temporary tax in 1699 but became permanent in 1701. It was essentially an income tax levied at fixed but different rates upon twenty classes or grades in the population. Nearly all classes except the peasantry managed to obtain either legal immunity from the *capitation* or practical relief by various means of tax evasion. In 1761 it was formally acknowledged that the *capitation* had become merely a supplement to the *taille*. The *dixième* was first levied in 1710 but allowed to lapse at the end of the War of the Spanish Succession; it had been a ten percent tax upon all kinds of income. The second *dixième* was levied in 1733 and terminated in 1736. It was renewed in 1741, only to be suppressed again in 1750. In that year, Machault, the royal controller-general, proposed to replace the *dixième* with a *vingtième*, a five percent income tax

While the latter two were by no means negligible as sources of revenue, each displayed a strong tendency to gravitate around the *taille*. Since it was the *taille* which largely determined the form and function of the General Receipts, attention will be concentrated here upon it.

The permanent establishment of the royal *taille* in 1429 had been a milestone on the march of the French kings to absolute political power; it was the symbol of the royal *arbitraire*.[21] To many of the peasantry, the assessment and collection of the *taille* appeared as the one direct link between them and the king. Yet the fact that the *taille* even in the eighteenth century was levied directly in the name of the king only in the *pays d'élection* and not in the *pays d'état*, such as Brittany, Languedoc, and Burgundy, was symptomatic of the still-decentralized nature of much of the Bourbons' realm.[22] Moreover, due to the exemptions

which was to be permanent and not merely a wartime expedient. The government succeeded in applying the tax only after a bitter struggle with the privileged classes during which the clergy succeeded in re-affirming its right to exemption from direct taxation. In 1756 a second *vingtième*, designed as a temporary war tax, was added; in 1760 a third was added. In 1761 the third *vingtième* was suppressed but the government proposed to make the second, like the first, a permanent rather than a temporary tax. It succeeded only by permitting widespread exemptions among the privileged classes and by allowing privileged places, like the *pays d'état*, to compound. The result was that the *vingtièmes* were corroded by privilege; like the *capitation* they tended to be paid only by the peasantry. In 1790 the *vingtièmes* yielded 56,966,077 livres plus 18,000,000 livres in compoundings from the places which had purchased immunity. See Marion, *Les Impôts directs*, pp. 49-61, 65-69, 75-78, 82-86, 87-112.

21 Clamageran, *Histoire de l'impôt*, I, 483-489.

22 In the eighteenth century the ancient provinces of France fell into two rough political classifications: *pays d'état* and *pays d'élection*. In the *pays d'état*, whcih generally were situated on the frontiers and had been subjected to royal power only relatively recently, periodic meetings of the medieval *états*, or assemblies of representatives of the three legally recognized estates, had been allowed to continue. In general, the *pays d'état*, the most important of which were Brittany, Languedoc, Provence, Burgundy, Franche Comté, Lille, and Béarn, did not bear the royal *taille* and enjoyed numerous other fiscal advantages over the *pays d'élection*. The activities of the General Receipts were largely confined to the *pays d'élection*. It should be pointed out that, although the royal *taille* was not levied upon the *pays d'état*,

from the payment of the *taille* enjoyed by the privileged ecclesiastical and noble estates, the *taille* was the fiscal incarnation of the castelike character of old-regime society.

The royal *taille* was a tax directly assessed against individual peasants in the *pays d'élection*.[23] This assessment was accomplished in five steps.[24] First, the central government [25] determined the global amount to be paid by the *pays d'élection* as a whole in the course of a

---

provincial *tailles* were levied in the name of the several *états*. The product went directly to the provincial treasury rather than to the royal treasury.

[23] In the eighteenth entury there were three major variations on the *taille*. The *taille personnelle,* levied generally in the *pays d'élection* and in a few places outside that area, was a tax assessed upon the individual personally, rough account being taken of his ability to pay. The *taille réelle,* assessed against the value of real property, was generally levied in the *pays d'état* and hence not by the instruments of the central government but by provincial authorities. It was collected to the account of the provincial *état*. During the eighteenth century attempts were made sporadically to reform the *taille personnelle*. The result was a *taille tariffé* in scattered localities. This study is concerned only with the *taille personnelle* and its bearing upon the functions of the General Receipts. See Marion, *Les Impôts directs,* pp. 5, 18-21.

[24] Moreau de Beaumont, *Mémoires concernant les impositions,* II, 71-74.

[25] In the eighteenth century the central government of France consisted of the king, a series of interlocking councils and special commissions, and various departmental or ministerial bureaus. In theory, the *conseil de finance* and its two permanent commissions, the *grande* and the *petite directions des finances,* exercised supreme authority over all fiscal and financial matters. In practice, the actual authority was wielded by the controller-general, legally only a kind of superior clerk but in reality the equivalent of a finance minister. Effectively the controller-general made fiscal and financial policy and saw to its enforcement by the local units of government. The *conseil de finance* was usually in the position of ratifying decisions and acts made by the controller-general. Since in the eighteenth century nearly all matters of internal policy quickly resolved themselves into financial problems, the controller-general was more than a finance minister; he was also a kind of minister of the interior dealing with nearly all aspects of civil government. The controller-general headed the *contrôle-général,* a rambling, badly joined series of *bureaux de finance* among whose staffs the work of the "department" was distributed. The controller-general was also in charge, indirectly, of the royal treasury. See Viollet, *Le Roi et ses ministres,* pp. 78, 228-238, and Aucoc, *Le Conseil d'état,* pp. 54, 60-61.

fiscal year [26] and then broke this sum down into the amounts to be paid by each of the twenty-four generalities [27] subject to the tax. Next, the amount due from a given generality was further broken down into the amounts to be paid by each of the elections [28] into which

[26] The global amount of the *taille* was called a *brevet;* actually there were two *brevets* for each fiscal year. The first contained in addition to the *taille* proper, a series of supplementary taxes which had been attached permanently to the *taille.* The second comprised a variety of other accessory taxes, many of which were applied to local expenses. These accessories varied from time to time and place to place. In 1768 the first *brevet* was permanently fixed to the amount of 40,107,239 livres. It was not until 1780 that the second *brevet* was also fixed, to the amount of 24,000,000 livres. In the last decade of the old regime the *taille* was invariable in total amount, being a sum in the vicinity of 65,000,000 livres. See Marion, *Les Impôts directs,* p. 2, *n.* 1, and *Dictionnaire des institutions,* p. 526.

[27] The generality was the major subdivision of civil government in eighteenth-century France. In 1789 there were thirty-four generalities, twenty in the *pays d'élection* (Caen, Rouen, Amiens, Soissons, Paris, Châlons, Orléans, Alençon, Tours, Poitiers, La Rochelle, Bourges, Moulins, Lyons, Riom, Grenoble, Montauban, Limoges, Auch, and Bordeaux) and fourteen in the *pays d'état* (Aix, Dijon, Rennes, Toulouse, Montpellier, Perpignan, Lille, Valenciennes, Metz, Nancy, Strasbourg, Besançon, Pau, and Corsica). The generality was of medieval origin. In the fourteenth century certain royal fiscal officers, called *généraux des finances,* were assigned to conduct financial affairs in specific parts of France. These jurisdictions were called generalities. In the fifteenth century there were four generalities, each then headed by a *trésorier de France.* In 1542 the *pays d'élection* were divided into sixteen generalities each headed by a *receveur-général des finances,* a fiscal officer whose duties were to centralize the receipts of all, or general, royal taxes levied upon his generality. In the course of the seventeenth and eighteenth centuries the number of generalities was increased, and special royal civil officials, called intendants, were seated in them. At the same time in the *pays d'états,* jurisdictions similar to the generalities but called intendancies (because the generality was originally a fiscal division and because royal taxation was not extended to the *pays d'états,* there were no generalities—in a technical sense—in those provinces) were created. See Marion, *Dictionnaire des institutions,* p. 257.

[28] The elections were ancient fiscal and administrative jurisdictions antedating the generalities. In origin, the word referred to a medieval practice whereby the local inhabitants elected certain officials, called *élus,* who were charged with apportioning the royal direct taxes. In time, the *élus* were formed into a fiscal court of first instance with competence to try cases arising from the collection of royal taxes levied upon its jurisdiction. The *élus* also possessed civil

the generalities were divided. This was accomplished by the central government with the assistance of the intendant [29] who governed the generality. The fourth step in the assessment of the *taille* consisted in assigning each parish of the election its share of the tax, a task which, in the eighteenth century, was almost entirely in the hands of the intendants.[30]

The final step in the assessment of the *taille*, that of apportioning to each parochial taxpayer his share of the parish's obligation, was the most exacting. Yet it was confided to a temporary agent who was often ignorant and generally harassed by all the pressures of neighborhood jealousy and intrigue. This was the parish collector, who, in theory, was elected to his office by the inhabitants of his parish, but who, in fact was most often simply designated by the intendant. The post of collector was arduous, unremunerative, and widely detested. Working without accurate information as to the real economic con-

---

authority in certain affairs and acted as general agents for the monarchy. By the seventeenth century the elective character of the *élus*, long vestigial, was eliminated. The offices became venal and in function were confined to fiscal matters of a juridical nature. The courts of the *élus* still functioned in the eighteenth century as jurisdictions of first instance hearing suits concerning the *tailles* and the *aides*. The court of the *élus* also possessed the police power to enforce its decisions. Each election normally contained several parishes and each generality usually comprised several elections.

[29] In eighteenth-century France the intendants, one seated in each generality (or intendancy), were the real governors of the kingdom. They possessed civil, fiscal, and police powers for the execution of all laws and orders emanating from the central government in Paris. They administered justice, verified accounts of fiscal agents, supervised the apportionment and collection of direct taxes. They controlled the movement of troops within their generalities, mustered the militia, and directed the police. They enjoyed considerable authority over religious and educational institutions. They supervised agricultural and industrial production and regulated the public markets. They undertook public works, repaired roads, built bridges. Direct agents of the king, the intendants were responsible to the king through the various councils. But increasingly in the late seventeenth and eighteenth centuries they were most responsive to the orders of the controller-general.

[30] Marion, *Les Impôts directs*, p. 4.

dition of his fellow parishioners, the collector attempted to estimate the ability of his neighbors to pay and allotted each with a quota of the total share of the parish. He then drew up a tax roll and proceeded with the business of collecting the *taille*.[31] Once the task of actual tax collection started, the direct part of the regular civil administration in the management of the *taille* ceased. The work of the General Receipts, a part of the fiscal service, began.

The primary fiscal task of the General Receipts was to supervise the collectors, to receive from them (and to force them to remit if necessary by appeal to the police power of the election courts) the yield of the *taille*, to centralize the tax money first in local, then in generality *caisses*, and finally to remit the funds to the royal treasury. For this purpose no complex bureaucratic machinery was required.

The structure of the General Receipts was simple. It comprised two sorts of officials: the Financial Receivers, of which there were two for each election, and the General Receivers, of which there were two for each generality. The Financial Receivers supervised and enforced the collection of the *taille* in the parishes, received the yield, and remitted to the General Receivers. For these labors they were entitled to retain from four to six deniers of each livre handled. The General Receivers supervised the Financial Receivers, verified their accounts, received from them the receipt of the *taille*, and in turn remitted to the royal treasury. The General Receivers retained as their remuneration the same proportion of the funds passing through their *caisses* as did the Financial Receivers.[32]

[31] Villain, *Le Recouvrement des impôts directs,* pp. 22-29. The collector received a small percentage of the yield for his trouble.

[32] The General Receipts, in addition to handling the funds of the *taille,* acted as a general remittance agency for various other royal funds destined for the treasury. The General Receipts handled the receipt of the *dixièmes-vingtièmes, dons gratuits* of the clergy, subventions and compoundings of the *pays d'état* and the municipalities. The organization of the General Receipts experienced some changes during the eighteenth century. In 1718 it was suppressed but revived again in 1720. Again in 1780 Necker revolutionized the General Re-

The dual task of supervision of collection and remittance of funds was only the formal function of the General Receipts. For the General Receipts, like the General Farms, was not simply a fiscal agency. It was also a financial institution. Like the General Farmers, the General Receivers were financial intermediaries who loaned their private credit to the king. The most significant duty of the General Receipts was not merely to remit tax money but also to advance those sums in anticipation of their collection.

In order to understand this financial aspect of the General Receipts, the manner in which the receipt of the *taille* reached the treasury must be considered. Once assessed with his share of the *taille,* the taxpayer was legally allowed from eighteen to twenty-four months in which to acquit himself of his obligation to the king. This was the fiscal year of the *taille.* Payment was due from taxpayer to collector and from collector to Financial Receiver at regularly stated intervals within the fiscal year. But innumerable obstacles prevented a rigid adherence to the schedule, and often three or four calendar years were required before all parishes could acquit themselves of a single fiscal year's tax.[33]

The monarchy could not patiently await the final recovery before spending the sums involved; therefore, the government relied upon the General Receivers to provide a steady receipt to the treasury. The General Receivers advanced the future yield of a given fiscal year at 4 or 5 percent discount before they themselves actually received the sum in question. This tax anticipation was accomplished on the basis of contractual agreements between each of the General Receivers and the royal treasury. The General Receiver contracted to pay the government a

ceipts by reducing the number of General Receivers from forty-eight to twelve. But in 1781 the original corps was restored. See Necker, *De l'administration,* I, 56-57; Duval, *Elémens de finances,* pp. 11-13; *Encyclopédie méthodique: Finances,* III, 451-471.

[33] *Encyclopédie méthodique: Finances,* III, 661; Marion, *Les Impôts directs,* p. 16,

stated receipt for a given period, usually quarter-annually, thus smoothing out the normal irregularities in the collection and remittance of the *taille*. Even though the receipts of the General Receivers might be sporadic or delayed during a given period, the government was assured that its receipt would be constant and predictable.[34]

This system was capable of intensive exploitation. As in the case of the General Farms, the General Receipts also managed local expenditures, called charges, for the treasury. Charges on the General Receipts were applied both to the level of the Financial Receivers and to that of the General Receivers. Even in normal times the amount of the charges deducted by the General or Financial Receivers, on order of the government for the disbursement of sums locally, absorbed a large part of the cash receipt from the *taille* (and from the *dixièmes-vingtièmes*). [35] In times of financial emergency the government need only increase the amount of the charges to a point beyond that due from the *taille* for a given fiscal year, or for a given contract period, to have created a debt with the General Receivers. Such an operation was covered by the issuance of *réscriptions* by the General Receivers. The *réscriptions* were fundamentally the same as the *billets des fermes*. The principal and interest of these *réscriptions* were assigned for payment against some future year's collection.[36] Thus the General Receipts functioned as an institution designed to service the short-term credit needs of the treasury.

The operation of this system of short-term credits depended upon the financial strength of the General and Fi-

[34] Moreau de Beaumont, *Mémoires concernant les impositions,* II, 76; Duval, *Elémens de finances,* p. 13; Villain, *Le Recouvrement des impôts directs,* pp. 35-37. The financial relation of the Financial Receivers and the General Receivers was also contractual.

[35] Necker, *Le Compte rendu,* pp. 10-11. In 1780, of a total of 149,000,000 livres due from the General Receipts, only 29,000,000 livres actually were budgeted to be received in cash. The remainder was accounted for by charges.

[36] Duval, *Elémens de finances,* p. 86; *Encyclopédie méthodique: Finances,* III, 495.

nancial Receivers. They had to be men of wealth and high credit standing in the financial community. Upon their ability to borrow from the investing public rested the ability of the government to anticipate the yield of direct taxation. The government assured itself of the wealth of its General Receivers and, at the same time, drew additional financial assistance from the process by a technique characteristic of administrative practice in the old regime. The offices of both the General and the Financial Receivers were venal.

The fundamental motive behind the system of venality (sale of public offices) was the need of the government for loans. The late Valois and Bourbon monarchy, in its search for lenders, discovered the almost catholic desire of the French bourgeoisie to hold public offices that were at once honorific and profitable. A venal office bought outright for cash satisfied both the need of the treasury for money and the wish of the purchaser for a safe investment earning a moderate but steady rate of return. In order to attract such investors, the office could be made to carry important social prerogatives and privileges, such as exemption from the *taille,* or even patents of nobility. The definitive establishment in 1604 of the right to deed a purchased office, subject only to a moderate taxation, was the final inducement to middle-class investors to buy offices and so place their money at the disposal of the king. From that date onward, venality of public office was an integral part of the financial system of the monarchy. Its economic, financial, social, and even political effects were far-reaching.[37]

The financial mechanism of venality was relatively simple. An inheritable venal office was an instrument of perpetual government indebtedness. The purchaser paid the government a lump sum, known as the *finance* of the office. This *finance* represented the capital or principal of the permanent loan which the purchaser was advancing

---

[37] Bigo, *Bases historiques de la finance moderne,* pp. 4-5; Göhring, *Die ämterkäuflickeit im ancien régime,* pp. 305-306, 317-349.

to the treasury. In turn, the government attributed to the office certain salaries or perquisites known as *gages*. Generally the *gages* were assigned against the receipt of a specific taxation. The *gages* were, in effect, the annual interest earned by the *finance*, but were great or small depending upon the amount of the capital invested, the importance or brilliance of the office, and the urgency of the government's need to obtain money at the time of the sale. The *gages* were guaranteed so long as the government did not suppress the office. But most of the offices could not be suppressed so long as the government could not reimburse the *finance* or, in modern terms, repay the capital investment. With the introduction of the principle of inheritability, a system of perpetual loans had been established. Only rarely could the government manage to reimburse the officeholder. Therefore, once in possession of a venal office, an officeholder and his heirs were permanently fixed in their positions.[38]

The proprietorship of venal offices was the antithesis of bureaucratic tenure. In measure as the positions were permanent, the government lost control over the actions of the owner. It was difficult to make a venal officer sensitive and responsive to orders from a superior because he was neither dependent upon his chief for salary nor subject to dismissal.

Venality of office permeated nearly all branches of the judicial, civil, and fiscal administration of the old regime. But it took special root in the fiscal and financial services. No other part of the government witnessed so great a proliferation of venal offices. Only the venal magistracies of the great Parlementarian nobility could equal in amount of *finance* the offices of the General and Financial Receivers. No offices bore such rich *gages;* none offered greater opportunity for profiting from the functions of the office itself. These offices were so highly regarded by the financial class and had become such an important source of money to the treasury that the monarchy early created two

---

[38] Hennet, *Théorie du crédit*, p. 27.

offices where one would have been sufficient to perform the
required duties. Thus, in each of the twenty-four generalities which paid the *taille* there were two General Receivers; in each of the two hundred and two elections
there were two Financial Receivers. Each General Receiver and each Financial Receiver served only on alter-
nate years, yet each paid the same *finance* for the purchase
of his office. Each *finance* returned the same amount in
gages. In 1788 the total capital invested in all the offices
of the General Receipts was 65,399,000 livres. In the
same year the government paid a total of 2,801,400 livres
in *gages* or interest on this capital in the General Receipts.[39]

The basic functional resemblance between the General
Receipts and the General Farms is obvious. Technically
each was a tax-collecting, tax-remitting mechanism; yet
each operated also as an agency for the disbursement and
transfer of government funds and as a lending institution.
Together they reveal the highly decentralized nature of the
fiscal service of the old regime.[40] For, although each existed only by virtue of royal authority, each was an autonomous agency whose relationship with the central
government was contractual rather than bureaucratic.
The royal controller-general did not, and could not, command the General Receivers and General Farmers as subordinates. Rather he negotiated with them seeking not
obedience but bargaining advantages. The General Receivers and General Farmers were not modern civil ser-

---

[39] Moreau de Beaumont, *Mémoires concernant les impositions,* II,
181; *Encyclopédie méthodique: Finance,* III, 463-464, 667-679;
Braesch, *Finances et monnaie révolutionnaires,* II, Table between pp.
200-201. The General Receivers also posted a surety bond on which
they received interest. In 1788 the total of these surety bonds was
10,000,000 livres and the annual interest 500,000 livres.

[40] The General Farms and the General Receipts were only twin
giants among a crowd of similar institutions in the fiscal service, all
which displayed the same characteristics. Among these latter were
in 1780 the *fermes des postes et méssageries,* the *ferme des affinages,*
the *régie des monnaies,* the *régie des poudres,* the *régie du droit de
marc d'or,* and the *régie des revenus casuels.* See Necker, *Le Compte
rendu,* pp. 107-110.

vants, but chiefs of quasiprivate financial corporations. The General Receipts and the General Farms were used primarily as instruments of financial manipulation. Both were dedicated to the policy of tax anticipation. The same financial pressures distorted the original fiscal functions of both institutions. To the government the main importance of the General Receivers and the General Farmers was not their managerial or administrative skill, but their financial strength and willingness to place at the king's disposal their own private credit. So long as that credit was indispensable to the monarchy, neither the General Receiver nor the General Farmer could effectively be dismissed from his office or position.

In the eighteenth century the General Receipts was in age the senior fiscal and financial institution. But the General Farms was the most powerful from the point of view of the value of its financial assistance to the royal fisc. The history of the General Receipts extended back to the Middle Ages, but, although tax-farming and tax-farmers were ancient, the General Farms and the General Farmers were of comparatively recent formation. Confined to the *impôts de perception*, the development of tax-farming was a function of the growth of the money economy and of the increasing importance to the monarchy of indirect taxation. It is with these matters that the succeeding chapter is concerned.

2. The Formation and Establishment of the General Farms

In the late Middle Ages great varieties of consumable goods were made the object of indirect taxation. This taxation was of a local nature. The monarchy levied a medley of excises, duties, and tolls, with no regard to the establishment of uniform schedules for the entire kingdom. Rates of taxation and objects taxed varied from province to province, city to city, parish to parish. Territorial privilege relieved one locality of a tax which its neighbor bore. No unified fiscal code existed. Each tax in each region was the subject of a special accumulation of edicts and writs.

The situation was further complicated by the practice of leasing the rights to the collection of each local tax to a separate tax-farmer. The individual tax-farms thus created were limited to small areas whose boundaries fluctuated and coincided only rarely with those of other political, civil, or fiscal subdivisions. Each petty tax-farm operated under a different lease embodying its own peculiar terms and conditions. Large-scale tax-farming enterprises in which several leases might be held by one man or group of farmers were exceptional. The leases ran for but one year. Continuity of management within a tax-farm was difficult, coordination among the tax-farms even more so.[1] Moreover, capital accumulation for investment in the affairs of the royal fisc was limited. The upper bourgeoisie generally had not yet developed the habit of extensive investment of savings in government finance. Tax-farming tended to be undertaken casually by speculators, rather than professionally by persons devoting all their energies to it.

In the fourteenth and fifteenth centuries the attitude of the monarchy encouraged this state of affairs. Its administration, localized in a rudimentary money economy, was still largely decentralized. Revenue from the *perceptions* was regarded, even in the early sixteenth century, as incidental to that deriving from the *impositions*.[2] The receipt of each isolated tax-farm was moderate; lease prices and bondsmoney were small.

Up to the mid-sixteenth century the monarchy discouraged the development of large amalgamated tax-farms. The government's chief interest in tax-farming was to profit quickly from a speculative up-bidding of lease prices rather than from an intensive exploitation of credit potentialities of the system. Consequently, the monarchy made open, public, competitive bidding at auction its primary method for the awarding of leases on its tax-farms. Responsibility for managing royal tax-farming affairs fell to purely local officials, at first the bailiffs and senechals, later the *élus*. These officials favored short-term leases and frequent public auctions in the hopes thereby of continually forcing the lease prices upward. The king resisted the formation of syndicates of tax-farmers wealthy enough to engross several or all tax-farms in a given locality for fear that they might combine to eliminate competition. The king also regarded powerful tax-farming companies with suspicion on the well-founded grounds that they might corrupt his own officials. For much the same reasons, the monarchy

---

[1] Dupont-Ferrier, *Les Institutions financières*, II, 76-77; Roux, *Les Fermes d'impôts*, pp. 19-20.
[2] Douçet, *Les Institutions de la France*, II, 592.

sought to exclude nobles, ecclesiastics, and royal agents
from participation in the tax-farms. In order to maintain competitive conditions and to prevent collusion, the
king desired that his tax-farmers be drawn from the
"môyen estat" rather than from the richest orders of society. He wanted men who were neither too wealthy or
powerful to bribe his officials nor too poor to bear the
risks of the tax-farming enterprises.[3] To keep tax-farming within the reach of such persons the government
time and again limited the value and extent of the tax-
farms and tried to restrict the capital sums of joint tax-
farming ventures.

THE TRANSITION FROM MEDIEVAL TO EARLY MODERN
TAX-FARMING

In the sixteenth and seventeenth centuries conditions changed. In a time of considerable economic growth
marked by an acceleration of commercial activity, the
fiscal and financial needs of the centralizing monarchy
grew in proportion to its political and military ambi-
tions. Government expenditures mounted. The *impôts
de perception* acquired a new importance. Established
indirect taxation was heavily surtaxed; new taxes were
added in great number. In the late sixteenth and early
seventeenth centuries revenue from indirect taxation of
all kinds increased both absolutely and relatively to revenue from direct taxation. Equally important was the
growth of the budgetary deficit and the consequent search
for lenders. The establishment of the *rentes sur l'Hôtel
de Ville* in 1522 marked the beginning of a new policy of
borrowing. The financial crisis of 1559 and the breakdown of older sources of credit deriving principally from
the merchant-bankers of Lyons forced the monarchy to
rely on techniques of borrowing until then comparatively

[3] Clamageran, *Histoire de l'impôt,* II, 92; Dupont-Ferrier, *Les Institutions financières,* II, 79-82, 293, 303. The bidding was conducted
by the light of a burning candle. So long as the candle burned, new
bids were accepted. The last and final bidder received the farm. He
was called the *adjudicataire.*

undeveloped. Sales of public offices multiplied. Tax-farming, along with every other possible means of antici-pating the yield of future taxation, was now fully exploited. From the time of the stablishment of the Bourbon dynasty (1589) it was clear that these, and similar flimsy financial expedients were to be the chief means of bridging the chasm between income and expenditure.[4]

During the same period profits from trade and industry accumulated in the hands of the commercial bourgeoisie. Second only to the possession of land, participation in state financial operations attracted the savings of the suc-cessful bourgeois, great or small. The return on funds invested in the royal debt was high even in the face of the demonstrable bad faith of the monarchy. Above all, like the proprietorship of land, the ownership of *rentes* and venal offices or a claim to a share in one of the financial companies that dealt in the royal debt implied a superior social status. Thus capital tended to be drawn from the processes of economic growth into the financial affairs of the royal fisc.[5]

A class of native French professional manipulators of government debt developed as the financial intermediary between the bourgeoisie and the monarchy. These were the *gens d'affaires,* the financiers. The financiers bor-rowed money from the more venturesome bourgeois and loaned it to the king in return for financial conces-sions and monopolies. They bought up blocks of venal offices at discount and resold them to the public for pri-vate profit. They purchased government paper and held it for speculative rise. They dealt in the commissary serv-ice of the royal army. They speculated with the leases on the royal tax-farms. The *partisans* (from the *partis,* or financial syndicates into which the financiers grouped themselves) and the *traitants* (from the *traités,* or con-

---

[4] Forbonnais, *Recherches et considérations,* I, 258, 441; Sée, *His-toire économique,* I, 87.

[5] Bigo, *Bases historiques,* p. 5; D'Avenel, *Histoire de la fortune française,* pp. 65-73.

tracts they signed with the government) flourished after the financial crisis of 1559. Each successive stage in the growth of the royal deficit increased their influence. From the time of Henri IV the financiers were a dominant section of the bourgeoisie.[6]

In this financial, political, and economic context, the fragmented character of late-medieval tax-farming was wholly inadequate. Both the government and the financiers felt the need for larger, more centralized tax-farming units embracing all taxes of similar type levied upon a province rather than a parish or upon the entire kingdom rather than upon separate provinces. Such great tax-farms could effect administrative savings by reduction of duplicate bureaucracies. They were more easily controlled by the increasingly powerful central government. They offered the opportunity to regularize and extend the practice of systematic assignment of expenditures to specific revenues. Above all, such large tax-farms served as more adequate bases for the manipulation of the credit potentialities of the tax-farming system.

Thus, from the middle of the sixteenth to the last quarter of the seventeenth century, the evolution of tax-farming led away from the many local tax-farms typical of the Middle Ages toward the establishment of a few large, consolidated tax-farms operating on a regional and finally on a nation-wide basis. Such a great centralized tax-farm was called a *ferme-générale*.[7] All *fermes-générales* were essentially amalgamations of older individual farms, the terms of whose leases were comprehended in a single general lease. But each *ferme-générale* tended to be restricted to a certain kind of taxation. By the mid-sixteenth cen-

---

[6] Pagès, *La Monarchie d'ancien régime*, p. 12; Martin, *L'Histoire du crédit*, pp. 19-20; *Encyclopédie, ou dictionnaire raisonné*, XVI, 53; Hauser, "Les Caractères généraux de l'histoire économique de la France du milieu du XVI e siècle à la fin du XVIII e," *Révue historique*, LXXIII (1934), 317-319.

[7] *Encyclopédie méthodique: Finances*, II, 117. The French *ferme-générale* is used here to distinguish the large but still separate tax-farms from the giant General Farms of 1681.

tury four major groupings of analogous taxes were distinguished among the welter of *perceptions*.   These were: the *gabelles*, or taxes on salt; the *traites*, or customs duties; the *aides*, or excises and sales taxes; and the *domaines*, or the revenues of the old *finances ordinaires*.   By the mid-seventeenth century, there was established, at least in outline, a *ferme-générale* corresponding to each of these four categories of indirect taxation.   The establishment of a single tax-farm combining all four of these older *fermes-générales* was the logical culmination of this century-long development.   This was accomplished in 1681, when Colbert created the *fermes-unies et générales*, for which organization the term General Farms has been adopted for purposes of this study.

This late-sixteenth- and seventeenth-century movement toward the consolidation of tax-farming around a few centralized *fermes-générales* was accompanied by changes in the character of the tax-farmers themselves.   As the various tax-farms grew in size, the lease prices mounted and the amount of credit which the government demanded increased.   The small individual tax-farmer, often only casually interested in the royal finances, was not capable of mustering the capital required of such great enterprises. The need was for large companies of professional tax-farming financiers.   Such companies, drawing upon the resources of numerous partners, could accept lease after lease on a given *ferme-générale*.[8]   Assured of a long-term control over a *ferme-générale*, the company of tax-farmers could acquire skill in the management of the developing bureaucratic organization.   It could also build up a permanent capital reserve to sustain it over periods of faltering tax yield.   From such capital reserve, the government could draw valuable financial assistance in times of emergency.   Thus, as the tax-farming units grew fewer but larger, the number of tax-farmers declined, but permanently constituted syndicates of tax-farming financiers emerged.   By the last quarter of the seventeenth century

[8] Delahante, *Une Famille de finance*, I, 191-193.

royal tax-farming was approaching a condition of monopoly [9] in which a few large, consolidated *fermes-générales*
had absorbed nearly all local tax-farms while three or four
syndicates, interlocking tax-farming companies, dominated
the entire system. When the General Farms was established in 1681, the membership of these companies was
merged to form the single Company of General Farmers.

The development of large-scale tax-farming operations
necessarily entailed changes in the method by which the
monarchy controlled and directed the tax-farming process. In the early sixteenth century the government
withdrew its medieval injunctions against the formation
of tax-farming companies. By the seventeenth century it
specifically invited nobles to participate in the tax-farming syndicates. Simultaneously, the tax-farms were
withdrawn from the supervision of local officials and
control over the tax-farming system was concentrated in
the royal council. In practice, this meant that the actual
direction of tax-farming was exercised by the chiefs of
the financial service, at first the *trésoriers de France,* then
the two *intendants des finances,* later the *superintendant
des finances,* and finally, after 1665, the controller-general.[10] As the adjudication of tax-farming leases was centered in the capital and as their terms became more intricate, open competition in bidding for leases at public
auction proved impossible to manage. From at least the

[9] Smith, *An Enquiry into the Nature and Causes of the Wealth of
Nations* (ed. The Modern Library), pp. 853-854. "To farm any considerable branch of the public revenue requires either a great capital
or a great credit; circumstances which would alone restrain competition for such an undertaking to a very small number of people. Of
the few . . . a still smaller number have the necessary knowledge or
experience; another circumstance which restrains the competition still
further. The very few who are in condition to become competitors
find it more for their interest to combine to-gether; to become co-
partners instead of competitors, and when the farm is set up to auction to offer no rent, but what is far below the real value."

[10] Esmein, *Cours élémentaire,* pp. 580-581; Perrot, *Les Institutions
publiques,* pp. 432-433.

late sixteenth century leases on all major tax-farms were awarded as a result of direct secret negotiations between the financiers and the finance ministers.

But it was characteristic of the old regime never to allow the ancient formalities to lapse. As a legal fiction, the medieval practice of auctioning a tax-farming lease persisted to 1780. Theoretically, a lease on the General Farms was always let to a single individual called the *adjudicataire-général* (the word *adjudicataire* literally meaning a person who came into possession as a result of purchase by auction) who was "celui qui est le plus offrant ou le dernier enchérisseur." [11] Moreover, old French law never was adjusted to recognize the juridical existence of the Company of General Farmers. It had no means of distinguishing the fictitious person of a financial organization which was in form a partnership rather than a corporation. Consequently, leases continued to be signed only by the *adjudicataire-général* who alone was regarded, legally, as the titular General Farmer.[12] On the whole, tax-farming financiers preferred anonymity to publicity; François Legendre was the last actual financier publicly to lend his name to a tax-farming lease, the Lease Legendre of 1668. After that time, the titular General Farmer was never a member of the Company of General Farmers. He was only a straw man whose sole duty was

---

11 *Répertoire universel et raisonné de jurisprudence*, I, 166; Bosquet, *Dictionnaire raisonné des domaines*, II, 342-344. In the eighteenth century, *after* all negotiations were settled between the government and the Company of General Farmers, notices were posted in all royal jurisdictions, courts, and councils announcing a forthcoming auction on the General Farms and inviting the public to submit bids. At the appointed time and place, the motions of an auction were acted out before a burning candle; only after a second round of notices inviting the public to raise the bid of the Company were posted was the lease finally closed. All of this was, of course, a mummery, yet in 1759 the government broke a lease on the General Farms for its own purposes and used as an excuse the fact that the full formalities of public auction had not been followed during its negotiation.

12 Esmein, *Cours élémentaire*, p. 582 *n*.1; Bosquet, *Dictionnaire raisonné des domaines*, II, 366.

to give the Company a collective personality at law and to provide, by the use of his name, a means of distinguishing one lease from another.[13]

THE TAX-FARMS FROM THE SIXTEENTH CENTURY
TO THE TIME OF COLBERT

The process of consolidating the tax-farming system around a comparatively few *fermes-générales,* just described in broad terms, was actually accomplished only slowly and hesitantly. It required firm and continuous governmental direction. But from the death of Henri II in 1559 to the majority of Louis XIV in 1660, the monarchy suffered many reverses. Periods of stable administration seemed only to punctuate a history of financial crises, religious strife, civil wars, and foreign conflict. Moreover, the government, even when relatively secure, was exposed to venal influences which found it profitable to maintain the archaic system of small tax-farms as a screen behind which to plunder the king's purse. In the formative years of the *fermes-générales* everything depended upon the resoluteness and honesty of the finance ministers. These qualities, save in Sully and Colbert, were notable in the characters of the finance ministers chiefly by their absence.

The first *ferme-générale* to achieve recognizable form dealt with the internal customs duties, or *traites,* of the central provinces of France. In 1583 Henri III reorganized the twenty-one small tax-farms in which the customs duties of the provinces surrounding Paris had been leased since 1574 and consolidated them into five large tax-farms, each let to a separate tax-farming company. Thenceforth these five farms were known as the *cinq*

---

[13] *Encyclopédie méthodique: Finances,* I, 13. The Company paid the *adjudicataire-général* an annual honorarium of 6000 livres for his services. After 1668 he was usually the *valet de chambre* of the royal controller-general. A different individual was required for each lease. When, as happened in 1751, the *adjudicataire-général* died in the course of a lease which he had signed, an entirely new contract, under another name, had to be negotiated.

grosses fermes. Next, in 1584, these five leases were canceled in favor of a new general lease combining the *cinq grosses fermes* into a single *ferme-générale.* This lease was awarded to one Réné Brouard, the active partner of a syndicate of Italian banking interests. The motive was purely financial. Upon signature of the lease, Brouard relieved the king of a major portion of his personal debts by making an immediate loan of 60,000 écus and advancing the first quarterly installment of the annual lease price, a sum of 398,833 écus, before the syndicate had collected a sou of revenue.[14]

However, the life of this first *ferme-générale* was extremely brief. Civil war disrupted operations, and by 1588 collection of customs duties had almost ceased. Brouard abandoned his lease and the *cinq grosses fermes* fell apart. Ten years later Sully, finance minister to Henri IV, managed to reunite the pieces in a new *ferme-générale.* In 1607 a royal edict declared the *cinq grosses fermes* to be inseparable.[15] But this *ferme-générale* did not embrace all the tariff systems of France. Until 1681 customs outside of the *cinq grosses fermes* continued to be leased to separate tax-farming companies in bewildering number.

The *ferme-générale des grandes gabelles* was the second such organization to be created in the sixteenth century. Prior to 1548 the various salt taxes and commercial concessions constituting the *grandes gabelles* were partly farmed to individual tax-farmers and partly managed by government *régies.* In that year, most of the *régies* were eliminated and the tax-farming system extended to all fiscal elements of the *grandes gabelles.* The monarchy

[14] Frémy, "Premières tentatives de centralisation des impôts indirects, 1584-1614," *Bibliothèque de l'Ecole des Chartes,* LXXII (1911), 603-615; Douçet, *Les Institutions de la France,* II, 587-594. In 1542 Francis I attempted to convert all tax-farms of the customs duties into *régies.* The financial crisis of 1559 ruined this early attempt at direct government management of the *perceptions.* By 1574 all *régies* were once again tax-farms.

[15] Roux, *Les Fermes d'impôts,* pp. 99-100.

deliberately chose tax-farming because it needed the tax-farmers' credit in order to establish advance payment of certain *rentes* secured by the salt taxes. By 1559 most of the *grandes gabelles* were combined in a tentative general lease which was extended in 1578 to include the totality of the levies. Yet, under this lease, the concessions under which salt carters provisioned each salt warehouse were still leased to individual contractors having no administrative or financial connection with the tax-farmers who leased the right to collect the taxes. The two functions of tax collection and salt furnishing were not brought together under one lease until 1598. In that year Sully succeeded in establishing a *ferme-générale des grandes gabelles*. But the *grandes gabelles* were only one part of the total system of salt taxes levied upon France. Outside the area of the *grandes gabelles,* at least ten individual tax-farms (such as those of the *gabelles de Lyonnais, Languedoc,* and *Roussillon*) continued to divide and subdivide salt taxes in endless transactions.[16]

The creation of a *ferme-générale* for the excises known as the *aides* was extremely slow. It was not until 1604 that Sully managed to piece together an organization known as the *ferme-générale des droits d'aides.* The accomplishment was but partial and tentative. Only a bare majority of the *aides* were actually included in this *ferme-générale.*[17]

Thus, despite Sully's endeavors to rationalize the collection of indirect taxation, his success was limited. He never was able to create a *ferme-générale* for the *domaines.* His *ferme-générale* of the *aides* remained incomplete. The *fermes-générales* for the *traites* and *grandes gabelles* were only core structures around which in time numerous independent farms might gravitate. Even in 1609 there remained at least forty-five tax-farms outside the *cinq grosses fermes,* the *grandes gabelles,* and the *aides,* each

<hr/>

[16] Douçet, *Les Institutions de la France,* II, 582-583; Beaulieu, *Les Gabelles sous Louis XIV,* pp. 12-13, 63; Roux, *Les Fermes d'impôts,* pp. 97-98.

[17] Milne, *L'Impôt des aides,* p. 107.

large enough to cover a province. Alongside these was an uncounted number of smaller organizations.[18]

Between the retirement of Sully and the advent of Colbert, tax-farming tended to relapse into a state of medieval fragmentation.[19] Government leadership in the movement to centralize the management of the *perceptions* faltered. The royal finances fell into dilapidation. The three *fermes-générales* which Sully had erected proved financially unstable. Although the *ferme-générale des cinq grosses fermes* remained consolidated no advance was made in the project of attaching various provincial tariff systems to the main body. The *ferme-générale des grandes gabelles* had a tendency to splinter as the farmers could muster more or less capital to meet the demands of government for advances. The *ferme-générale* of the *aides* was reduced to a skeletal condition by the gradual stripping away of its most valuable elements. During the regency of Marie de' Medici there were fifteen tax-farmers of the Paris *octrois*. So confusing was the severalty of agents that, in 1631 and again in 1635, the royal council ordered the different farmers to use the same clerks. Only the most indistinct of lines separated these farms. There were constant usurpations and endless litigation among the financiers. The situation was further confused by the existence of an unlimited right of subfarming and even subsubfarming.[20] During the reign of Louis XIII and the regency of Anne of Austria, whenever

---

[18] Forbonnais, *Recherches et considérations*, I, 113-118.

[19] Lavoisier, *Oeuvres*, VI, 126-127; Milne, *L'Impôt des aides*, p. 134; Roux, *Les Fermes d'impôts*, p. 132; D'Avenel, *Richelieu et la monarchie absolue*, II, 257.

[20] In subfarming the titular *adjudicataire* or tax-farmer broke his farm or farms into parts and sublet each to a secondary or subfarmer, the *sous-fermier*. In subsubfarming the subfarmer broke his subfarm into parts and leased them to tertiaries or *arrières-fermiers*. Thus the farmer turned over to a second party a segment of the rights which he had leased in the first instance from the king. Generally the total of the subfarm lease prices exceeded the amount of the lease price owed by the titular farmer to the king. By subfarming the tax-farmer could realize a profit without exerting any effort in the actual work of collection. On a modified scale this practice was allowed to continue down to 1756.

new taxes or even surcharges on the old were levied, they were generally given a name, placed in individual farms, and leased for whatever lump sum the government could obtain. They were absorbed into the existing *fermes-gén-érales* only slowly if at all. Occasionally, during this period, individual financiers made attempts to add farm to farm until they held large numbers of leases. But such combinations were ephemeral No attempt was made to unify the holdings financially or bureaucratically. The retirement or bankruptcy of the individual left the structure to collapse into its original parts. The great *traitant,* Antoine Feydeau, for example, cunning in threading his way among the court cliques, was powerful enough to control the entire *ferme-générale* of the *aides* and the *ferme-générale des grandes gabelles* for a few years. The enterprise involved millions of livres and offered the possibility of a lasting consolidation of the tax-farms. But Feydeau received no positive assistance from the government and was forced to rely upon mercenary courtiers to obtain and defend his leases. The factions at court shifted, and Feydeau ended in bankruptcy and flight. His tax-farming combination disintegrated.[21]

COLBERT AND THE ESTABLISHMENT OF THE GENERAL FARMS

It was not until 1661, when Colbert assumed control of the financial and economic affairs of Louis XIV, that the movement to consolidate the tax-farms was once again given firm leadership. Colbert had few illusions about tax-farming. Ideally he preferred state-directed tax commissions. But his immediate task was to raise the king's revenue. He proposed to accomplish this not by increasing the rate of the *taille* but through an accentuated reliance upon indirect taxation. For this purpose, the credit and administrative skill of the tax-farmers was in-

[21] Heuman, "Un Traitant sous Louis XIII: Antoine Feydeau," *Etudes sur l'histoire administrative et sociale de l'ancien régime,* pp. 185-189.

dispensable. Therefore, he set about the task of introducing order and regularity into the shifting complex of the tax-farms.

Colbert instituted a surveillance over tax-farming activities surpassing in severity any previous attempt. He drove hard bargains while conducting honest, well-publicized negotiations with the tax-farmers. He forced them to remit their lease prices within the time limits stipulated in the leases. He demanded precision and insisted that the farmers keep regular weekly accounts. Government clerks were given the task of continually supervising the financiers' bookkeeping.[22]

But Colbert's chief policy was not merely to police the existing confusion. His object was first to reconstruct the dilapidated *fermes-générales* and then to combine them all under one inclusive lease. He meant to unify the collection of the *perceptions* by means of a single, giant tax-farm let to a single tax-farming company.

The almost defunct *ferme-générale* of the *aides* was first to be reorganized. In 1663 Colbert negotiated the Lease Rouçelin which included for the first time all of the royal taxes on wines. In addition, for administrative purposes, he attached to the *ferme-générale* numerous other excises which technically were not *aides* and which had always been leased as separate, individual tax-farms. After 1663 the *ferme-générale* of the *aides* always had appended to its title the legend *et autres droits y jointes*.[23] Next, in 1664, Colbert signed the Lease Martinet combining the *ferme-générale des grandes gabelles* with the bulk of the tariffs outside the *cinq grosses fermes*. At least three separate tax-farming companies were eliminated in the process.[24]

In April, 1668, François Legendre, one of the foremost financiers of the day, leased all of the separate farms of the *petites gabelles* and merged them into a single *ferme-*

---

[22] Forbonnais, *Recherches et considérations,* I, 371; Beaulieu, *Les Gabelles sous Louis XIV,* p. 116.
[23] Milne, *L'Impôt des aides,* p. 134.
[24] Lavoisier, *Oeuvres,* VI, 127.

générale des petites gabelles. Then Legendre organized a company of financiers which offered Colbert 39,100,000 livres per year for six years for a general lease including: the *ferme-générale des grandes gabelles* and the farms of the *traites* currently under the Lease Martinet of 1664; the *ferme-générale des cinq grosses fermes;* the *ferme-générale des droits d'aides et autre droits y jointes;* and numerous other more minor farms. Colbert accepted. All current leases were canceled and the Lease Legendre was signed September 1, 1668. Legendre then joined his *ferme-générale des petites gabelles* to the structure to form the *Fermes Unies,* the immediate predecessor of the General Farms of 1681. The result of the merger, in terms of treasury income, was a guaranteed receipt of 43,740,000 livres per year for six years, a sum far in excess of that which the various farms divided and let separately had ever produced.[25] Colbert, now assured of a steady income from the *perceptions,* in 1669 dropped the rate of the *taille* to the low figure of 33,832,000 livres and planned further reductions for the future.[26]

The program was frustrated by the advent of the Dutch War (1672-1678). The *taille* mounted once again, and the events of war were soon reflected in the uncertain attitude of the financiers toward their new tax-farming organization. In 1674, the leases on the *Fermes-Unies* expired and Colbert opened negotiations with the tax-farmers. The financiers were not sanguine about the prospects of a 43,000,000 livre enterprise resting upon taxes acutely sensitive to war. Consequently, the farmers offered sums for the *Fermes-Unies* which Colbert considered far too slight. Reluctantly he broke the amalgamation in three units and farmed each to a separate company. The fiscal results were not ungratifying. The lease on the *grandes gabelles* and the *cinq grosses fermes,* farmed as a unit, was let for 25,959,000 a year for the duration of

[25] *Ibid.,* VI, 127-128; Forbonnais, *Recherches et considérations,* I, 406-407; Marion, *Dictionnaire des institutions,* p. 232.
[26] Clamageran, *Histoire de l'impôt,* II, 618-619.

the war and for 27,200,000 a year during peace. The lease on the second unit, comprising the *aides* and various appended taxes, was let for 18,700,000 livres during the war and 18,800,000 during peace. The lease on the third unit, the *petites gabelles*, went for a flat 4,500,000 livres. Thus Colbert obtained a maximum of 50,450,000 livres in assured net receipts, some 7,710,000 livres more than the Legendre leases had provided. [27] But Colbert regarded the arrangement as temporary. He awaited the time when the three units might once again be combined under a general lease.

On August 10, 1678, peace was reestablished between France and the United Provinces. On June 27, 1680, the leases on the three tax-farming units of 1674 expired. Colbert, finding the financiers now more amenable, recreated the *Fermes-Unies* under the Lease Boutet. In December, 1680, the leases on the individual farms of the *domaines de France,* the *domaines de Flandres,* and certain lands ceded by the treaties of Nyjmwegen expired. Colbert now perceived his opportunity. The Lease Boutet was canceled; all *domaines* were gathered for the first time into a *ferme-générale des domaines.* On July 26, 1681, by means of the Lease Fauconnet, Colbert finally brought into being a single tax-farming organization controlling nearly all the indirect taxation levied in France.

The Lease Fauconnet of July 26, 1681, created the General Farms of old-regime France.[28] It contained the three *fermes-générales* which, since the sixteenth century, had been engrossing the multitudes of individual tax-farms: the *ferme générale des grandes gabelles;* the *ferme-générale des cinq grosses fermes;* the *ferme-générale des*

---

[27] Lavoisier, *Oeuvres,* VI, 128; Clamageran, *Histoire de l'impôt,* II, 653; Roux, *Les Fermes d'impôts,* pp. 207-208.

[28] The Lease Fauconnet did not bear the full name *fermes-unies et générales des domaines et droits du roi.* The Lease Pointeau of 1691 was the first to carry this imposing title. But the difference was purely verbal. The Lease Fauconnet was the actual start of the eighteenth-century General Farms. See Roux, *Les Fermes d'impôts,* p. 214.

droits d'aides et autres droits y jointes. It comprised also a new *ferme-générale des domaines.* Together these four great tax-farms comprised one hundred and thirty-seven taxes.[29] Several other individual farms remaining outside the General Farms in 1681 were soon attached to the giant. The addition in 1685 of the *ferme-générale des petites gabelles* and of the *ferme des droits de domaines d'Occident et Canada* completed the practical monopoly of the General Farms over the *perceptions.*[30]

Financially the Lease Fauconnet set the pattern for future developments. The lease price was 56,670,000 livres per year for six years. The addition in 1685 of the *petites gabelles* and of the *domaines d'Occident* brought the effective annual lease price up to 64,124,000 livres. This sum was guaranteed by a Company of General Farmers which posted 8,000,000 livres in bondsmoney.[31] The new company assumed the obligations of its predecessors and accepted responsibility for all the outstanding charges, *assignations* and *billets de ferme.* The Company of General Farmers was still not fully matured in 1681, but the monopolization of tax-farming by a few great financiers was clearly forecast.

The Lease Fauconnet fixed the administrative framework of the General Farms for almost one hundred years. Externally the General Farms presented a facade of unity. But internally it remained essentially an amalgam of previously established administrative units. The General Farms was a compound of the older *fermes-générales,*

[29] Forbonnais, *Recherches et considérations,* I, 532-566 gives full account of all elements included in the Lease Fauconnet of 1681.

[30] The monopoly was never complete; some minor farms always existed apart. Moreover the General Farms grew in size and scope after 1685. At certain times rich taxes promulgated after 1685 were at first farmed to separate organizations. Thus the registry taxes levied in 1693 were farmed as a *ferme-générale des contrôles des actes et exploits* which did not become a part of the General Farms until 1719. The Tobacco Monopoly was often detached from the General Farms; it was firmly a part of the structure only from 1730 onward.

[31] Lavoisier, *Oeuvres,* VI, 129.

each with a distinctive function, tradition, and organization. Merged into the General Farms of 1681, these *fermes-générales* never quite lost their identities.

Upon the signature of the Lease Fauconnet, Colbert took the opportunity to clarify the traditional practices of tax-farming. In July, 1681, the minister issued the *Titre commun pour toutes les fermes.*[32] The *titre commun* distilled in one code the experience of hundreds of years of royal tax-farming. It set the judicial forms which, while often modified or simply disregarded, nonetheless were the legal basis of tax-farming for the rest of the old regime. However, the *titre commun* contained nothing in the way of innovation; it was only a recodification of regulations and customs which were essentially medieval in spirit and substance.

Colbert was as interested in codifying the legislation of the taxes themselves as he was in defining the usages of tax-farming. But in this endeavor he met with considerably less success. His attempt to produce a general ordinance for the *tailles*, which he started in 1670, never matured. Beyond the general ordering of the internal tariffs contained in the edict of 1664 which consolidated the duties of the *cinq grosses fermes*, Colbert accomplished little in the way of codification of the tariffs. His effort to unify the law of the royal *domaines* was equally unsuccessful.[33] Colbert's chief labors in the field of indirect taxation were expended upon regularizing the vast corpus of often contradictory edicts, decrees, and writs

---

[32] *Recueil générale des anciennes lois françaises,* XIX, 279-281, has the complete text.

[33] Lavisse, "Louis XIV de 1643 à 1689," *Histoire de France illustrée,* VII, Part One, 186-187, 193-195, 203-204. The ordinance of 1687, prepared by Colbert but issued after his death by his successor Le Pelletier, was a summation of administrative and legal practice in connection with the customs-duties. Ostensibly it concerned only the *cinq grosses fermes,* but in practice it was used as the fundamental statute for all matters concerning the internal and external tariffs. It is printed in its entirety in *Recueil alphabétique des droits de traites uniformes,* IV, 53-253.

which formed the legal foundations of the *gabelles* and *aides*. The *Ordonnance sur le fait des gabelles* [34] and the *Ordonnances sur le fait des aydes* [35] were issued in May and June of 1680. For over one hundred years these ordinances served without major alteration as the governing statutes of the two most important *impôts de perception*. Neither was more than a compilation of existing legislation. Little was accomplished in the way of fundamental reform of the twisted diversity and uneven applicability of the *aides* and *gabelles*. However, the advantages of the new codes were considerable. For the first time all laws concerning these taxes were written down in one place for easy reference. The will of the king was now explicit, and a basis for future legal interpretations now existed. Colbert had succeeded in compressing the antique confusion of the *aides* and *gabelles* into a summary form endowed with a certain clarity of language. [36]

The establishment of the General Farms was, in 1681, a progressive step. If indirect taxation was now irrevocably committed to the tax-farming system, at least that branch of the revenue had been stablized. The financial resources of scattered individuals and small companies were now focused upon a single institution with which the government could deal on a responsible basis. For the first time one clear line of accountability existed between the royal treasury and the *impôts de perception*. With an assured receipt from the General Farms the essential procedure of tax anticipation could be regularized, given intelligent and moderate direction from the govern-

[34] "Ordonnance sur le fait des gabelles," *Ordonnances de Louis XIV, Roy de France et de Navarre, sur le fait des gabelles et des aydes, donnés, à S. Germain en Laye aux mois de May et Juin 1680,* pp. 3-106. See also *Recueil générale des anciennes lois françaises,* XIX, 239-242 (extract).

[35] "Ordonnances sur le fait des entrées, aides et autres droits," *Recueil générale des anciennes lois françaises,* XIX, 242-249 (extract). There were two ordinances on the *aides,* one applicable within the jurisdiction of the Paris *Cour des Aides* and the other applicable within the jurisdiction of the Rouen *Cour des Aides.*

[36] Forbonnais, *Recherches et considérations,* I, 498-512.

ment. The merger of the General Farms held the promise of a more orderly fiscal administration. Combining the
personnel, procedures, and physical equipment of numerous companies and farms, the amalgamation effected savings in costs and reduced duplication of employees. Although the General Farms could not correct the inherent
confusion of the tax laws, it could go far in applying those
laws with an increasing measure of regularity and cer-
tainty. Finally, there could be no doubt that the consolidation was justified from the point of view of the royal
treasury. During Colbert's tenure of office the annual
lease prices mounted from year to year. In 1661 the
leases signed by Fouquet, Colbert's predecessor, had given
the royal treasury some 36,918,000 livres. In 1662 the
new leases signed by Colbert had already risen to 44,164,-
000 livres. The increase was steady until in 1683, leases
on all tax-farms totaled 65,892,000 livres, of which 64,-
124,000 livres derived from the General Farms alone.[37]
This was an increase over 1661 of 78 percent. Unques-
tionably numerous factors were involved in this general
upswing of receipts from the indirect taxes: Augmentation of the rates of old taxes and the levying of new ones,
greater circulation of taxable articles, increased consumption of goods, variation in the currency, changing price
levels were contributaries. But the most important single
factor was the establishment of the General Farms and the
strict accountability which Colbert imposed upon it.

THE GENERAL FARMS FROM THE DEATH OF COLBERT
TO THE FLIGHT OF JOHN LAW

The course of the General Farms between the death of
Colbert in 1683 and the bursting of the Mississippi Bub-
ble in 1720 was marked by seeming contradictions. On
the one hand, the General Farms as a bureaucratic organization flourished and became a permanent institution
in the realm. Yet, on the other hand, the Company of
General Farmers passed through a period of trial. During

---

[37] Clamageran, *Histoire de l'impôt*, II, 633.

much of this time the General Farms functioned not under tax-farming leases but as a state-directed *régie*. For a time the tax-farming process, strictly defined, ceased and the Company of General Farmers disintegrated. Wars, economic crises, violent price fluctuations, bad harvests and declining revenues ruined French finances after the death of Colbert and brought to a close the first period of consolidation of the General Farms.

As early as 1687, only four years after the death of Colbert and six years after the Lease Fauconnet, the movement toward a General Farms was temporarily reversed. In that year Le Pelletier, Colbert's successor, divided the General Farms, this time into two major units. One, containing the *gabelles* and *traites*, was leased for six years to a syndicate of twenty-nine financiers operating under the collective name of Domerque. The second, comprising the *aides* and *domaines*, was let to another syndicate of eleven farmers represented by a certain Charrière. Already, in 1687, the coming precipitous decline in tax yield was foreshadowed. These two leases combined yielded the government slightly less than had the Lease Fauconnet, 63,000,000 livres as against 64,124,000 livres.[38]

Pontchartrain, the next controller-general, was convinced that the action of Le Pelletier was misguided. In 1691, he suppressed the Leases Domerque and Charrière two years before their expiration dates and insisted upon a reestablishment of the General Farms. From the point of view of the financiers the future seemed ominous. The War of the League of Augsburg was three years old in 1691, and already a sharp drop in tax collections was noticeable. In the face of declining yields in most of the major titles of taxation, the financiers were hesitant in entering upon a new lease which would bind them to a fixed lease price for six years. The government was, however, adamant; it needed to demonstrate its financial

---

[38] Forbonnais, *Recherches et considérations,* II, 29-30; Marion, *Dictionnaire des institutions,* pp. 223-233.

strength and well-being before the eyes of Europe. It needed also to assure itself of a secure source of short-term credits. Accordingly, the Lease Pointeau of 1691 was signed. Under its terms the entire range of taxes which had comprised the Lease Fauconnet were reunited. The General Farms was reinstated. The same forty tax-farmers who had managed the Leases Domerque and Charrière formed a company to take the General Farms under the Lease Pointeau. The annual lease price was set at 61,000,000 livres for the war years and a promised 63,-000,000 livres for the peace years. This was a reduction from the combined leases of 1687; even so, the financiers were convinced that the Les Pointeau was destined to cause them loss.[39]

The Lease Pointeau was a financial disaster for the tax-farmers. Throughout its six years, the *gabelles*, *traites*, and *aides* reported nothing but plunging receipts. The Company of General Farmers could meet its remittances to the royal treasury only by borrowing on its own credit. The government, afraid openly to admit its financial plight by renegotiating the lease price in the middle of operations, secretly promised to indemnify the Company for its loss at some more propitious time after the war. In the meantime, the Company made up the deficits between the installments on the lease price it owed the government and the amounts which it managed to collect from the taxpayers by borrowing from the public and loaning to the king at high rates of interest. The issuance of *billets de ferme* was the chief technique employed. At the end of its term the Lease Pointeau revealed a deficit of 50,683,497 livres; the combined six-year remittance to the treasury was short to that amount. The figure represented the amount of the "loan," or the amount of taxation anticipated against tax yields of the future, which the General Farmers had made available to the king. The Lease Pointeau obviously produced no profits. But, the

[39] Clamageran, *Histoire de l'impôt*, III, 9; Lavoisier, *Oeuvres*, VI, 130; Pion, *La Ferme-générale des droits et domaines du roi*, p. 9.

government, in order to induce the financiers to continue in its service, compensated them for their labors by awarding them an immediate gratification of 800,000 livres, to be divided equally between the forty participants of the Company of General Farmers.[40]   Under these conditions the Lease Pointeau had been converted to a concealed *régie*.

In 1697 a new lease under the name of Templier, to run for six years, was signed with the Company of General Farmers.   The restoration of peace made for a more favorable contract than had been expected, even though the Lease Templier set the annual lease price at 58,750,-000 livres, still a sum considerably below the minimum of wartime annual lease price of the Lease Pointeau.[41]   Provision was made for the liquidation of the government's debt to the Company by means of an orderly schedule of advance deductions from the annual lease prices in the favor of the financiers.

The outbreak of the War of the Spanish Succession in 1701, however, ruined the hopes for recovery and made a shambles of the finances of the monarchy.   During the course of the long war and its attendant economic difficulties, tax loss accumulated.   Despite a general increase in tax rates, the receipt from the General Farms declined from 58,750,000 livres in 1699 to 47,000,000 livres in 1715.   This last sum, because of variation in the currency, was actually considerably less in real terms.   From 1690 (the most prosperous year of the reign from the fiscal point of view) to the end of the reign of Louis XIV, the recovery of indirect taxations dropped some sixteen and a half percent.[42]   Yet even these figures are illusory because they are stated in terms of contracted lease prices. The actual amounts collected from the taxpayers experi-

---

[40] Clamageran, *Histoire de l'impôt,* III, 10-12; Lavoisier, *Oeuvres,* VI, 130-131.

[41] Forbonnais, *Recherches et considérations,* II, 92; Roux, *Les Fermes d'impôts,* p. 272.

[42] Clamageran, *Histoire de l'impôt,* III, 77.

enced an even greater decrease. The Farmers were able only partially to meet their installments on the lease prices out of actual yield. The deficits continued to be covered by the flotation of *billets de ferme* and by assignation of various government credit instruments against the future yield of the *gabelles* and *aides*.[43] Only the credit of the Company kept the system afloat, and increasingly the financiers were reluctant to participate in tax-farming leases.

In 1703 the Lease Templier expired. The government could persuade the Company to accept a new Lease Ferreau only on a three-year basis. Moreover, the Company refused to include the *cinq grosses fermes* in the lease. Consequently, the *traites* were financially detached from the General Farms and placed in *régie*. The Lease Ferreau, therefore, contained only the *gabelles, aides,* and *domaines* and guaranteed an average annual lease price of only 41,700,000 livres.[44]

The year 1706 witnessed not only the rapid disintegration of the financial and fiscal structure of the state but the onset of severe economic crisis compounded of famine harvests, violently fluctuating prices, currency revaluations, and disrupted commercial activities.[45] In that year the Lease Ferreau expired, and the government could scarcely induce the financiers to accept a new contract. The new Lease Isembert included only the *aides, gabelles,* and *domaines*. The annual lease price was fixed at 40,-000,000 livres, 1,700,000 less than in 1703.[46] Yet even with this low figure and the imposition of general surtaxes on the *aides* in 1705, the farmers continued to sustain loss which only constant government subsidies redeemed. Times were so uncertain that the Lease Isem-

---

[43] Sagnac, "Le crédit de l'état et les banquiers," *Révue d'histoire moderne et contemporaine*, X (March-July, 1908), 259.

[44] Clamageran, *Histoire de l'impôt*, III, 78; Roux, *Les Fermes d'impôts*, p. 281.

[45] Sagnac, *La Formation de la société française moderne*, II, 205, 217-218.

[46] Clamageran, *Histoire de l'impôt*, III, 79.

bert was contracted for only one year. It had to be renewed each year amid great confusion.[47]

By 1709 the depth of the crisis was plumbed. All expedients seemed exhausted and the state was sustained only by an enormous floating debt. This debt consisted of a mass of government paper: *rescriptions, assignations, billets de ferme, rentes,* even paper money. It was issued without plan or accountability against taxes insufficient in revenue to back it. It was negotiated at sharp discounts. As the debt increased, the recovery of taxes diminished. The net receipts from the *aides, gabelles,* and *domaines* included in the Lease Isembert fell to 31,000,-000 livres. At this point the Company of General Farmers, which had been operating the General Farms on a year-to-year basis, refused to renew the leases. The *aides, domaines,* and *gabelles* openly joined the *traites* in *régie.* In a strict sense, tax-farming was suspended. The major components of the General Farms were now being administered, with great difficulty, directly in the king's name under various tax-commissions.[48]

These tax-commissions, however, were not indicative of any attempt to place the collection of the *impôts de perception* upon a new legal foundation. The government regarded them as temporary and extraordinary expedients, the result of national calamity. The government never ceased to offer the General Farms to the tax-farmers. Thus the General Farms did not cease to exist; the Company of General Farmers merely found it no longer profitable to continue exploiting the General Farms on its own account. The risks were too great.

But the General Farmers as individual financiers did not disappear from the scene. Many continued to administer the General Farms in *régie* as commissioners. Others

[47] Lavoisier, *Oeuvres,* VI, 132; Forbonnais, *Recherches et considérations,* II, 164.

[48] Forbonnais, *Recherches et considérations,* II, 220; Carré, "Louis XV, 1715-1774," *Histoire de France illustrée,* VIII, Part Two, 181; Pion, *La Ferme-générale des droits et domaines du roi,* p. 14; Roux, *Les Fermes d'impôts,* pp. 291-292.

acting privately, continued to lend the king their personal credit. There was, however, a considerable infiltration of new men into the old financial corps. These were the grafters who battened on the confusion of accounts and fraudulent deals in military supply and the speculators with easy money acquired in transactions in grain and other necessities.[49]

Moreover, the mere fact that the General Farms was in *régie* from 1709 to 1714 did not extinguish the Company of General Farmers. Even though officially unconnected with the General Farms, a nucleus of the Company remained organized to advise the controller-general on fiscal affairs and to support the tax-commissions with credit. Together with the financiers of the General Receipts, the tax-farmers possessed the only resources capable of filling the vacuum of public credit. The financial connections between the Company and the state had grown too intimate to be dissolved on short notice. Each was inextricably bound in debt to the other. The Company could not retire without collapsing the paper house of loans, advances, *billets*, anticipations. For the same reason, the state could not let it withdraw. Therefore, each awaited the opportunity to resume the business of tax-farming.[50]

A cautious effort was soon made. The worst of the economic crisis was passed by 1711, while peace came at last in the spring of 1713. The recovery of taxes quickened; tax-farming once again seemed a profitable enterprise. Therefore, in September, 1714, the major *régies* were reconverted into the Lease Nerville, the object of which was to collect the tax arrears which had been accumulating since October, 1709. The *gabelles*, *aides*, *traites*, and *domaines* were all included for a sliding-scale lease price ranging from 26,603,000 livres for the first

[49] Besson, *Un Chapitre de notre histoire financière*, p. 30; Martin, *Histoire du crédit*, pp. 142-155.
[50] Forbonnais, *Recherches et considérations*, II, 350-351; Marion, *Histoire financière*, I, 72; Carré, "Louis XV, 1715-1774," *Histoire de France illustrée*, VIII, Part Two, 173.

year to 44,099,328 livres for the last, with the king getting
three fourths of the profits of the sixth year.   Only in this
way could currency be brought to the treasuries of the
government and the Farms with which to back the enormous quantity of depreciated government paper.   While
still actually more of a *régie* contract than a farming
lease, the Lease Nerville marked the first step toward a
restoration of the General Farms to a tax-farming system.
In 1715 the next step was taken.   A full lease on the General Farms was once again negotiated.   The Lease Edme
Bonne was signed with the Company of General Farmers
for an annual price of 46,300,000 livres for six years.
But the new contract was no sooner made than the death
of Louis XIV required cancelation of the whole arrangement.[51]

The demise of the king brought to the surface the bankruptcy that underlay the regime.   The royal fisc was literally ruined.   The total debt was about two billions;
there were 600,000,000 livres of depreciated government
paper bearing a confusion of interest rates assigned to
taxes capable of producing 165,000,000 livres at best.
Much of this floating debt had been bought at discount
and was held by speculators hoping for payment in full.
The actual yield of taxation had fallen off 30 percent in
a quarter of a century.   Future yields to the year 1722
had already been spent.   There were no reliable accounts,
and everywhere there was confusion, profiteering, and
fraud.   All fiscal and financial institutions were saddled
with debts and charges far beyond the yield of the taxes
they administered.   The king's personal credit was exhausted.   Private credit was, moreover, also disrupted.
The burden of debt and the attraction of the royal fisc as
a center for speculation left commerce and agriculture
without funds with which to repair the damages of war.[52]

[51] Forbonnais, *Recherches et considérations*, II, 371-372; Roux, *Les
Fermes d'impôts*, p. 294.
[52] Marion, *Histoire financière*, I, 15, 63-65.   Exact figures on financial conditions at the end of the reign of Louis XIV are impossible to
arrive at.   Various authorities differed at the time and still differ to

To this economic and financial distress, the death of Louis XIV added political and administrative difficulties. Louis XV was a child of five, and the exercise of his sovereign authority was entrusted to the duc d'Orléans as regent until the young monarch's majority. The regent, in order to consolidate his position, permitted the court aristocracy actively to undertake the conduct of government. In place of the professional ministers through whom Louis XIV had ruled, a series of interlocking high councils, dominated by the great nobles, was substituted. The Council of Finances, composed of amateurish courtiers, had few constructive proposals with which to meet the twin problems of state bankruptcy and economic depression. It turned to traditional procedures. The currency was revaluated. A *visa* [53] operation reduced the short-term government paper from 600,000,000 livres to 250,000,000 livres at an even 4 percent interest; the holders suffered loss of 20 to 50 percent. The *rentes* were reconstituted at great loss to the bourgeoisie. A *chambre de justice* [54] taxed the financiers to the amount

---

the present. See also Vuitry, *Le disordre des finances et les excès du speculation à la fin du règne de Louis XIV et au commencement du règne de Louis XV,* pp. 193-200; Harsin, *Les Doctrines monétaires et financières en France au XVIe au XVIIIe siècles,* pp. 134-135; Clamageran, *Histoire de l'impôt,* III, 119; Soudois, "Difficultés monétaires au début du XVIIIe siècle," *Journal des économistes,* III, IV (1925), III, 184-185.

[53] A *visa* was a method of liquidating the floating debt. A commission, called a *visa,* was established with power to examine, refinance, and refund all government paper, payment on which had been suspended. The *visa* scrutinized all kinds of government indebtedness. It inquired into proper ownership and the means by which the present bearer had acquired the paper. It then decided whether to allow the claim to stand, having power to reduce the rates of discount and interest.

[54] A *chambre de justice* was an ancient institution in France. It was an extraordinary tribunal created and used to fine and tax persons charged and convicted by it of fraud. The accused was hailed before the *chambre,* forced to account for his wealth, and then allowed to buy pardon and freedom by payment of fines. Usually the small operators were fleeced while the great financiers and speculators escaped with fines which were only a fraction of what they had made in *les affaires,* in the finances of the state.

of 219,000,000 livres; it was believed, with much justice, that the *traitants* had made enormous profits at the government's expense.[55]

Then turning to the problem of raising revenue, the Council of Finances negotiated a new lease on the General Farms with the Company of General Farmers. Under the terms of the Lease Manis of 1715 the General Farmers guaranteed the government 48,500,000 livres for the first year and, as an expression of confidence, contracted to raise this price to 50,000,000 livres during the fourth, fifth, and sixth years of the lease. The whole was conditional upon an immediate advance of 4,000,000 livres. Of the 48,500,000 livres due the government as the first year's lease price, however, 3,500,000 livres were to be applied against the debt which the state owed to the financiers who had been involved in the Ferreau, Nerville, and Isembert leases. The rest was entirely consumed in discharging government obligations; *rentes, billets des fermes*, and other charges which the Farmers had underwritten. The new lease was favorable to the government if compared to the Bonne contract, while the total of all farmed taxes exhibited a 7 percent increase in the course of the one year alone, a result both of the firmness of the government and of a general easing of economic and financial conditions in the country.[56]

The Lease Manis was, however, hardly more enduring than its predecessors. Between 1716 and 1721 France passed through a tempest that left no branch of the financial and fiscal service unaltered. The failure of the *visa* and the *chambre de justice* to provide a real solution to the financial problem, and the sterility of the noble councils in offering effective political and economic leadership, induced the regent to favor more daring means. He was attracted to the proposals of John Law, Scotsman, adventurer, monetary theorist, and financier extraordinary.

[55] Marion, *Histoire financière,* I, 66-78.
[56] Forbonnais, *Recherches et considérations,* II, 372-374; Roux, *Les Fermes d'impôts,* pp. 310-312; Clamageran, *Histoire de l'impôt,* III, 148-149.

John Law offered to place the entire financial and fiscal system on a new and radical basis. He proposed to unite public and private credit in one central state bank, whose assets, ultimately, were to consist of shares of stock in a single chartered joint-stock trading company monopolizing the overseas commerce of France. The fiscal system was to be unified and taxes simplified. The company would assume the state debt. One basis for all credit operations in France would be created. Stripped of its extravagances, Law's plan was not essentially dissimilar to the operation of the national debt in early eighteenth-century England. In essence, the Scot proposed that a modern joint-stock trading company should replace the old financial corps as manager of a national, as opposed to a royal and personal, debt.[57] The financial corps (General Farmers, General Receivers, the swarms of venal financial officials, and the crowd of agents and sympathizers that hung upon their influence and affluence) regarded the Scot with suspicion. He made no secret of his plans, and it was obvious that their successful execution entailed the disruption of the monopoly over the royal fisc enjoyed by the entrenched financial companies.

John Law's bank was founded in May, 1716, as a private joint-stock enterprise. Its entrance into the field of public debt was soon foreshadowed. Depreciated government paper was accepted in payment for shares; the bank's notes were declared legal tender in payment of taxes, and their acceptance without discount was forced upon the General Farms and the General Receipts. The financiers protested to no avail. John Law was firmly supported by the regent. He proceeded to elaborate his "System." [58]

The Scot founded the Occident Company in August,

---

[57] Harsin, *Les Doctrines monétaires,* pp. 136, 143-157, 166-170. In June, 1719, Law addressed to the Regent a memoir entitled "Le denier royal," in which his fiscal program was outlined. See "Le denier royal," ed. Harsin, *Annales de la société scientifique de Bruxelles* (1927), No. 2, pp. 37-57.

[58] Du Hautchamp, *Histoire du système des finances sous la minorité de Louis XV pendant les années 1719 et 1720,* V, 74-78; Levasseur, *Recherches historiques sur le système de Law,* pp. 55-56.

1717, on a joint-stock basis. The Occident Company received as a concession from the regent monopoly rights to the exploitation and commerce of the Mississippi colony of Louisiana, as well as the monopoly of the Canadian fur trade. On the anticipation of profits from this empire John Law floated 200,000 shares of 500 livres each, payable exclusively in depreciated government paper. The shares sold well, but the company still possessed only slender resources. The bulk of the capital acquired through the sale of the shares was almost worthless, and the enterprise's solid assets rested upon 4,000,000 livres in *rentes* supplied by the government and upon the hope of profits from the Louisiana trade.[59]

The financial world now perceived its opportunity: it launched a rival company founded on far less ephemeral assets. Led by Joseph Pâris-Duverney, the financiers offered the government 48,500,000 livres a year for six years for a new lease on the General Farms. As this was an increase over the annual lease price of the Lease Manis of 1715,[60] the government accepted. The Lease Manis was canceled, and a new lease was signed with Aymard Lambert, straw man for the syndicate led by the brothers Pâris. The financiers, once in legal possession of the General Farms, promptly transferred their rights to a new joint-stock company that offered the public 100,000 shares at 1,000 livres each, on which were promised dividends of 12 to 16 percent to be paid out of profits from tax-collections. Not only was the capital thus equal to that of Law's Occident Company, but the financiers copied the Scot's organization as well. A board of share-

---

[59] Harsin, *Les Doctrines monétaires*, p. 161.

[60] Although the figure 48,500,000 livres was the same as the lease price of Manis, and less than that contracted for during the third year of that lease, still in real terms the offer of the Anti-System financiers was superior. This was because, whereas the Lease Manis contained the two surtaxes of four *sous pour livre* of 1705 and 1715, these special and fruitful surtaxes had been suspended in 1717 by John Law. Hence the financiers offered more for considerably less potential yield. See Marion, *Histoire financière*, I, 96, n. 1.

holders, open to all holders of at least fifty shares, was designated the policy-making organ of the enterprise.[61] This novel tax-farming company was dubbed the "Anti-System."

The Anti-System was serious competition to John Law's Occident Company. Its shares sold brilliantly. The public had more confidence in an enterprise whose profits were to come from the proven gold mine of the tax-farms than in one whose assets were discounted government bills and whose profits lay in the future development of the Louisiana wilderness. Behind the Pâris brothers rallied the tax-farmers, their agents and allies, the speculators, the court bankers—all whose profession of *gens d'affaires* was threatened by the revolution in the management of state credit implied by the close connections between bank, company, and council of state. Determined to wipe out the System, they attacked its chief prop, public confidence. In possession of millions of livres of bank notes and other government paper which had been forced upon the General Farms and the General Receipts in lieu of hard-cash tax money, the financiers organized heavy demands for gold upon the bank, the actual reserve of which was only a fraction of its outstanding obligations.

The Scot met the challenge first by fixing the value of the bank notes by law and then by debasing the gold content of the *louis d'or*. The run on the bank was halted. He then replied to the long-term threat of the Anti-System. The regent granted the Occident Company the highly profitable monopoly of the royal mint. Next, the *ferme-générale des tabacs* was leased to John Law's Occident Company. Then the several small companies that held the monopolies of France's Eastern and African trade were engrossed by the Company. In May, 1719, the Occident Company was transformed into the Indies Company. Previously the bank, in late 1718, had already

[61] Forbonnais, *Recherches et considérations,* II, 589-590.

been transformed into a royal bank of issue devoted to the service of the fisc. The need for tax anticipations financed through the expensive mechanisms of the General Farms and the General Receipts had been eliminated. The king's credit had been taken out of the hands of the intermediaries who had held it so profitably for so long.[62]

Law was now in possession of several immediately lucrative enterprises (the mint and the *ferme générale des tabacs*) and of the potentially profitable French colonial empire. Through the bank sufficient paper money could be issued to supply the demands of those crowding to buy shares in the company, the value of which would be borne up by profits from its several activities. Two dividends of 6 percent were declared, implying a profit of 18,000,000 livres. The price of shares mounted in the Rue Quincampoix.

At this point Law moved to complete the design he had long had in mind: to combine his bank and company into a single join-stock enterprise that would assume the state debt and supply industry and commerce with the credit and cash with which to finance economic growth and expansion.

The Indies Company offered to take the General Farms for an annual lease price of 52,000,000 livres and an immediate loan of 1,200,000 livres at the low rate of 3 percent interest. The government hastened to comply. The Lease Lambert held by the company of the Anti-System was canceled. A new Lease Pillavoine was signed with the Indies Company. The threat of the Anti-System was eliminated. The Indies Company had replaced the Company of General Farmers. The General Farms

[62] Du Hautchamp, *Histoire du système,* V, 191-201; Weber, *La Compagnie française des Indes,* p. 306; Harsin, *Les Doctrines monétaires,* pp. 161-165. The government bought out the bank's share holders for cash and thus became owner of 6,000,000 livres of capital in the form of shares in the Company which guaranteed the bank notes issued. Thenceforth all bank notes were authorized by the Council of State, and in effect France was possessed of a regular paper currency.

(nearly one half of the tax-revenues of France) was now part of John Law's System. Upon the profits of its tax collection was based the greatest single part of the profits of the Indies Company.[63]

Encouraged by an almost immediate rise in the price of the Indies Company's shares on the exchange, Law proceeded during September and October of 1719 to add to the General Farms all of the individual farms, such as the *ferme-générales des droits de contrôle*, the *ferme des gabelles de Franche Comté*, and numerous others which had never previously been parts of the General Farms. At the same time (October, 1719) the Indies Company absorbed the functions of the General Receipts. The yield of the *tailles* now passed directly to the company, which in turn paid it into the royal treasury, deducting a small profit for its operation.[64]

Thus the Indies Company became the sole collector of taxes, the sole minter of money, and the monopolist of French colonial trade. The next step, that of taking over the royal debt, proceeded. The operation, while complicated, was along the lines already laid down by the Scottish financier. Shares in the company were sold to the amount of the capital of the outstanding *rentes*. The *rentes* and other evidences of government indebtedness were accepted as payment for the shares. Dividends from the stock were to replace interest payments from *rentes*. The government assigned 48,000,000 livres of the annual lease price of the Lease Pillavoine to the Indies Company (which itself held the lease) for that purpose. The operation commenced in September, 1719, and continued rapidly throughout 1720.[65]

For the first time in French history, between late 1719

---

[63] Du Hautchamp, *Histoire du système*, V, 225-232; Harsin, *Les Doctrines monétaires*, pp. 174-178.

[64] Levasseur, *Recherches historiques*, pp. 115, 118; Harsin, *Les Doctrines monétaires*, p. 166; Clamageran, *Histoire de l'impôt*, III, 181-182.

[65] Harsin, *Les Doctrines monétaires*, pp. 170-172; Marion, *Histoire financière*, I, 96.

and late 1720, all state revenues and the means of their collection were joined under one directing administration which controlled also the treasury and its adjuncts. When in January, 1720, Law was designated controller-general and in February, 1720, the bank and the company were merged to form a single institution. the foundations for a unified financial and fiscal service were set. Events moved too fast for anything but a sketch of the structure to appear, but in the short time at his disposal the Scot laid down the basis for a complete reorganization.

The general administration of the General Farms was placed in the charge of thirty directors nominated by John Law. He drew the personnel almost exclusively from the ranks of the former General Farmers or subfarmers. The taxes were regrouped into bureaus which disregarded the traditional boundaries of the old farms. An attempt was made to combine the levies according to their administrative requirements. In the field the best of the personnel of the General Farms was employed to reorganize, simplify, and improve the measures of collection and surveillance. Similar efforts to rationalize the General Receipts were made. The ultimate plan was to merge both General Receipts and General Farms into a single agency of twenty specialized bureaus.[66]

Law's administration of the fisc aimed not merely at administrative unification. The Scot set about suppressing or reducing numerous complicated and irritating taxes, some of ancient, some of recent origin. Taxes on fish, playing cards, and paper were suppressed, while those on pit coal, leather, and raw silk were greatly reduced; a 30 to 40 percent reduction was applied to taxes on various comestibles and on wood. The sale of tobacco was made free, although the growing of the plant in France was prohibited. Customs duties heavily favored the product of Louisiana. The Parisian *aides* were simplified; taxes on wine were unified and collected solely at the city *en-*

---

[66] Levasseur, *Recherches historiques,* pp. 116, 118-119.

trées. These suppressions and reductions continued on into May, 1720. In the sphere of the *impositions* Law could accomplish relatively little. The only visible effect of his administration was two attempts in 1719 to develop regularized tax rolls for the *tailles* in La Rochelle and Normandy.[67]

Law's reorganization of the fiscal service was never more than tentative. Every expansion of the Indies Company was accomplished by issuance of new stock. Every financial maneuver called for an expansion of credit in the form of bank notes. Speculative fever mounted, reaching a peak in February, 1720. Public confidence then wavered. It was gradually understood that the prices for which shares sold on the exchange bore no reasonable relation to their earning power. In March the drop was noticeable; in June and July a landslide was in progress. By the end of 1720 the System had collapsed, and John Law was in exile.[68]

THE REESTABLISHMENT OF THE GENERAL FARMS

The rapid elaboration of the System followed by its even more abrupt conclusion left a profound impression upon the country. During five years of economic dislocation and state bankruptcy coming hard on the heels of war, France had been buffeted by financial, economic, and, to an extent, political and social change. The country had experienced the most intense inflation in its history. The deflation which followed was painful but not disastrous. Many speculative fortunes were wiped out or gravely reduced by the puncturing of paper values in the crash of the Indies Company's stock. The operation of a second *visa* cut into speculative gains still further. But solid investors emerged still in possession of the fundamentally gilt-edged securities of a reorganized Indies Company. The rentiers were trimmed, but the government

[67] Marion, *Histoire financière,* I, 105-106; Levasseur, *Recherches historiques,* pp. 117, 184-185; Clamageran, *Histoire de l'impôt,* III, 200.
[68] Harsin, *Les Doctrines monétaires,* pp. 178-190.

had managed to free itself of much of its floating indebtedness even though its financial structure was snarled and twisted.[69]

A psychological and political reaction was among the chief results of the System. The deflation was in the charge of the conservative financial cliques which regarded the fisc as a monopoly entrusted to customary corps. A profound distrust of state banks and fiduciary money was predominant among the royal administrative and financial classes. The conservative Parlements, the court nobility, and the financiers now dominated the government. These groups sought stability and a return to assured, traditional institutions. There was a desire for peace, rest, and a measure of old-fashioned prosperity for all orders according to their stations.[70] The solid reforms were swept aside with the unsound ephemera of the System. Much that was valuable was thrown over by the board: the central state bank; the concept of a funded national debt independent of the personal credit of the monarch; the idea of a system of public credit appealing directly to the sources of national wealth in the growing capitalist enterprise; the regrouping and systematization of the fiscal service and the projected reform of taxation; the notion of an integrated direction to economic life free of obsolescent mercantilist restrictions. The System was quickly dismantled. The reinstitution of the Company of General Farmers and of the General Receipts was part of this scene. Five years experience with change had convinced those in control that the established routines were best.

After the flight of John Law, cash revenue was the immediate need of government. Its credit was nonexistent; the compulsion to anticipate the yield of both direct and indirect taxation was strong. If the public was chary

---

[69] *Ibid.*, pp. 191, 200-210; Marion, *Histoire financière*, I, 99-104, 109-112; Soudois, "Difficultés monétaires au début du XVIIIe siècle," *Journal des économistes,* III, 186.

[70] Sagnac, *La Formation de le société française moderne,* II, 6.

of lending directly to the state, the credit of the accustomed financial intermediaries was still high. The reestablishment of the old financial system seemed imperative. Among the first acts of Le Pelletier de la Housaye, the new controller-general, was to restore the structure of the General Receipts. Several millions in advances were drawn at once from the venal offices. Next the General Farms was reassembled and offered to the financiers.[71]

However, the tax-farmers were wary. John Law's administration had upset the normal bureaucratic structure of the General Farms. The financiers did not wish to bear the expense of overhauling the damaged machine at a time when economic and fiscal uncertainty made the prospects of profit extremely dubious. Consequently, they offered the government, in return for a six-year lease, an annual lease price of only 40,000,000 livres for the first two years and 44,000,000 livres for the rest. The offer was unacceptable in view both of the sums which Law had drawn from the General Farms (52,000,000 livres minimum) and of the potential yield in a reviving economy (in 1726 substantially the same financiers offered 80,000-000 livres for the General Farms).[72]

Unable to induce the tax-farmers to increase their bid, the government reluctantly abandoned for the moment the attempt to lease the General Farms. A commission was created for its management, not from any desire to eliminate tax-farming, but as a necessity born of the refusal of the financiers to engage in tax-farming on terms other than their own. By writ of January 5, 1721, the *régie* Cordier was created to administer the General Farms on the king's account.[73]

The *régie* Cordier comprised forty financiers (the same number which since 1691 had been the customary consti-

[71] Forbonnais, *Recherches et considérations*, II, 639; *Encyclopédie méthodique: Finances*, III, 456; Marion, *Histoire financière*, I, 108.

[72] Soudois, "Difficultés monétaires au début du XVIIIe siècle," *Journal des économistes*, III, 180; Marion, *Histoire financière*, I, 141.

[73] Lavoisier, *Oeuvres*, VI, 132; Roux, *Les Fermes d'impôts*, p. 309; Clamageran, *Histoire de l'impôt*, III, 241.

tuency of the Company of General Farmers), organized into a financial and managerial company. As a company, this syndicate signed a contract with the government stipulating the conditions of its management of the General Farms. Each member of the company posted with the government 140,000 livres in bondsmoney, on which the government was to pay 5 percent interest per year. Thus the total bondsmoney amounted to 5,600,000 livres loan or advance. The government agreed to bear the full costs of collection: salaries of employees, rent on necessary buildings, purchase and processing of stocks of salt and stamped paper. Each of the forty commissioners received a salary of 18,000 livres per year. The contract bore the name of one Cordier, a figurehead who signed the agreement on the part of the company of commissioners. The contract ran for only one year; at the end of each year up through 1723 it was renegotiated. Joseph Pâris-Duverney was directed to supervise and control the activities of the commissioners. In 1723 the commission was converted into a *régie intéressée*. In that year the financiers induced the government to insert a bonus clause in the contract by the terms of which the commissioners guaranteed to pay the treasury two sous on every livre short of a net tax yield of 57,000,000 livres, while the government was bound to pay them a bonus of one sou on every livre collected above that figure. The conditions of this clause were back-dated to the year 1721 and were continued in each annual contract through the year 1725.[74]

The story of the *régie* Cordier is one of confusion mixed with fraud and governmental negligence. Despite the intentions of Joseph Pâris-Duverney carefully to supervise the financiers' activities, the *régie* Cordier was a gold mine to the commissioners. The financial manipulation of the commission laid the foundations of the fortunes enjoyed by the dynasties of General Farmers which dominated the fiscal service during the reign of Louis XV.

[74] Marion, *Histoire financière*, I, 142; Roux, *Les Fermes d'impôt*, pp. 311-312.

It was during the *régie* Cordier that the financiers enhanced the unsavory reputation for "insolent luxury" and unmitigated greed which their predecessors had established, and which their successors could not shake off for the rest of the eighteenth century. It was the mismanagement of the *régie* that convinced many influential persons that, for all its drawbacks, outright tax-farming was the preferable method of administering the General Farms.

Joseph Pâris-Duverney attempted to subject the commissioners to strict accountability. He devised a new method of accounting which required the financiers to establish a fully articulated system of double-entry bookkeeping. He made all financial accounts reviewable by the finance ministry. But Pâris-Duverney was helpless before the bribery and corruption which penetrated through the court to the highest officials. The fiscal service was laid open to those seeking quick profits from speculation in the tax-farms.[75]

The instability of the commission provided the opportunity for such speculation. The *régie* Cordier displayed a tendency to splinter. In 1722 the *régie* was divided into three parts, each concerned with a different range of taxes. In 1723 it was brought back together but almost immediately splintered once again. This time the core levies, *gabelles, aides, traites*, and *domaines* remained under the *régie* Cordier, but between 1723 and 1725 several secondary commissions, administering a fluctuating number of taxes under a variety of contracts and subcontracts, appeared. So great was the confusion that the government often did not know which tax was being managed by which commission. The essential reason for this instability was the fact that these secondary commissions were excellent bases from which to raid the royal fisc. Relying upon the good offices of Mme de Prie, the mistress of the Duc de Bourbon and herself a daughter of the financial class, the financiers manipulated the *régies* to

---

[75] Marion, *Histoire financière*, I, 121.

their own profit.   The commissioners would detach a tax, sign a contract with the government containing a bonus clause based upon an outrageously low estimated yield, and proceed to milk the *régie* for what it was worth.[76]

In this situation Pâris-Duverney's accounting control broke down.   Accurate accounts on the actual yield of the taxes and the costs of operation became impossible to obtain.   Efficiency and economy of management became increasingly difficult.   Contrary to the financiers' original professed expectations, the yield of the indirect taxes during the five years immediately following the collapse of the System mounted with great rapidity.   The financiers now looked forward to a full-fledged tax-farming lease.   Moreover, they were convinced that in time the government, weary of the confusion and in need of the credit of a Company of General Farmers, would accept such a lease on the Company's terms,   The commissioners therefore, had no incentive to economize on the costs of collection nor to report accurately the true state of the tax yield.   When the time came to bargain for a favorable lease on the General Farms, high costs and low yields could be the strongest arguments for a moderate annual lease price.   Consequently, the financiers inflated administrative overhead.   Since the government bore the costs, payrolls could be bloated with unnecessary personnel whose wages increased the costs of operations.   At the same time, indifference to tax evasion was encouraged.   Once in possession of a real lease on the General Farms, the tax-farmers could then easily dismiss the supernumerary personnel and collect the taxes with severity.[77]

The greatest source of profit to the commissioners of the *régie* Cordier, however, lay in the inaccuracy of the government's knowledge of the true yield of the taxes. Because of this, the bonus clause of the contract of 1723

[76] Lavoisier, *Oeuvres,* VI, 132-133; Duclos, *Mémoires sécrètes,* II, 289; Narbonne, *Journal des règnes de Louis XIV et Louis XV,* p. 143.

[77] Roux, *Les Fermes d'impôts,* pp. 310-312; Marion, *Histoire financière,* I, 142.

made the management of the commission an extremely lucrative enterprise. That clause provided for a sou per livre bonus on anything collected over the sum of 57,000,-000 livres, net yield. But in 1721 the net yield of all taxes in the *régie* Cordier was approximately 61,000,000 livres. In 1725 the net yield had risen to about 91,500,000 livres. Thus, as the yield of the taxes mounted, the commissioners' bonus increased. Over the five-year period of the *régie* Cordier, it has been estimated that the forty commissioners divided a bonus in the vicinity of 21,000,-000 livres.[78]

In 1725 the Bishop of Fréjus, soon to be Cardinal Fleury, entered his long tenure as chief minister of Louis XV. Fleury was an aged man of pacific temper bent upon establishing for France an era of peace abroad and conservative prosperity at home. He disliked scandal and disturbance. He avoided change. In place of reform, he proposed an orderly and economical management of the inherited system of government. The chaotic, malfunctioning *régie* Cordier distressed him. He regarded it as an inefficacious innovation. Fleury viewed the General Farms and the Company of General Farmers as ancient and normal institutions. He was not impressed by the fact that the General Farms had been in *régie* since 1709 without serious interruption. He was not unaware of the faults of tax-farming and tax-farmers, but he felt that he could both profit from and control their activities. As a landholder, the Cardinal was accustomed to the farming of his personal and ecclesiastical revenue. He had observed that the revenue-farmer who was left to his own devices and allowed a fair profit managed the revenue-farms with greatest efficiency and benefit to the proprietor. He could see no reason why this experience could not be applied to the revenues of the king. He had need of the tax-farmers' credit to obviate the necessity of levying new taxes which might arouse the ire of the Parlements and the Church.

[78] Clamageran, *Histoire de l'impôt*, III, 232; Marion, *Histoire financière*, I, 145; Roux, *Les Fermes d'impôts*, p. 130.

Moreover, he was not at all unfavorable to creating a kind of aristocracy of finance (the "forty columns of the State," as he called the General Farmers), acting as a counterpoise to the aristocracies of the sword and the robe, an aristocracy which would owe its being to Fleury himself.[79]

The ascendancy of Fleury made the discontinuance of the commission and the reestablishment of the Company of General Farmers a foregone conclusion. The *régie* Cordier was suppressed by declaration of July 9, 1726, in which it was described as a "novelty which has inverted the order which . . . the late King had so wisely prescribed." [80] On August 19, 1726, the Lease Carlier was signed. The Company of General Farmers, comprising forty financiers, most of whom had been commissioners of the *régie* Cordier, contracted to pay an annual lease price of 80,000,000 livres for six years in return for the right to exploit the four titles of indirect taxation included in the General Farms. In addition, it posted 8,000,000 livres in bondsmoney, payable at the formal registration of the lease in the courts and reimbursable at the expiration of its term.[81]

The signature of the Lease Carlier marked the definitive reestablishment of tax-farming in old-regime France. From 1726 until the final dissolution of the system by the National Constituent Assembly in 1791, the General Farms was continuously let to the Company of General Farmers. It is to an examination, first, of the structure and operation of the General Farms as managed by the tax-farmers and, second, of the financial role of the Company of General Farmers in its relation to the royal government that attention will now be directed.

[79] Duclos, *Mémoires sécrètes,* II, 371-372; D'Argenson, *Journal et mémoires,* II, 21; Clamageran, *Histoire de l'impôt,* III, 241.

[80] Quoted in Marion, *Histoire financière,* II, 243.

[81] Lavoisier, *Oeuvres,* VI, 133, 136; Clamageran, *Histoire de l'impôt,* III, 241.

3. The Fiscal Components of the General Farms

In the preceding discussion, it was observed that when the Company of General Farmers rented the General Farms from the king, it acquired temporary control over two elements essential to any tax-farm. The Company leased royal rights to the exploitation of the principal *impôts de perception*; it also leased the administrative machinery which had been elaborated to enforce those rights. The General Farms was a body of royal fiscal statutes on the basis of which the taxes were levied and collected; it was also a permanently established bureaucracy. In the eighteenth century that bureaucracy fulfilled many functions in the service of the royal treasury, but all rested upon the primary function of tax collection. Any analysis of the post-1726 General Farms must, therefore, begin with some detailed consideration of the taxes and of the techniques employed in their collection.

All leases on the eighteenth-century General Farms included reference to literally hundreds of different taxes, some as old as tax-farming itself, others of modern origin. These levies represented the utmost in diversity of type and disparity of rates and objects taxed. Yet it was customary to group each of these taxes under one of four or five major categories: the *gabelles,* the *tabacs,* the *traites,* the *aides,* and the *domaines.* Except for the *tabacs,* each of these categories contained a complex of several different taxes, rather than a single levy. In the language of the fiscal service, these four or five tax groups were called the receipts of the General Farms, the term "receipt" being taken to mean both the actual revenue received from a particular group of taxes and the body of tax-rights upon which the particular category of taxes was based. Thus in 1726 the General Farms comprised four major tax groups or receipts: the receipt of the *gabelles,* of the *traites,* of the *aides,* and of the *domaines.*

During the course of the period 1726 to 1783 there were several changes in, and additions to, the receipts of the General Farms. Some of these changes involved taxes of such minor importance as to be of no great consequence to the over-all structure of the General Farms. However, some were of major significance, such as the addition of the tobacco monopoly.

In 1730 the Company of General Farmers leased the *ferme-générale des tabacs* from the Indies Company to which organization the government had assigned the rights to the monopoly sale of tobacco in France after the collapse of John Law's System. From a practical administrative point of view, the *tabacs* may be considered as the fifth receipt of the General Farms from that date onward.[1] Legally, however, the *tabacs* was not a part of the General Farms until 1747.[2]

Up to 1732 the group of taxes known as the *droits de domaine d'Occident et Canada* were farmed by the Indies

[1] *Bail des fermes royales-unies fait à M. Jacques Forceville le 16 Septembre 1738: Régistré en la Chambre des Comptes le 31 Décembre 1738 et en la Cour des Aydes le 22 des mesmes mois et an,* Arts., 1-223 *(gabelles),* 224-405 *(traites),* 406-472 *(aides),* 473-489 *(tabacs),* and 490-522 *(domaines).* The Lease Forceville was the last lease printed and published in full during the eighteenth century. It was regarded as the standard lease. After 1738 leases were published only as extracts indicating simply those clauses which were different from the Lease Forceville.

[2] Weber, *La Compagnie française des Indes,* pp. 551-564. Up to 1747, the Company of General Farmers continued to pay the lease price of the *tabacs* to the Indies Company rather than to the royal government.

Company. In that year these export-import duties on French colonial trade were added to the lease on the General Farms. The *domaine d'Occident* was administered as a part of the *traites*, but until 1780 it was always maintained as a distinct receipt for accounting purposes.[3]

From 1738 the Company of General Farmers leased the various tax-farms of the duchies of Bar and Lorraine from the dethroned Stanislas, King of Poland, father-in-law of Louis XV. These farms were legally and administratively separate from the General Farms. Upon Stanislas' death the duchies reverted to the realm of France, and their tax-farms were included in the 1762 lease on General Farms.[4] For a few years thereafter *Bar et Lorraine* was maintained as a separate receipt within the General Farms. But by 1780 the taxes which it included were distributed among the five established major receipts of the *gabelles, tabacs, traites, aides,* and *domaines.*

In 1780 a major reorganization of the administration of the *impôts de perception* occurred. The financial and political causes and effects of this reorganization will be discussed in a subsequent place. But for the purpose of this chapter its administrative outline must be considered. Under the terms of the *règlement* of January 9, 1780, and of the Lease Salzard of July 5, 1780,[5] the organization of the General Farms was divided into three separate units. The first, which continued to bear the name of the General Farms, retained only the receipts of the *gabelles, tabacs,* and *traites.* The second division was called the *régie-générale des aides* and included the bulk of the taxes comprising the old receipt of the *aides.* The third unit was called the *administration-générale des domaines* and included the majority of revenues contained in the old receipt of the *domaines.* The General Farms continued to be let to the Company of General Farmers on a much-

---

[3] *Bail fait à Forceville,* Arts., 541-550 (*domaines d'Occident*).
[4] Roux, *Les Fermes d'impôts,* p. 351.
[5] *Recueil générale des anciennes lois françaises,* VII, 333-340; *Encyclopédie méthodique: Finances,* I, 73-81.

modified tax-farming lease. The General Commission of the *aides* and the General Administration of the *domaines* were both *régies intéressées,* the costs of their operations being borne by the government. They were entirely independent of any administrative connection with the General Farms. This reorganization of the General Farms was not a temporary expedient. It was regarded as a permanent reform. It endured to the Revolution with one exception. In 1783 the *traites* was removed from the lease on the General Farms and placed in *régie.* The General Farmers, however, served as commissioners.[6]

In addition to splitting the General Farms into three segments, the reorganization of 1780 also accomplished a considerable redistribution of taxes among the various administrative bodies. Several *octrois* and internal tolls which had formerly been considered as part of the receipt of the *aides* were left within the General Farms when the General Commission of the *aides* was formed. The greatest of these was the *entrées de Paris.* From 1780 onward the *entrées de Paris* was a separate accounting category within the General Farms. The content of the General Administration of the *domaines* was richer than that of the old receipt of the *domaines* by the addition of several fiscal elements which had never been part of the lease on the General Farms. Chief among these were the rights to the exploitation of the royal forests known as the *eaux, bois et forêts.* These rights had always been administered by commissions and revenue-farms separate from the General Farms.[7] Thus, as a result of the reorganization of 1780, the receipts of the *aides* and *domaines* were considerably altered in detailed composition.

From 1726 to 1789 indirect taxation in general and those taxes contained within the General Farms in particular represented a fiscal revenue of enormous and con-

<hr>

[6] Necker, *De l'administration,* I, 40-43, 76-77; *Encyclopédie méthodique: Finances,* II, 125.

[7] Marion, *Histoire financière,* I, 319; Braesch, *Finances et monnaie révolutionnaires,* II, 211; Necker, *Le Compte rendu,* pp. 50-53.

stantly increasing value to the monarchy. Roughly the same range of *perceptions* which in 1725 brought the government an estimated net revenue of approximately 99,000,000 livres [8] increased in 1788 to approximately 243,546,000 livres.[9] In 1725 total direct taxation channeled to the royal treasury by the General Receipts produced a net revenue of approximately 87,500,000 livres.[10] In 1788 the General Receipts netted about 179,373,000 livres.[11] In 1725 the global sum of all fiscal resources available to the monarchy was approximately 204,000,000 livres.[12] In 1788 it was approximately 459,919,500 livres. Of this last figure, direct taxation (gross revenue) accounted for 29.24 percent while indirect taxation (gross revenue) clearly constituted 32.47 percent or higher, if the resources of the General Administration of the *domaines* are taken to be largely in the nature of indirect taxation.[13]

[8] Clamageran, *Histoire de l'impôt*, III, 232. This figure includes *gabelles, aides, domaines,* and *traites* in the *régie* Cordier of 1725 and also the *eaux, bois et forêts* and numerous other *régies* and individual tax-farms. It does not include the *tabacs,* estimated at about 2,000,000 livres.

[9] Braesch, *Finances et monnaie révolutionnaires,* II, tables between pp. 200-201, 210-211. This figure includes: The General Farms (*gabelles, tabacs, entrées de Paris* and the 1783 *régie des traites*) at a lease price of 150,106,875 livres; the *régie-générale des aides* which yielded a gross of 51,000,000 livres; the *administration-générale des domaines* (including *eaux, bois et forêts*), which yielded a total of 50,340,000 livres gross; divers minor tax-farms and *régies* yielding 1,197,552 livres gross. The 243,546,328 livres net revenue is the sum of all these figures less about 14,857,000 livres in clear-cut administrative costs borne by the government.

[10] Clamageran, *Histoire de l'impôt*, III, 232.

[11] Braesch, *Finances et monnaie révolutionnaires,* II, table between pp. 210-211.

[12] Clamageran, *Histoire de l'impôt*, III, 232.

[13] Braesch, *Finances et monnaie révolutionnaires,* table between pp. 210-211 and pp. 210-212. In this calculation the contributions of the *pays d'état* are included, taxes in those parts being largely of the direct variety. Hence the percentage 29.24 must be corrected to 24.60 percent if attention is concentrated upon royal direct taxation. The question of the *domaines* is difficult, perhaps insoluble. Braesch does not consider the *domaines* of 1788 as being revenue from taxation either direct or indirect. This present writer takes exception to this

Because the five receipts of the General Farms never contained all the *impôts de perception* levied in eighteenth-century France, the total net revenue from the General Farms was always slightly less than the total revenue from all indirect taxation. However, the difference was not great and the general course of indirect taxation as a whole from 1726 to the Revolution may be adequately measured in terms of the annual lease prices received from the General Farms by the royal treasury.[14] Between 1726 and 1786 the Company of General Farmers signed an unbroken succession of twelve leases with the government.[15]

The first four leases, running from 1726 through 1749, showed only a moderate disposition to rise in annual lease price. In 1726 the lease price was 80,000,000 livres an-

point of view. It is true that a large, but indeterminate, part of the revenue lumped under the title *domaines* derived from seignorial and feudal fines, dues, and fees, profits from agricultural exploitation or leases on royal real estate, and from profits from such sources as the *eaux, bois et forêts,* not one of which may properly be called taxation. Yet the core of the *domaines* was the extremely fruitful registry taxes on legal documents, which were in the nature of indirect taxation. If the *domaines* are to be taken as largely of a tax nature, then an additional 7.86 percent must be added to the proportion of fiscal revenue stemming from indirect taxation in 1788. In any case, it is clear that indirect taxation toward the end of the old regime represented considerably more than one half of the tax revenues available to the monarchy.

[14] It should be emphasized that an annual lease price was only a net revenue recorded on the books of the royal treasury. The gross yield of the taxes was considerably higher than the annual lease price, the difference being the costs of collection and the profits of the Company of General Farmers.

[15] The twelve leases were: The Lease Carlier, August 20, 1726; The Lease Desboves, September 9, 1732; the Lease Forceville, July 1, 1738; The Lease La Rue, October 15, 1743; the Lease Girandin, October 28, 1749 (and the Lease Bocquillon, to which was subrogated the Lease Girandin upon Girandin's death on March 6, 1751); the Lease Henriet, August 31, 1756; the Lease Prévost, July 6, 1762; the Lease Alaterre, November 24, 1767; the Lease David, October 1, 1774; the Lease Salzard, July 5, 1780; and, finally, the Lease Mager, 1786. The dates indicated are those on which the leases were signed. Leases normally went into effect about six months after signature. See *Répertoire universel de jurisprudence,* VII, 340-341; *Encyclopédie méthodique: Finances,* I, 13-14 and also Appendix p. 285.

MAP OF THE DISTRIBUTION OF THE GABELLES
(From: Necker, *Le Compte rendu au roi*)

MAP OF THE DISTRIBUTION OF THE TRAITES
(From: Necker, *Le Compte rendu au roi*)

nually for six years.[16] In 1732 it was set at 84,000,000 livres,[17] in 1738 at 91,830,000 livres,[18] and in 1744 at 92,000,000 livres.[19] In 1750 a new lease of that year evidenced the first significant increase; 102,765,000 livres annually for six years.[20] In 1756 the annual lease price was set at 110,000,000 livres for six years,[21] which was raised to 124,000,000 livres in 1762,[22] to 132,000,000 livres in 1768,[23] and finally to 152,000,000 livres in 1774.[24]

[16] Marion, *Histoire financière*, I, 143; Clamageran, *Histoire de l'impôt*, III, 241.

[17] Marion, *Histoire financière*, I, 150-151; Roux, *Les fermes d'impôts*, p. 324. This figure includes the lease price of *tabacs* (4,000,000 livres), the receipt going to the Indies Company and not to the government.

[18] Marion, *Histoire financière*, I, 152; Clamageran, *Histoire de l'impôt*, III, 254. This figure includes the lease price of the *tabacs* (8,000,000 livres), the receipt of which still went to the Indies Company.

[19] Marion, *Histoire financière*, I, 177; Clamageran, *Histoire de l'impôt*, III, 293; Roux, *Les Fermes d'impôts*, pp. 330-331. This figure includes the lease price of the *tabacs*, the receipt still going to the Indies Company. The lease price mentioned was the peacetime, or maximum, price. The war price of 91,153,000 livres was actually in effect until 1748. It was the practice to have a peace price and a war price, the latter also being lower than the former for all leases signed during a war or in anticipation of war.

[20] Marion, *Histoire financière*, I, 177-178; Clamageran, *Histoire de l'impôt*, III, 314; Roux, *Les Fermes d'impôts*, p. 335. The actual annual lease price under Girandin was 101,149,000 livres. But to this was added certain of the profits of subfarming, which the government sequestered. This added about 1,500,000 livres a year to revenues from the General Farms, thus making an effective lease price of 102,765,000 livres. The figure now includes *tabacs* receipt to the government.

[21] Marion, *Histoire financière*, I, 180; Clamageran, *Histoire de l'impôt*, III, 362; Roux, *Les Fermes d'impôts*, pp. 329-341.

[22] Marion, *Histoire financière*, I, 212; Clamageran, *Histoire de l'impôt*, III, 353; Roux, *Les Fermes d'impôts*, pp. 350-351. This figure was the maximum or peace price. The war price, in effect for the two years 1762 and 1763, was 118,000,000 livres. It included also for the first time the receipts from *Bar et Lorraine*, 2,623,000 livres.

[23] Marion, *Histoire financière*, I, 224; Clamageran, *Histoire de l'impôt*, III, 401; Roux, *Les Fermes d'impôts*, p. 359.

[24] Marion, *Histoire financière*, I, 274; Clamageran, *Histoire de l'impôt*, III, 442; Roux, *Les Fermes d'impôts*, p. 367.

In 1780 the lease price on the General Farms (now including only the *gabelles, traites, tabacs,* and *entrées de Paris*) was set at a minimum figure of 122,900,000 livres for six years, to which should be added the lease price of the *domaines d'Occident,* set at 4,100,000 livres. The result was a minimum total of 127,000,000 livres.[25] In 1786 the last lease on the General Farms set the annual lease price at a minimum figure of 144,000,000 livres, not including the *traites,* which since 1783 had been placed in *régie.*[26] In 1780 Necker estimated the yield of the General Commission of the *aides* to be a minimum of 42,-000,000 livres and the yield of the General Administration of the *domaines* to be about the same, from which figures the costs of collection must be deducted.[27] In 1788 the General Commission of the *aides* contributed a net receipt of 49,041,000 livres and the General Administration of the *domaines* a net receipt of 43,715,754 livres.[28]

Many factors contributed to this enhancement of the value of the *impôts de perception* after 1726. Population was steadily, if slowly, growing throughout most of this time. The production, circulation, and sale of taxable goods increased, while, on the long term, general prices mounted, especially after about 1733. The actual increase in the rate of taxation also was of great importance. Within the context of an expanding economic and demographic situation, the addition of surtaxes to the base rates [29] of existing taxes [30] largely accounted for the aug-

[25] Marion, *Histoire financière,* I, 319; Rous, *Les Fermes d'impôts,* p. 384. The pricing arrangements of the Leases Salzard and Mager were completely different from any preceding leases.

[26] Marion, *Histoire financière,* I, 372; Roux, *Les Fermes d'impôts,* p. 399.

[27] Necker, *Le Compte rendu,* p. 106.

[28] Braesch, *Finances et monnaie révolutionnaires,* II, 72, and table between pp. 210-211. The figure for the General Farms includes the *traites* and the *domaines d'Occident* then in *régie,* the budgeted receipt of which together was 28,440,000 livres.

[29] From 1726 to 1789 the base rates of none of the major receipts were changed. For the *gabelles* and the *aides,* the base rates were established by the ordinances of 1680. The ordinance of 1687 similarly fixed the base rates of the internal *traites.* The base rates of the

mentation of the yield of the five receipts of the General Farms.[31]

In the eighteenth century surtaxing was accomplished by the imposition of *sous pour livre*. A *sou pour livre* surtax upon an existing tax meant that an extra sou was added for every livre of the base collected. Since a sou was one-twentieth of a livre, a *sou pour livre* surtax increased the rate of a tax by 5 percent. When a *sou pour livre* was promulgated, it was applied generally to all royal taxations, except as specifically stated in the enabling legislation that created the surtax.

In 1705 two *sous pour livre* were levied on all taxes including *gabelles, traites, aides,* and *domaines.* Numerous exemptions were made, however, in favor of specific localities, while not all the components of these four receipts were subjected to the surtax. In 1715 two additional *sous pour livres* were imposed, making a total of four surtaxes or a 20 percent increase over the base rates established prior to 1705. Again numerous specific taxes and areas were exempted. In 1717 John Law caused the existing four *sous pour livre* to be suspended, but in 1718 they were reimposed. From 1718 to 1747 no further *sous pour livre* were added. For almost the entire first half of the reign of Louis XV the five receipts experienced no increase in rate. From 1747 onward, however, there was a strong tendency not only to impose additional *sous pour livre* upon the four already established in 1718, but to reduce the areas of exemption granted in 1705 and 1715. In 1747 numerous taxes which had been exempted

main registry taxes (*domaines*) were fixed by statute in 1722, while the base rate of the tobacco tax was settled in 1721.

[30] Although during the period 1726 to 1789 several objects—paper, cardboard, starch, oil and soap, playing cards, printed cotton cloths, tallow and candles, heating and building wood—were newly taxed, these levies were of no great fiscal importance. See Milne, *Histoire de l'impôt des aides,* p. 174.

[31] Increased efficiency on the part of the General Farms, on the one hand, and, on the other, the ability of the government to negotiate leases more favorable to itself after 1749, also contributed to the increase in receipts.

in 1705 and 1715 were brought under the existing four *sous pour livre* surtax. In 1760 an additional *sou pour livre* was added to nearly all taxes, thus increasing the rate over that of 1718 by 5 percent and the entire rate of such important levies as the *gabelles, traites,* and *aides* by 25 percent over the base rates fixed prior to 1705. In 1763 a new *sou pour livre* was promulgated to apply only to the *gabelles* and *entrées de Paris.* In 1771 two additional *sous pour livre* were imposed and the *sou pour livre* of 1763 was applied to all farmed taxes. Almost without exception all *perceptions* now bore a surtax of eight *sous pour livre.* For ten years there was no change, until finally in 1781 two additional *sous pour livre* were added to the existing eight. At the same time all *sous pour livre* were made uniformly applicable to all *perceptions* without exception.[32] There was no further increase in the rate of indirect taxation from 1781 to 1789.

Thus from 1705 to 1781 the actual rate of the taxes included in the General Farms was increased by ten *sous pour livre* or 50 percent. Emphasis should be placed upon the observation that of the ten *sous pour livre* four were levied between 1705 and 1715 and that between 1715 and 1760 there was no further increase, aside from the narrowing of the areas of exemption which began in 1747. But from 1760 to 1781 six of the total of ten *sous pour livre* were added.[33] The greatest proportion of the in-

---

[32] *Encyclopédie méthodique: Finances,* III, 555-556; Clamageran, *Histoire de l'impôt,* III, 71, 148, 199, 363-364, 435.

[33] The actual increase to the individual taxpayer was likely to be more than a flat 50 percent. This was due to the method employed in applying the surtaxes to the base rate. Most taxes were not single units, but complexes of several taxes which had been gathered together and given a collective name and applied at one time. But the individual taxes of which the complex was composed remained as distinct entities. Thus when a wine merchant paid the fixed rate of the *entrées de Paris* he actually was paying three distinct taxes at the same time; the *aides,* taxes in favor of the *hôpitaux,* taxes in favor of the city. The practice was not to add these three together and then add a flat 50 percent for the surtaxes, but rather to calculate the surtax on each tax separately as the total was being added. In effect the individual was paying surtaxes on the surtaxes.

crease was concentrated in the twenty years preceding 1781. It was during those years that the revenue from the General Farms mounted drastically from lease to lease. Throughout the last thirty years of the old regime the royal monopolies of the *gabelles* and *tabacs*, the customs duties of the *traites*, the sales taxes of the *aides*, and the registry taxes of the *domaines* returned continuously increasing receipts to the treasury and profits to the Company of General Farmers.

4. The Royal Salt Monopolies: Gabelles

The group of taxes on the consumption of salt in France, known collectively as *les gabelles*, was one of the most important sources of revenue at the disposal of the French monarchy.[1] In 1726 the *gabelles* accounted for 26,500,-000 livres of the 80,000,000 livres annual lease price of the Lease Carlier. Out of the 124,000,000 livres deriving from the Lease Prévost of 1762, the *gabelles* contributed 35,197,000 livres. In the Lease David of 1774 the *gabelles* formed a receipt of 45,602,583 livres out of a total of 152,000,000 livres annual lease price. By 1788 the net yield of the *gabelles* had risen to 58,560,000 livres out of a total net yield from all receipts formerly within the General Farms of about 243,496,300 livres.[2]

The expression *gabelles* was an administrative abbreviation for the most complicated fiscal system, or medley of systems, in old-regime France. There was no single tax bearing on salt but rather a series of diverse levies, some of which were consumption taxes, some sales taxes, and some circulation taxes or tolls. There was no single method of collecting these various imposts but rather

---

[1] Stroum, *Les Finances*, I, 304.

[2] Clamageran, *Histoire de l'impôt*, III, 242; Roux, *Les Fermes d'impôts*, p. 352; Lavoisier, *Oeuvres*, VI, 180; Braesch, *Finances et monnaie révolutionnaires*, II, 72.

a variety of methods of which the most important was the technique of monopoly sales. But there was no single monopoly; rather there were a number of monopolies, each embracing a different part of the country, the only administrative connection between them being the fact that the sole monopolist in the post-1726 period was the Company of General Farmers.

In the eighteenth century France was partitioned, for purposes of the *gabelles*, into six major regions, each region having a distinctive system for managing the fiscal-commercial affairs of the salt trade. These major regions were: the *pays de grandes gabelles*, the *pays de petites gabelles*, the *pays de salines*, the *pays de quart bouillon*, the *pays rédimés des gabelles*, and the *pays francs*.[3] Each of these regions was itself a jumble of minor divisions and subdivisions, each operating under different codes, different modes of selling salt, and collecting the salt taxes. The mass of confusing detail concerning the *gabelles* was a source of bafflement even to the experts of the General Farms; it is possible now, in brief compass, only to discuss the broad character of the six major regions.

THE *Grandes Gabelles*

The *grandes gabelles* embraced that northern and central region of France, centering about Paris and Orléans and drained by the rivers Seine and Loire, from which the monarchy drew the major portion of its taxation revenue. The area was approximately circumscribed by the *traites* of the *cinq grosses fermes*;[4] it bore the sales taxes of the *aides*; it was contained within the *pays d'élection* in which the royal *taille* was imposed. The *grandes gabelles* was the largest and most important of the six major regions. It consistently contributed the greatest share of the total revenue from the receipt of the *gabelles*. In 1788, for example, the government received a lease price of 39,500,000 livres for the *grandes gabelles*, 14,000,000

[3] *Encyclopédie méthodique: Finances,* II, 317.
[4] See maps, facing pages 82 and 83.

livres for the *petites gabelles* and 5,060,000 livres for the rest of the salt taxes combined.[5] Perhaps because of its superlative fiscal value, the *grandes gabelles* was the region to which the government and the Company of General Farmers devoted most time and attention. The ordinance of 1680, which codified the law of the *gabelles,* was almost exclusively concerned with the *grandes gabelles.*

In the *grandes gabelles* the salt trade was confined to an exclusive royal monopoly, rights over which were leased to the Company of General Farmers as part of the General Farms. The salt taxes (the *droits de gabelles,* accessory taxations of a local nature, and the *sous pour livre* surtaxes) [6] were collected as part, the greatest part, of the monopoly price which the consumer was compelled to pay for salt purchased at a General Farms' store. The rate of the salt taxes was extremely high. No economic proportion existed between the monopoly price and the price which might have obtained had the market in salt been free. At Paris, in 1713, the free market price, the price without taxes, of a minot of salt was four livres ten sous; the same minot was sold at a monopoly price of forty-five livres, the amount of the taxes included being forty-one livres ten sous.[7] With the addition of the late

---

[5] Braesch, *Finances et monnaie révolutionnaires,* II, 72.

[6] The *droits de gabelles* were the royal consumption taxes proper fixed in rate for different localities by the ordinance of 1680. In addition to these, the monopoly price of a given quantity of salt contained additional taxation of variable amounts: certain taxes called *crues locales* were levied in favor of municipalities and provinces but collected by the General Farms; certain other taxes called *droits manuels,* levied to provide funds for the *gages* of certain venal judicial offices connected with the administration of justice in the *grandes gabelles,* were collected by the General Farms and paid by it to the magistrates in question; the *sous pour livres* surtaxes were applied to all of these taxations. This accumulation of taxation was piled upon the economic costs of producing, handling, selling the salt to yield the monopoly price for a given locality. See Moreau de Beaumont, *Mémoires concernant les impositions,* III, 54-57; *Encyclopédie méthodique: Finances,* I, 673, II, 407; Beaulieu, *Les Gabelles sous Louis XIV,* pp. 49-53, 59.

[7] Beaulieu, *Les Gabelles sous Louis XIV,* p. 61. A minot was a measure containing about 39 litres.

eighteenth-century *sous pour livres* surtaxes, the differential between a free market price and the monopoly price increased.

But a uniform monopoly price did not prevail throughout the entire *grandes gabelles*. In 1780 at least twelve basic price systems were in effect, each containing several local variations. Prices ranged from sixty livres seven sous the minot in the Ile de France to fifty-four livres fifteen sous the minot in Normandy and Perche. Furthermore, several places existed as privileged enclaves in the midst of the *pays de grandes gabelles*, some blessed with the right to buy salt at prices as low as three livres ten sous the minot,[8] while everywhere privileged persons, called *franc-salés*,[9] were entitled to purchase salt free of taxation.

The channels of distribution through which the General Farms supplied and sold salt to the *grandes gabelles* were established in great detail by the ordinance of 1680. Demand for salt in the *grandes gabelles* was extremely inelastic and responses in the mechanism of the salt supply were governed by the fiscal considerations of government, rather than by economic marketing conditions. The whole management of the salt supply revolved not so much around a desire to augment sales, as around the General Farms' fear of being defrauded by its own employees, by royal officials, and by the general public. In consequence the salt supply was conducted according to highly formalized, bureaucratic regulations from which any deviation was suspect. The entire system was subject to a

[8] See map, facing page 82.

[9] Officers of justice, finance and police, members of religious communities and many other persons were in degree *franc-salé*. This liberty from the *droits de gabelles* was a cherished franchise. Often considered as a supplement to official salaries, it was conceived to carry with it an indication of honorific status in society. As classes the clergy and the nobility were not privileged in regards the *gabelles*. But members of these classes had no difficulty in obtaining individual privileges of *franc-salé*. In the late eighteenth century the government began clearly to restrict the *franc-salé* privilege to narrower and narrower groups. See *Encyclopédie méthodique: Finances*, II, 289-290.

rigorous routine of inspections, controls, and searches applied by General Farms agents to every stage in the supply from producer to ultimate consumer. Salt for the *grandes gabelles* came only from the salt marshes of the county of Nantes. In the eighteenth century the salt works were privately owned. Up to 1760 the proprietors sold their product to various entrepreneurs who in turn resold it to the General Farms. In 1760 the entrepreneurs were eliminated in order to tighten the control of the General Farms over the salt trade. Thenceforth the owners of the salt works were required to sell directly and exclusively to the Company of General Farmers at prices fixed, after negotiation, by government order. Technically the Company bought all salt in the name of the king, financing the purchases by means of advances which ultimately were deducted from the annual lease price. The Company received 5 percent interest on these advances in lieu of an ordinary commercial profit from the salt trade.[10]

From the salt works supplies of salt destined for the *grandes gabelles* proceeded by ship to coastal depots located at the mouths of rivers leading into the *grandes gabelles*. There the salt was placed in registered, sealed sacks and transferred to river barges. Each coastal depot was assigned the exclusive supply of several specific interior depots located at the navigable limits of the river. At the interior depots the salt was reloaded, after intensive inspection to determine that none had been stolen en route, in wagons for shipment overland along strictly defined and constantly patrolled routes to specifically designated inland warehouses called *greniers à sel*.[11]

[10] Lavoisier, *Oeuvres*, VI, 149-150; *Encyclopédie méthodique: Finances*, I, 50, II, 262. Only salt from the Nantais marshes could legally be sold in the *grandes gabelles*. Even the use of salt licks on private land was forbidden.

[11] *Encyclopédie méthodique: Finances*, I, 493, II, 261-266. The ships, barges, and wagons used in the salt supply were privately owned by concessionnaires of the General Farms. The costs involved were paid by the Company but were ultimately deducted from the an-

The *greniers à sel* were the basic fiscal-judicial institutions of the *gabelles*. Physically a *grenier à sel* was a
warehouse rented as part of the General Farms by the
Company of General Farmers. This building served as
the seat of two organizations distinct in personnel and
function, yet related in common purpose. One was the
court of the *jurisdiction des gabelles*, a royal fiscal tribunal
of first instance, presided over by venal magistrates, having jurisdiction over the *gabelles* in an area usually the
same as a royal election and embracing several parishes.[12]
The other was the *bureau des gabelles*, the local office of
the General Farms for management of the salt trade
within the limits of the court jurisdiction. In 1763 there
were, in the *grandes gabelles*, 244 *greniers à sel*.[13]

The *bureau des gabelles* was in the charge of a high-
ranking General Farms' agent called a receiver. He was
responsible and accountable for the supply, storage, and
sale of salt, and he had general charge of all General
Farms functions and personnel stationed at the *grenier*.
Under his orders, an extensive staff of General Farms'
employees (clerks, warehousemen, guards) maintained

nual lease price. The depots were manned by General Farms' employees headed by *inspecteurs* and *vérificateurs* who supervised the entire supply procedure. In addition certain royal officials also verified
and countersigned the invoices and clearance papers without which
the salt could not move on its journey. The amount of paper work
involved in moving a shipment of salt was formidable.

[12] *Répertoire universel de jurisprudence*, VIII, 318. By the eighteenth century the older *chambres de sel* were being rapidly replaced
by the courts of the *jurisdiction des gabelles*. Appeal ran from these
newer courts to the Paris *Cour des Aides*. The magistrates of the
jurisdictions were venal, the *gages* of their offices being paid by the
droits manuels. They were *franc-salés* and privileged in respect to
the *taille*. The precise organization of the court varied considerably
from *grenier* to *grenier*. In general the presiding justice was the
président, assisted by *grenetiers* and *lieutenants*. The court officers
were *greffiers, procureurs, contrôleurs, huissiers* and *sergents*. Some
of these, particularly the *contrôleurs*, retained vestigial authority over
certain phases of administration of the salt trade. See also *Encyclopédie, ou dictionnaire raisonné*, VII, 942.

[13] *Dictionnaire géographique*, III, 535. In 1785 there were 253
greniers à sel in the *grandes gabelles*. See *Encyclopédie méthodique:
Finances*, II, 425, 429-430.

the salt stocks, sold the commodity to the consumers, and policed the *grenier* jurisdiction for violation of the regulations of the salt monopoly. Business at the *bureau des gabelles* was conducted on the basis of highly stylized bureaucratic routines. No salt was sold without the signature of the receiver and proper releases from the *grenier* magistrates. Records of inventory and sales and accounts of money received and expended (the receiver acted as a local paymaster for the General Farms) were maintained in duplicate registers and account books, the whole subject to inspection and audit without advance notice by special agents of the General Farms' headquarters in Paris. The primary intent of this system of bookkeeping controls was not to maintain clear and accurate records; it was to foil the General Farms' own employees in any illegal attempt to sell the king's salt below the monopoly price.[14]

The *grenier* was the chief retail outlet for the sale of salt in the *grandes gabelles*. However, throughout the region the General Farms granted licenses, called *regrats*, to petty retailers in rural districts enabling them to sell small quantities in shops detached from the *grenier*, at a price slightly above that prevailing in the *grenier*. The receiver was responsible for these salt vendors; he audited their accounts, supervised their activities, and supplied them with salt.[15]

The relationship of the consumers to the salt monopoly was governed by a fiscal technique unique to the *grandes*

---

[14] *Encyclopédie méthodique: Finances,* I, 334, 337, III, 793. The number of employees per *grenier* was extremely variable, each *bureau des gabelles* being organized in a somewhat different manner. The receiver headed the list, being followed by *commis à la déscente de sel* who supervised warehouse stocking, by the *jurés mesureurs de sel* who weighed the salt upon delivery and sale; by the *minotiers* who kept the scales and measures and assisted the receiver in distribution, by the *magasiniers* who guarded the salt inventories and maintained the salt registers, by *briseurs, remureurs* and *porteurs de sel* who were hired day laborers and finally by the guards. See also *Répertoire universel de jurisprudence,* IV, 93-94.

[15] *Encyclopédie méthodique: Finances,* III, 479-480.

gabelles. In the *grandes gabelles* the salt taxes functioned not solely as *perceptions*, indirect taxes, but as *impositions*, direct taxes. The consumer was not only forced to purchase his salt at a high monopoly price exclusively from the General Farms, he was also compelled by law to purchase a minimum quantity of salt annually. This minimum quantity was called *sel d'impôt*. The amount of *sel d'impôt* which each taxpayer must purchase in the course of a year was assessed against him directly and personally in much the same manner as the royal *taille* was assessed against the individual *taillable*.[16]

Each year the royal controller-general fixed the total amount of *sel d'impôt* to be bought in the *grandes gabelles* and apportioned to each *grenier* its share. The royal intendants and the magistrates of the *grenier* court then allotted quotas of salt to each parish. The assessment of the individual tax payer with his personal share of the *sel d'impôt* was the next step.[17] This final apportionment was accomplished by two entirely different systems, depending upon the type of *grenier* jurisdiction in which the taxpayer resided.

In the *grandes gabelles* there were three kinds of *greniers à sel: greniers d'impôts, greniers de ventes volontaires*, and *greniers mixtes*. The *greniers d'impôts*, of which there were 35 in 1785, were situated along the frontiers of the *grandes gabelles*, forming a continuous belt that encircled the entire region. The rigorous procedures which characterized them were designed to protect the operations of the monopoly in the interior by rendering as difficult as possible the smuggling of cheap salt to

---

[16] Moreau de Beaumont, *Mémoires concernant les impositions,* III, 80-81; Beaulieu, *Les Gabelles sous Louis XIV,* p. 39.

[17] *Encyclopédie méthodique: Finances,* II, 335, 556-557. The taxpayer was defined in law as anyone over seven or eight years of age (the figure depended upon the peculiarities of each *grenier*). The taxpayers were grouped into family units comprising fourteen members each. The head of such a family unit was responsible for the payment of the tax, that is, for the purchase of the *sel d'impôt* assessed against each member of his family.

consumers from places outside the *grandes gabelles*. The *greniers mixtes*, of which there were 37 in 1785, formed a supplementary barrier in back of the *greniers d'impôts*. The *greniers de ventes volontaires*, of which there were 181 in 1785, lay in the center of the *grandes gabelles*, isolated from the rest of the country by the *greniers d'impôts* and *mixtes*.[18]

In the parishes of the *greniers d'impôts* the collector of the *taille* automatically served also as the collector of the *gabelles*. It was his responsibility to break down the parish quota of *sel d'impôt* into the amounts which each family head must purchase. To accomplish this, the collector drew up a tax roll containing the names of the parish taxpayers and the amount of *sel d'impôt* each was required to purchase. He then went to the *grenier* court and registered the tax roll with the magistrates. He personally obtained from the receiver of the office of *gabelles* the amount of salt called for in the registered tax roll and freighted it back to his parish. He personally distributed the salt to the family heads and collected the monopoly price. Within six weeks after the registration of the tax roll the collector was obligated to remit to the receiver one half of the sum due from his parish; the remainder was due in quarter-annual installments. The collector stood as bondsman for his parish; in case of nonpayment the General Farms brought suit against him. In turn, the collector brought suit against the delinquent taxpayer. Such suits were heard before the *grenier* magistrates. In remuneration for his labor and expense, the collector was entitled to a fixed compensation. He was allowed two deniers per livre of the price of each minot of salt dispensed, plus two sous for each league of distance he must travel to and from the *grenier* and five sous per minot for freight and handling charges. He was permitted to deduct these sums from the remittance due at the end of

---

[18] *Encyclopédie méthodique: Finances*, II, 408-409, 413-424. The *greniers mixtes* were an indeterminate type, tending in the eighteenth century to be absorbed into the category of the *ventes volontaires*.

the last quarter of the fiscal year.[19]   In turn, these costs of collection were deducted from the annual lease price which the Company of General Farmers paid to the royal treasury.

In the parishes of the *greniers de ventes volontaires* the final assessment of the individual taxpayer was accomplished by the *grenier* magistrates.   The parish collector played no part in the procedure.   Here apportionment of the *sel d'impôt* was a direct corollary of the assessment of the *taille*.   According to usages peculiar to each *grenier de ventes volontaires,* the amount of the *taille* paid by a *taillable* was taken as a standard against which to judge the amount of *sel d'impôt* assessed against him.   As a rule, the amount of *sel d'impôt* assessed against a parish of the *greniers de ventes volontaires* tended to be less than that allotted to a parish of the *greniers d'impôts*.   Hence, the individual quotas were less.   Moreover, the taxpayer was allowed greater freedom of choice in selecting the time when he wished to discharge his obligation.   This relief to the taxpayer was offset, however, by the circumstance that each family head must personally travel to the *grenier* to obtain his salt.   He personally bore the expense of its shipment to his home.[20]

Throughout the eighteenth century the total amount of assessed *sel d'impôt* increased almost imperceptibly, although the amount of the monopoly price augmented greatly after 1760 under the impact of the *sous pour livre* surtaxes.   In the period between 1681 and 1777 the weight of *sel d'impôt* sold annually increased only from 1,968 muids to 2,176 muids.   The latter figure was fixed in 1777 and remained unchanged until the Revolution.[21]

Sel d'impôt was, of course, not the only salt sold within

[19] Beaulieu, *Les Gabelles sous Louis XIV,* pp. 42-43, 46; *Encyclopédie méthodique: Finances,* II, 560-563.

[20] Moreau de Beaumont, *Mémoires concernant les impositions,* III, 69, 80.

[21] *Encyclopédie méthodique: Finances,* II, 316; Clamageran, *Histoire de l'impôt,* III, 202-203.   A muid contained forty-eight minots and weighed about 936 pounds.

the *grandes gabelles*. Once the taxpayer had acquitted his yearly obligation to buy *sel d'impôt*, he was free to purchase an unlimited amount of additional salt at his designated *grenier* or from a licensed salt-vendor. Such salt was called *de vente volontaire*, and was generally offered at a monopoly price of a livre per minot less than *sel d'impôt*. In order to encourage the purchase of *sel de vente volontaire*, the use of *sel d'impôt* was hedged by numerous restrictions. By law, *sel d'impôt* could be used only for *pot et salière*—that is, for kitchen, table, or personal consumption. Conversely, *sel de vente volontaire* could be used only for *grosses salaisons*—that is, for the feeding of cattle, curing of meats, and industrial purposes. Special authorization was required to use *sel d'impôt* for purposes other than *pot et salière*. In the eighteenth century it was usual for the *grenier* magistrates to grant such permission. But to obtain it, the consumer must travel to the *grenier* and face a formidable amount of bureaucratic formality. An individual detected in the act of using *sel d'impôt* for purposes other than *pot et salière* without authorization was subject to the same severe punishments that were meted out to those who bought salt from smugglers at less than the monopoly price. By like token, the use of *sel de vente volontaire* for other than *grosses salaisons* exposed the taxpayer to rigorous chastisement in the form of fines or imprisonment in the galleys. Yet, despite these restrictions, the sale of *sel de vente volontaire* in the *grandes gabelles* increased in the period 1681 to 1780. In the former year 7,886 muids of *sel de vente volontaire* were sold. In 1780 the amount had nearly doubled. After 1756 the sale of *sel de vente volontaire* increased by a thousand muids every six years.[22]

[22] *Encyclopédie méthodique: Finances,* II, 316-317, III, 358, 515, 761-768. Clamageran, *Histoire de l'impôt,* III, 202-203. The increase in sale of *sel de vente volontaire* was despite the rise in price due to the *sous pour livre* surtaxes. It bespeaks the rise in population, increase in industrial activity and perhaps the prosperity of the countryside at certain times during the period.

THE *Petites Gabelles*

The *pays de petites gabelles* lay in the south and southeast of France, in a broad territory watered by almost the entire course of the river Rhône and including such great provinces as Languedoc, Provence, Dauphiné, and Lyonnais.[23] Throughout this region, the *droit de gabelles* was levied, and the salt trade was monopolized in the king's name by the General Farms. But the General Farms' control over the salt trade was not as absolute in the *petites gabelles* as it was in the *grandes gabelles*. In various localities municipal, provincial, and even ecclesiastical authorities still exercised supervisory rights over its terms and conditions. The laws of the *petites gabelles* were largely uncodified and presented to view an imbroglio of regulations and customs, among which there were few points of similarity.[24]

In the *petites gabelles* the General Farms operated at least six different, individual monopolies, functioning under a confusion of monopoly prices of even greater variety than existed in the *grandes gabelles*. In general, monopoly prices were considerably lower (and hence the rate of the salt taxes was lower) in the *petites gabelles* than in the *grandes gabelles*. But the differentials among the several localities were far more glaring. In the Vallée de Barcelonette, on the Spanish border, the monopoly price per minot of salt was nine livres six sous, while in Maconais, adjacent to the *grandes gabelles,* it was fifty-seven livres ten sous; in Provence, to the east, the monopoly price ranged from twenty-two livres eight sous to twenty-seven livres six sous the minot, while in Languedoc, to the west

---

23 See map, facing page 82.

24 *Encyclopédie méthodique: Finances*, II, 320. The bulk of the *petites gabelles* lay in the *pays d'état* or other areas which still clung to the semblances of local autonomy. Furthermore administration of the salt monopolies in the *petites gabelles* had never been incorporated into a single *ferme-générale* such as had those of the *grandes gabelles,* except for a brief period just prior to the establishment of the General Farms in 1681.

of the Rhône, it was fixed at thirty livres seventeen sous in 1780.[25]

Salt for the *petites gabelles* came from the rich salt mines of the Mediterranean coast. These were the only legal source of supply. The works were in private hands; salt was procured for the monopoly on terms similar to those pertaining to the supply of the *grandes gabelles*. However, the system of salt supply was completely lacking in uniform procedures, each inland *grenier* to which the salt was ultimately delivered operating under its own peculiar usages.

In 1763 there were 135 *greniers à sel* in the *petites gabelles*, each having dependent upon it numerous salt vendors. In broad jurisdiction and personnel these *greniers* resembled their counterparts in the *grandes gabelles*. Each was the seat of a royal court or *jurisdiction des gabelles* (although provincial magistrates often shared judicial burdens with the royal justices). Each possessed a *bureau des gabelles* headed by a receiver and staffed by General Farms employees. Each served as the principal local warehouse and retail store for the sale of salt and as a center of surveillance and administration of the monopoly.[26]

Throughout the *petites gabelles* all salt was *de vente volontaire*. There was no assessment of *sel d'impôt*. Thus in the *petites gabelles* the *droit de gabelles* was plainly an indirect tax on the consumption of salt, avoidance of which was legally possible on the part of the taxpayer; he need simply choose not to buy any of the commodity. Legal salt could be purchased only at the *grenier* to which the individual consumer was assigned (or from a salt vendor licensed by that *grenier's* receiver). He must pay the regular monopoly price current there. But the amount and time of the purchase were left entirely to the individual to decide. In the *petites gabelles* the consumer was subject to the same intense supervision to prevent use of illegal salt, but compulsory purchase was absent.

THE *Pays des Salines* AND *Quart Bouillon*

The *pays des salines*, adjacent to the *grandes gabelles* on the northeastern frontiers of the kingdom, comprised the provinces of Lorraine (and Clermentois), Alsace, Trois Evechés, and Franche Comté, all newly joined to France in the seventeenth century. These places were subject to distinctive salt regimes and bore taxes which, in method of levying and collection, were in no ways similar to the *grandes* and *petites gabelles* taxes. In general, salt produced in the plentiful, privately owned but state-regulated salt mines and marshes of the territory was sold within the boundaries of the *salines* by merchants enfranchised by the General Farms. A *droit de gabelles de salines*, functioning as an excise, was levied upon the market price of salt (fixed by law) and was collected by General Farms' agents from the salt merchants. Prices of salt in the *salines* ranged from twelve livres ten sous in Alsace to thirty-six livres the minot in Trois Evechés.

The *pays de quart bouillon* corresponded almost exactly to the peninsula of Lower Normandy. Here a coarse grade of salt was evaporated from sea water and sold, by licensed salt merchants, in various cities in the area. A combination of tolls on the transportation of salt and excises on its sale constituted the *droit de gabelles* collected by the General Farms. With these taxes added the average price of salt in this region in 1780 was thirteen livres.[27]

Neither the *salines* nor the *quart bouillon* was of any great fiscal consequence. The General Farms' interest in these regions was almost exclusively regulatory. It

[27] See map, facing page 82. *Encyclopédie méthodique: Finances,* III, 421-432, 515-516. The *gabelles* of Réthélais, considered as a separate region by Necker in the *Compte rendu* was actually administered as a part of the *pays de salines* by the late-eighteenth century General Farms.

was content if it was able to prevent low-priced salt from Lower Normandy and Lorraine or Franche Comté from filtering into the *grandes gabelles* as contraband.

THE *Pays Rédimés des Gabelles*

The *pays rédimés des gabelles* were those provinces, located in the southwest of France, in the valleys of the Charente, the Dordogne, the Garonne, and the Gironde rivers, which had compounded or purchased their freedom from the *droits de gabelles* by payment of a lump sum in the days of Henri II (1547-1559). Hence, the *pays rédimés* paid no royal consumption taxes or excises on salt. Neither the royal salt monopoly nor the General Farms was operative in this area, two circumstances cherished by the inhabitants as among the most prized of provincial privileges.

All salt consumed legally in the *pays rédimés* derived from the Mediterranean salt mines. Upon being imported into the region by private salt merchants, it paid high import tariffs, called *droits de convoi* and *traites de Charente*, collected in lieu of the *droits de gabelles* at the provincial frontiers by the General Farms. Base prices of salt were fixed by royal ordinance and were surtaxed by the *sous pour livres* collected as additions to the *convoi* and *traite*. In 1780 salt was sold in the *pays rédimés* at prices drastically lower than in either the *grandes* or *petites gabelles*, with both of which regions the *rédimés* shared long-common borders. Prices ranged from seven livres the minot in parts of Périgord, Quercy, and Guyenne to eleven livres in parts of Auvergne.[28]

The general conditions under which the salt trade of the *rédimés* was conducted were laid down in the ordinance of 1680. At that time there were established some forty salt depots, scattered throughout the region, which served as wholesale distributing centers. The trade itself was dominated by large wholesale salt middlemen.

[28] See map, facing page 82; Necker, *De l'administration,* II, 41-45.

Seated at the depots, these middlemen financed and directed the various enterprisers who, linked in a commercial chain of supply that extended from the salt mines to the consumers, imported the salt, warehoused it, and retailed it throughout the *pays rédimés*. The middlemen (and other principals in the trade) were organized into guild like companies operating under franchises sold by various municipal and provincial authorities. The price of the franchises was high; much patronage and corruption went into the awarding of them.

The ordinance of 1680 marked out the trade routes to be followed by the salt merchants, stipulated the times during which salt could legally be shipped and sold, and prescribed conditions of storage and sale. Moreover, the General Farms had the right to station at each depot a controller to represent its interests. At each depot was a fiscal tribunal, similar to a *grenier* court, which handled litigation in cases dealing with salt matters. Violation of the regulations was regarded as a crime. But there was no adequate system of enforcement provided; the General Farms' controller had no police force at his disposal. The General Farmers had no voice in the nomination of the salt merchants to their franchises; there was no restriction upon their numbers and none upon the amounts of salt they could import and sell. Under these conditions, it was inevitable that the *pays rédimés*, with their low salt prices, should be centers of supply for an illegal traffic in salt smuggled into the *petites* and *grandes gabelles*. The legal trade in salt was moderately profitable, but the illicit supply of salt smugglers was extremely lucrative. It was generally recognized that a high proportion of the salt imported into the *rédimés* rapidly found its way into the black markets of the *grandes gabelles*. It was further recognized that the smugglers were financed by the salt merchants.[29]

---

[29] *Encyclopédie méthodique: Finances,* II, 497-503. The official names of the enterprisers were: the *fournisseurs,* who imported the salt; the *minotiers,* who were the middlemen at the depots; the *mar-*

As the fiscal value of the *grandes gabelles* mounted in the eighteenth century, this state of affairs became increasingly intolerable to the General Farms. At first, quietly and intermittently, the Company of General Farmers negotiated with various local authorities to extend General Farms' control over the salt trade. On a piecemeal basis, concessions were obtained that augmented the power of the controllers to supervise the salt merchants. In 1722 the central government recognized the changes and amended the ordinance of 1680 to allow the General Farms to restrict the number of middlemen at each depot to twenty and to limit the amount of salt which each might legally import. With this as a foundation, the General Farms continued to encroach upon provincial privileges until in the mid-eighteenth century the time seemed ripe for a more overt attempt to convert the salt trade of the *rédimés* into a royal monopoly.

In 1749 the royal controller-general, Machault, having just negotiated the Lease Girandin with sharply increased annual lease prices, issued a royal writ which canceled all existing franchises held by the salt merchants, voided the right of local authorities to sell such franchises in the future, and vested in the General Farms the right to nominate men of its own choosing to positions in the salt trade of the *pays rédimés*. In addition, the writ established distribution quotas under which consumers living in areas close to the borders of the *grandes* and *petites gabelles* were allotted yearly average consumption amounts and forbidden to purchase over those amounts. Similar quotas were set for the retailers and wholesalers supplying the frontier area. To control the quota system, the salt merchants were forced to maintain salt registers, open to the inspection of the General Farms' controllers, each of whom

---

chands de sel, who were secondary wholesalers; the *revendeurs,* who were tertiary wholesalers seated at warehouses called *salorges;* the *regrattiers,* who were the retailers. The trade in each locality of the *rédimés* was conducted along somewhat different lines, of which the discussion in this chapter is a generalization.

was now provided with a small police force. Armed with this writ, the General Farms undertook to rid the salt trade of men who too obviously had been supplying the smugglers and to substitute others more sensitive to the needs of the royal fisc.

After 1749 the General Farms, sporadically supported by the central government, and the entrenched salt merchants, supported by provincial authorities, engaged in an open struggle that grew in bitterness. Salt smuggling and the general tendency of the consumers to defraud the fisc grew in scope during the middle years of the eighteenth century, as the numerous *sous pour livres* surtaxes forced the price of salt up in the *grandes gabelles*. The General Farmers, at the peak of their influence in Versailles, obtained additional powers to control the situation. As new and stricter regulations were issued, provincial authorities, whose chief spokesman was the Parlement of Bordeaux, used every quiddity of the law to defend the provincial privileges symbolized by the salt trade and to obstruct the General Farms in its efforts to curb smuggling activity.[30]

Momentarily, these voices were silenced when in 1771 the royal chancellor, Maupeou, dissolved the Parlements and established a new judicial structure for the country.

[30] The twelve (or, after 1775, thirteen) Parlements of France constituted a system of appellate courts for civil and criminal cases. Of these, the Parlement of Paris pretended to act as a sort of supreme court and held first rank in honor and dignity. Most Parlements contained special bodies, called *cours des aides* and *chambres des comptes,* having competence over financial and fiscal affairs. In Paris, however, the *Cour des Aides* was a separate court second only to the Parlement in power and influence. These courts, by reason of venality of office, were in the possession of the highest members of the *noblesse de la robe.* They acted as self-appointed spokesmen for aristocratic and provincial privilege. Endowed with the right of remonstrance—a right which enabled them to delay temporarily the promulgation of royal legislation—and claiming to speak for the nation in the absence of an Estates-General, the Parlements acted with increasing boldness to obstruct royal legislation in the eighteenth century. So serious was this opposition that it was necessary in 1763 and again in 1771 to exile the magistrates and to void their functions. See Marion, *Dictionnaire des institutions,* pp. 422-439.

The General Farmers seized the opportunity to bring to a logical conclusion their project of controlling the salt trade of the *pays rédimés*. In 1773 the royal controller-general, Terray, issued a writ which swept aside the entire system of the salt trade in the *rédimés* and turned the wholesale trade in salt in that region over to the General Farms as a royal monopoly. The agitation in the provinces was intense. The disfranchised salt merchants and their financial backers, the consumers, and the salt smugglers joined the discontented nobility in denouncing this final infringement of ancient provincial immunities. It was widely feared that the General Farms, now monopolizing the salt trade, would connive to raise the price of salt in the *rédimés* to levels close to those prevailing in the *grandes gabelles*.

At this juncture Louis XVI succeeded to the throne. The former system of Parlements was restored, and those connected with the *pays rédimés* lost no time in remonstrating on the subject of the salt trade. At the end of 1774 Turgot, the new royal controller-general, issued a writ which voided that of 1773 and restored the salt merchants to their franchises. But the right of the General Farms to nominate and to control them was retained, nor were any of the control regulations developed since 1749 abandoned.[31] The salt trade of the *pays rédimés* remained on this basis to the end of the old regime. Although the General Farms had failed to monopolize the salt trade in that region, it possessed in 1789 powers over the *pays rédimés* vastly greater than had been provided for in the ordinance of 1680.

THE *Pays Francs des Gabelles*

The *pays francs des gabelles* constituted a group of widely scattered provinces which were never subject to a *droit de gabelles*. These places enjoyed a trade in salt free of any tax or import duty. Consequently, salt prices hovered near to open market prices. In Brittany, to the

---

[31] Turgot, *Oeuvres*, IV, 159-164. The writ of 1774 is printed in full in this work. See also *Encyclopédie méthodique: Finances*, III, 503.

west, the price of a minot of salt ranged from one livre ten sous to three livres in 1780. In Navarre, to the south, the price was three to four livres. In Artois, in the north, the price was seven to eight livres the minot. In Gex, to the east, it was six livres.[32] In all cases, the price was determined almost solely by economic costs of production and distribution, although it was fixed by local authorities. The General Farms had interest in the *pays francs* only insofar as salt from them threatened to leak into the *grandes* and *petites gabelles* as contraband.

From this point of view, the duchy of Brittany was the most important *pay franc*. In Brittany the salt trade was organized in a manner similar to that of the *pays rédimés*. However, the crowd of salt merchants and dealers operated without franchises and almost without regulation. The General Farms maintained controllers at the salt depots, but these officials possessed no real powers. Theoretically, the General Farms had the right to control the retail trade along the borders of the *grandes gabelles*. Practically, the exercise of this right was frustrated by lack of any means of enforcement. Throughout the eighteenth century the powerful Brittany Estates and the Parlement of Rennes successfully resisted all meaningful attempts to impose a workable *police de gabelles* upon the duchy. To the end of the old regime, Brittany, whose inhabitants had unlimited, unrestricted access to the lowest-priced salt in France, was the chief entrepot of the illegal trade in that commodity and the main salt-smuggling base.[33]

THE PROBLEM OF SALT SMUGGLING

Salt smuggling was the central problem of the administration of the *gabelles*. It was the inevitable result of the extreme and purely arbitrary price differentials among the various regions and their innumerable subdivisions.

[32] See map, facing page 82. Although the expression *provinces franches* appears on this map, the expression *pays francs* was more commonly used.

[33] *Encyclopédie méthodique: Finances*, III, 505-510.

Everywhere in the *grandes* and *petites gabelles* the tax-payers engaged in passive *faux-saunage*—that is, the purchase of illegal salt smuggled to them from a neighboring *grenier,* or from the *pays rédimés* or *pays francs.* The increasing volume of active *faux-saunage*—that is, the actual selling and transporting of smuggled salt—was a normal economic response to the clandestine demand.[34]

Salt smuggling was ubiquitous within and around the *grandes gabelles* and *petites gabelles.* But the most active centers were those areas where the *pays rédimés* and the *pays francs* faced the *grandes gabelles.* This was especially true of the Brittany border. In Brittany salt was sold freely in unlimited amounts for from two to three livres the minot; in Maine and Anjou, across the frontier in the *grandes gabelles,* the monopoly price was fifty-six livres three sous to fifty-eight livres nineteen sous for the same minot. Salt smugglers, almost immune from arrest while in the duchy, could buy their stocks from the Brittany villagers at from three to four livres the minot and sell it across the border at prices ranging from thirty to thirty-six livres the minot. The supply of the smugglers involved hundreds of people. In 1784 Necker estimated that one Brittany parish alone furnished an average of three hundred minots of salt a month and that in the border areas of the *pays francs* some sixty thousand persons, of all social classes, shared in the profits of the illegal commerce. The trade itself was practiced by men, women, and children; by civilians, soldiers, and by the General Farms' own personnel. Even dogs were trained to carry light loads of salt into the *grandes gabelles* from Brittany. Most of these smugglers were poor peasants who turned desperately but irregularly to smuggling to supplement their meager livings. Some were hardened professionals enjoying the financial backing of respectable bourgeois, established salt merchants, even of nobles. Most salt smugglers operated individually or in small groups. Others moved in armed troops of from five to forty men, preceded by spies and scouts and led by

[34] *Répertoire universel de jurisprudence,* VII, 318-322.

famous chieftains.[35] Figures on the actual number engaged in salt smuggling are, of course, unobtainable, but
an indication may be found in the numbers of those
arrested, charged, or convicted of the crime. During the
first three years of the Lease Salzard (1780), an annual
average of 2,342 men, 896 women, and 201 children were
convicted of the crime of salt smuggling in the vicinity of
Laval and Angers, on the Brittany border. This figure
does not include the thousands apprehended but against
whom it was considered not worth while to press charges.
The value of illegal salt seized and of horses and wagons
confiscated amounted to a yearly average of three hundred and eighty thousand livres toward the end of the
old regime.[36]

Against the threat of salt smuggling, the General Farms
offered an elaborate defense based upon a rigid system of
surveillance and coercion backed by drastic penal codes.
The chief instrument of that surveillance was the General
Farms' own "milice financière," [37] the corps of *gardes
des fermes et des gabelles.* The corps of guards was not
exclusively used to police the *gabelles.* It served also as
an auxiliary force to prevent all kinds of smuggling, fraud,
and tax evasion affecting as well the *tabacs* and the
traites. But the apprehension of salt smugglers was one
of its major occupations.[38] Some consideration of the

[35] Calléry, "La Fraude des gabelles sous l'ancien régime; d'après
les mémoires de M. De Châteaubrun, 1730-1786, *France judicataire,*
Part one (1881-1882), pp. 387-393; Necker, *De l'administration,* II,
21-24.

[36] *Encyclopédie méthodique: Finances,* II, 337-338. In 1784 Necker
computed the yearly average of arrests in Laval and Angers at 2,300
men, 1,800 women, 6,600 children, 1,100 horses, and 50 wagons.
Many of the arrests were actually rearrests of women and children
repeating the same crime over and over. See Necker, *De l'administration,* II, 34, and also Mollien, *Mémoires d'un ministre,* I, 105.

[37] *Encyclopédie méthodique: Finances,* II, 352.

[38] The original seventeenth-century nucleus of the corps was the
brigades des gabelles. With the establishment of the General Farms
in 1681, various police forces employed in the *traites* were merged
with the brigades to form one body. The corps combated smuggling
in all forms, contrabanding through the international tariff frontiers
as well as smuggling of salt and tobacco. Although the details of
their service in the *traites* and *tabacs* differed from those of their

general organization of the force is necessary at this point. The corps of guards was the greatest aggregate of personnel in the General Farms. In 1768 the General Farmer E. M. Delahante reckoned the corps at 19,500 men. Of approximately 24,000 regular agents listed by Lavoisier at attached to the *gabelles, tabacs,* and *traites* in 1774, almost 21,200 were guards. Ten years later Necker placed the strength of the guards at 23,000.[39] The steady increase in number was a direct response to the growing volume of smuggling.

The corps was paramilitary in formation, discipline, and equipment. The primary tactical units were the brigades, small troops of from two to eight men, armed and uniformed like soldiers, led by a brigadier. There were two types of brigades, *sédentaires* and *ambulantes.* The former were assigned to the police of interior *greniers* and customs-houses. The latter were stationed along the fiscal frontiers, usually based on small villages commanding a segment of the exposed lines of the *grandes* or *petites gabelles* or of an internal tariff boundary. Most brigades were infantry, a few were mounted and some were crews of coastal, harbor, and river-patrol craft. Several brigades were usually grouped to form a division, commanded by a captain-general. In size the divisions ranged from 24 to 200 men. Almost the entire country was divided into strategic sectors called inspections, subdivided into posts. A division was entrusted with the duty of securing an inspection; a brigade was stationed at each post. In 1774 there were 352 divisions in the whole corps of guards, stationed in as many inspections throughout France.[40]

The guards were invested with extraordinary police

service in the *gabelles,* the general duties and functions were the same. Therefore, it was been felt best to limit the discussion of smuggling and the guards to their work in the salt monopolies.

[39] Delahante, *Une Famille de finance,* II, 96; Lavoisier, *Oeuvres,* VI, 155; Necker, *De l'administration,* I, 38, 106, II, 34.

[40] *Encyclopédie méthodique: Finance,* I, 144, 171, 330, II, 529-530; Pitre, *La Ferme-générale en Bourgogne,* pp. 150-152, 156, 161, 165, 171; Lavoisier, *Oeuvres,* VI, 155.

powers. They had an almost unlimited and arbitrary right of search over the premises, domiciles, and persons of all private subjects at any hour on any day without court warrant. They were empowered to stop and to search any vehicles on the roads and to seize any salt regarded as contraband, to impound wagons and horses used in the smuggling trade. The guards were authorized to draw up *procès-verbaux* [41] which, while legally only statements of evidence regarding a crime of salt smuggling, were in practice tantamount to arrest warrants. At all times the guards were permitted to use force of arms in pursuit of their duty and were entitled to whatever assistance the bailiffs and sergeants of the courts could render them; if necessary, the captains-general could command the services of the *maréchaussées* and the army to run down the salt smugglers.

Thus equipped, the brigades of the guards were permanently mustered for a kind of smoldering civil war endemic to the borders of the *grandes* and *petites gabelles*. They were maneuvered "to make war upon their compatriots; to defend Anjou, Maine, and Normandy against Brittany; to separate Languedoc from Guienne; to defend Picardy from Lorraine and Franche Comté; Bourbonnais and Berry from Auvergne and La Marche." Ambushes, skirmishes, and pursuits were not infrequent. Sometimes pitched battles were fought between bands of salt smugglers and the *brigades ambulantes*.[42]

However, such events were only spectacular episodes punctuating the routine of surveillance under which all procedures within the *greniers* were conducted. The *brigades sédentaires* systematically patrolled the *greniers* to

[41] *Encyclopédie méthodique: Finances,* I, 22-23, 58-59, III, 380-381, 513-515, 791-795. The detailed application of the rights of *visite* and *saisie* varied from place to place, but in substance were the same everywhere in the *gabelles* and indeed in the *tabacs* and *traites* as well. In the course of the eighteenth century the rights were made increasingly arbitrary and unrestricted.

[42] *Ibid.,* II, 317; Marion, *Histoire financière,* I, 19; Calléry, "La Fraude des gabelles sous l'ancien régime," *France judicataire,* Part One (1881-1882), pp. 401-403.

prevent legal salt from leaking from the General Farms' supply channels into the black markets. They guarded private salt licks in the interior. They scrutinized each step in the final assessment and sale of *sel d'impôt*. They watched the salt vendors and acted as spies among the population to ferret out evidences of fraud and tax evasion. By means of house-to-house searches [43] they attempted to frustrate the purchase of such illegal salt as might slip through the lines of the *ambulantes* on the frontiers.

Once apprehended the salt smuggler faced trial in the court of the *jurisdiction de gabelles*, before "judges who on their own accounts were free of the salt tax" [44] or in extraordinary administrative tribunals which increasingly in the late eighteenth century were used to speed the process of trying smuggling cases. [45]   The penal codes of the *gabelles* were ferocious in letter and spirit. The prototype was the ordinance of 1680. But the criminal provisions of this legislation were much amended in the course of the eighteenth century always in the direction of greater severity. Under the terms of these statutes fines for purchase or use of illegal salt were graduated from 200 to 1,000 livres. The punishments prescribed for active salt

[43] *Recueil de la Cour des Aides,* pp. 465-467 ; Necker, *De l'administration,* II, 34. Necker notes 3,700 seizures of illegal salt from private houses a year in Laval and Angers alone.

[44] Mollien, *Mémoires d'un ministre,* I, 65.

[45] *Encyclopédie méthodique: Finances,* I, 335-338. There were five of these tribunals, or *commissions* as they were called, established in the course of the eighteenth century: Valence, 1733; Saumur, 1742; Reims, 1762; Rouen, 1767; Paris, 1775 (which last dealt only in cases of tobacco smuggling). They dealt out a speedy, if summary, form of administrative justice unencumbered by traditional and costly procedures found in the ordinary courts. The regular magistrates detested the *commissions* as symbols of arbitrary statutory rule. Popular literature of invective against the General Farmers castigated them. But in fact their procedures were honest and cheap and their sentences were generally lighter than those inflicted by the ordinary courts. See *Recueil de la Cour des Aides,* pp. 13, 379, 516, and for an example of a popular broadside (Anonymous) *Sur les finances: Oeuvres posthumes de Pierre André,* pp. 33-39. This work was actually published in Limoges even though it bears London on the title page, and was most likely written at the request of the salt merchants of Limousin in the *pays rédimés.*

smuggling ranged from whipping, branding, and exile for men and women to consignment to the galleys for men. The bearing of arms against the guards, or even the use of fists to resist arrest, was regarded as a crime of rebellion against sovereign authority. Major cases of this sort were punishable by death on the wheel.[46] The antique brutality of the penal codes of the *gabelles* persisted to the end of the old regime. But, as Mollien noted, there was a great difference between the fierce letter of the law and the application. In the later eighteenth century the courts, especially the extraordinary tribunals, inclined toward an easy interpretation of the law. During the last two decades of the old regime the death penalty was seldom imposed and when pronounced was usually commuted to life imprisonment in the galleys. Branding and public whipping fell into disuse. In part, this moderate penal approach reflected the attitude of the Company of General Farmers. The tax-farmers were not humanitarians but administrators sensitive to the mounting costs of the struggle against smuggling. When the General Farms Director in Laval suggested the use of mounted guards rather than of footmen, the Company decided that the added expense of stabling the horses was not worth the slight increase in yield which might be expected from their use.[47] When the same Director induced the courts to revive public whipping of women in order to arrest their descent into crime, the Company counseled its abandonment. The Company rarely pressed charges against petty salt smugglers; the cost of collecting fines from poor peasants was not worth the effort. The late eighteenth-century Company of General Farmers sought to minimize rather than to eliminate smuggling and fraud. Rather than being the "sangsues du peuple" as popular imagination often envisioned them, the personnel of the

---

[46] *Encyclopédie méthodique: Finances,* I, 370, III, 442-443.

[47] Mollien, *Mémoires d'un ministre,* I, 65; Calléry, "La Fraude des gabelles sous l'ancien régime," *France judicataire,* Part One (1881-1882), pp. 396-397, 400

General Farms, from guards to General Farmers, frequently seemed to be "asleep on their pikes." [48] At the end of the old regime a spirit of moderation seemed to pervade the bureaucracy of the General Farms. But, if "the fisc humanized itself, it was merely as executioners who know when to stop the torture at just the point to spare the life." [49] Although Mollien discerned leniency in the administration of the laws, still he also noted that as late as 1783 over two hundred men were condemned to the galleys for active salt smuggling. In the same year, out of six thousand convicts in the hulks, over a third were condemned smugglers. [50]

THE COSTS OF OPERATION: *Gabelles*

It is impossible accurately to calculate the costs of operating the royal salt monopolies. No complete series of figures exists. But the chemist-financier Lavoisier, in his "Calculs des produits des différents baux de la ferme-générale," presented, probably for the information of the royal controller-general Turgot, certain statistics which, if taken only as approximations, may at least be indicative of the costs. [51] However, certain observations concerning these data must be made before they can be used.

The Lavoisier figures were not actual accounts of any one fiscal year of operation. Rather they were estimates of anticipated yields and costs based upon calculation of an annual average of yields and costs of the first four years (1768 through 1772) of the Lease Alaterre of 1768. It should be noted that the figures *do not* include tax-farming profits as an element of the costs of operating the General Farms.

For bookkeeping purposes two sorts of costs were identified. The first were called costs borne by the king, or

48 Delahante, *Une Famille de finance,* II, 102.
49 Mollien, *Mémoires d'un ministre,* I, 82.
50 *Ibid.,* I, 105.
51 Lavoisier, *Oeuvres,* VI, 149-153 and table p. 154. There is no reason to doubt the candor of Lavoisier's data, nor their accuracy within the limits of the use to which they were designed.

those costs directly assumed by the royal treasury.[52] Some of these costs were deducted out of gross yield independently of the annual lease price; others, the most important, were paid by means of advance deduction from annual lease price. The second order of costs were *frais de régie* or administrative costs borne directly by the Company of General Farmers. These costs were deducted from gross yield after the amount of the annual lease price had been discounted and before tax-farming profits could be reckoned. Together the king's costs and the costs borne by the Company reflect the cost of operating the tax-collecting machinery without regard to the specifically tax-farming relation that existed between the Company and the government.

According to Lavoisier, the annual average gross yield of the *grandes gabelles* (including the *pays de salines* of Lorraine and Franche Comté) for the first four years of the Lease Alaterre was 45,498,563 livres. Of this sum 2,143,994 livres was spent for the purchase of salt and 1,236,589 livres was spent to operate the system of salt supply. Rent on *greniers à sel* came to 208,678 livres while the *gages* of the *grenier* magistrates and the pay of the parish collectors came to 725,756 livres. These costs were all borne by the king advanced by the Company on which the tax-farmers received annual interest, a sum of 319,786 livres. For the *salines* of Lorraine and Franche Comté, the total of these costs came to 1,080,349 livres. In addition the king bore certain general costs of [53] the central administration of the General Farms. These costs

---

[52] By a strict definition no lease in the period 1726-1786 was completely a free tax-farming contract. There were always some costs borne by the king, and these had a tendency to mount across the century.

[53] The general costs borne by the king concerned the central administration of the General Farms. Included were many items of minor consequence. But the greatest and most important were the salaries of the General Farmers and the annual interest paid to them by the king on bondsmoney and other loans. These sums were considered as costs of operation and hence were prorated against each receipt on Lavoisier's data sheets.

were not specifically connected with the operation of the salt monopolies but were prorated against the yield of the *grandes gabelles* at 1,844,975 livres, thereby increasing the cost of operation on the books. The total costs borne by the king came to 7,560,119 livres.[54] As to costs assumed directly by the Company itself, an annual average of 3,283,655 livres was spent as *frais de régie* most of which was absorbed by the wages of *grandes gabelles* personnel and a prorated share of the cost of maintaining the corps of guards.[55] The total of all these costs came to 7⅛ percent of the gross yield. In other words it cost approximately one sou five deniers to sell one livre worth of salt in the *grandes gabelles*.

In the *petites gabelles* the costs borne by the king (purchase and handling of salt, rents on *greniers*, *gages*, and a prorated share of the general expenses) came to 2,942,102 livres out of a gross yield of 16,250,558 livres. Costs assumed by the Company (salaries and wages of guards prorated) came to 1,545,551 livres. In the *petites gabelles* 8½ percent of the gross yield was absorbed in costs of operation. Of every livre obtained by sale of salt, one sou eight deniers was expended as costs.

These costs do not seem excessive when the extreme complication and confusion of the *grandes* and *petites gabelles* are considered. In a purely administrative sense the Company of General Farmers and the permanent personnel of the General Farms managed the antiquated machinery of the salt monopolies as economically and as efficiently as the irrational construction of the mechanism would permit. But it must be reemphasized that none of these figures and percentages include the general tax-farming profits of the Company of General Farmers.

[54] No attempt has been made to recapitulate the details presented by Lavoisier. The figures presented serve only as representative of the kinds of costs borne by the king. Hence, the figures do not add up to the total of king's cost indicated in the text.

[55] Because the corps of guards was an auxiliary force serving the *tabacs* and *traites* as well as the *gabelles*, it was necessary to prorate each with a share of the cost of their maintenance.

5. The Royal Tobacco Monopoly and the Customs Duties: Tabacs and Traites

THE ROYAL TOBACCO MONOPOLY: Tabacs

Inclusion of the royal tobacco monopoly among the receipts of the General Farms did not occur until 1730.[1] But once established in the General Farms, the *tabacs* enjoyed

[1] The taxing of tobacco experienced many vicissitudes before it was stabilized by the General Farms in 1730. From 1629 to 1674 the tobacco tax was simply a high import duty. From 1674 to 1719 the tax was collected as part of the price of tobacco sold in a royal monopoly, rights to that monopoly being leased, in the form of a *ferme-générale*, to a variety of tax-farmers, including the General Farmers for a brief period between 1681 and 1697. In 1718 it was awarded to the Indies Company, which in 1719 abandoned the sales monopoly in favor of a tax in the form of a high import duty. By the end of 1720 the monopoly had been reestablished but let to a syndicate of tax-farmers distinct from the General Farmers and separate from the Indies Company. In 1723 the monopoly was reassigned to the Indies Company in return for the assumption by the Company of certain elements of the state debt. From 1723 to 1730 the Indies Company tried to manage the monopoly directly, without any real success. In 1730 the Indies Company leased its rights to the Company of General Farmers. Finally in 1747 the king resumed his proprietorship of the monopoly and leased it as a part of the General Farms. For all practical purposes the *tabacs* was a part of the General Farms from 1730 onwards. See Bonneau, *Les Législations françaises sur les tabacs sous l'ancien régime*, pp. 8-11, 25-29, 35-39, 42; Weber, *La Compagnie française des Indes*, pp. 304, 549; Moreau de Beaumont, *Mémoires concernant les impositions*, IV, 623-624, 636.

meteoric development among the indirect taxes.   In 1717 the *tabacs* was worth only 4,020,000 livres a year in lease price (the monopoly being farmed by a syndicate apart from the Company of General Farmers). In 1730 its value had increased to an annual lease price of only 7,500,-000 livres. But from 1730 to 1789 revenue from the *tabacs* more than quadrupled. In the Lease Mager of 1786 the *tabacs* was evaluated at a minimum of 27,000,-000 livres annual lease price. By 1789 revenue from the monopoly had increased to 30,500,000 livres. Credit for this great increase in the fiscal value of the tobacco monopoly is largely due the phenomenal growth of the tobacco habit among the eighteenth-century French. But important as a contributory factor was the efficient organization and management of the monopoly by the Company of General Farmers after 1730.[2]

The fundamental statute governing the tobacco monopoly was the royal declaration of August 1, 1721. By terms of this legislation the exclusive right to import and to sell tobacco, at wholesale and retail, was reserved to the king. It was this right which the Company of General Farmers leased as part of the General Farms. As a corollary, the cultivation of tobacco in any form was prohibited within the territories of the kingdom. The Company also leased the right to enforce this regulation. The royal monopoly applied everywhere in France except for a group of privileged provinces (Flanders, Artois, Hainault, Cambrésis, Alsace, and Franche Comté) along the northern and northeastern frontiers of the kingdom. In these places cultivation of tobacco was permitted except along a strip of territory bordering upon the monopoly

[2] Moreau de Beaumont, *Mémoires concernant les impositions,* IV, 614-615; Clamageran, *Histoire de l'impôt,* III, 216-217, 254-263, 402, 444; Marion, *Histoire financière,* I, 31; Braesch, *Finances et monnaie révolutionnaires,* II, 72; Stroum, *Les Finances,* I, 364-368. The framework of the administration of the *tabacs* was so firmly laid in the post 1730 period that its primary features survived the Revolution and were incorporated into the nineteenth-century state tobacco monopoly, regulations governing which, even in details of language, were directly descendant from the eighteenth-century General Farms.

area in which the General Farms had rights of supervision. The sale of tobacco within the privileged provinces was also free and untaxed.[3] Thus the tobacco monopoly, in contrast to the salt monopolies, was operative throughout almost the entire extent of France; the exceptions were neatly grouped rather than scattered as enclaves within the monopoly area.[4]

The declaration of 1721 also established the base prices, wholesale and retail, for the various grades of tobacco sold by the monopoly. These prices, with only minor changes due to regrading of tobacco types, remained in force to 1789, subject, of course, to the *sous pour livre* surtaxes. The base prices were uniform throughout the monopoly area. The *tabacs* displayed none of the extreme legal price differentials characteristic of the *gabelles*.[5] Further, unlike the fixed and rigid monopoly prices of salt, the base tobacco prices of the declaration of 1721 were intended only as legal maxima. The General

---

[3] Moreau de Beaumont, *Mémoires concernant les impositions,* IV, 624-632. In the course of the late eighteenth century several minor additions were made to the privileged provinces. These were certain places in the generality of Metz, the *pays de* Gex, and the city and territory of Bayonne. See also Necker, *De l'administration,* I, 59.

[4] The General Farmers rounded out the monopoly area by leasing monopoly rights to the import and sale of tobacco in the Papal territory of Avignon. See Marion, *Histoire financière,* I, 31.

[5] In 1758 the one outstanding price irregularity was eliminated. Prior to that date the price of tobacco was higher in certain parts of the south of France than in the north due to the existence of different standards of weight employed in the different regions. The declaration of 1721 indicated the maximum price per pound (*la livre*) but neglected to distinguish between those pounds based upon the *table* and those based upon the *marc*. When the *table* was used as a standard, then the pound contained fourteen ounces; when the *marc* was used, then the pound contained sixteen ounces. The *table* was the standard in the generalities of Toulouse, Montauban, Montpellier, and *pays de* Roussillon. In these places the General Farms sold tobacco at fourteen ounces the pound. Elsewhere the General Farms sold on the basis of the *marc,* sixteen ounces to the pound. Although the price per pound was uniform, in effect those regions based on the *table* paid about twelve percent higher prices than those based on the *marc.* This anomalous situation was eliminated in 1758 when for purposes of the tobacco monopoly the *marc* was declared to be the legal standard for all of France. See Bonneau, *Les Législations,* pp. 95-96.

Farms was at liberty to sell below the base price for administrative reasons. Consequently, the tobacco monopoly was much more flexible than the salt monopolies. It was more responsive to consumer demand and could be conducted more nearly like a commercial enterprise.

In the post-1730 period tobacco for the royal monopoly came largely from British America, although small amounts from Brazil and Spain were imported by way of Dutch middlemen. Up to the War of American Independence (1775-1783) Virginia and Maryland dried-leaf tobacco was purchased from colonial factors in England by agents of the General Farms. During the war the General Farms purchased directly in the tobacco producing states and later, in 1785, signed with Robert Morris a contract granting him the exclusive right to supply the monopoly with all its American tobacco. The contract was renewed in 1787 to the chagrin of commercial interests on both sides of the Atlantic interested in developing a free Franco-American trading market.[6]

Tobacco arrived in France by ship and was immediately sent to one of the royal tobacco factories operated on lease by the General Farms. These were located in the cities of Arles, Cette, Le Havre, Marseilles, Morlaix, Paris, Tonniens, Toulouse, Nancy, and Valenciennes. There the tobacco was graded, processed, and packed for distribution to the wholesale and retail outlets of the organization. Private freighters hauled the tobacco to general offices, large warehouses serving as the financial and adminis-

---

[6] It is not the purpose of this study to investigate the commercial and political transactions of the Company of General Farmers in the international markets. The reader is referred to the studies of Nussbaum, "American Tobacco and French Politics," *Political Science Quarterly,* XL (1925), 497-516, and "The Revolutionary Vergennes and Lafayette versus the Farmers-General," *The Journal of Modern History,* III (1931), 592-604; "Lafayette's Attack upon the Tobacco Farm in the American Committee of 1786," by the same author, is printed on pp. 605-613 of the same issue. For further information, consult Mathiez, "Lafayette et le commerce franco-américaine à la veille de la révolution," *Annales historiques de la révolution française, nouvelle série,* III (1926), 474-484, and Gottschalk, *Lafayette between the American and the French Revolution,* pp. 222-237.

trative headquarters of areas roughly equivalent to the royal generalities. The warehouse was in the charge of a General Farms agent called a general manager. On each general office was dependent a varying number of stores, secondary warehouses each in the charge of a manager assisted by a large staff of clerks, warehousemen, and guards. In 1774 there were 453 such stores serving as supply centers to the ultimate retail outlets, the tobacconists' shops scattered, more or less thickly according to need, throughout the sales territory of the store. The retail shops were managed by tobacconists as private enterprises, licensed, regulated, and supervised by the General Farms. The licenses were issued by the store's manager who was responsible to his superiors for the conduct of the tobacconists in his jurisdiction. The enormous increase in the tobacco trade from 1740 required a constantly expanding number of retail outlets. By 1785 Necker estimated that there were as many as ten thousand tobacconists in France, most of whose businesses hardly exceeded two hundred livres a year gross.[7]

The system of tobacco supply was as tightly controlled by bureaucratic regulations, accounting techniques, and constant inspections as was the salt supply of the *grandes* and *petites gabelles*. But the organization as a whole was managed more as a marketing enterprise. The General Farms used economic incentives, such as bonuses, to stimulate initiative among its employees in creating a grow-

[7] Moreau de Beaumont, *Mémoires concernant les impositions*, IV, 642-645; Lavoisier, *Oeuvres*, VI, 155, 657; *Encyclopédie méthodique. Finances*, II, 56, 109, III, 618, 633; Pitre, *La Ferme-générale en Bourgogne*, pp. 129, 138; Necker, *De l'administration*, I, 108. The Valenciennes and Nancy tobacco factories were located in the privileged provinces. They purchased tobacco from the free cultivators of the region, sending it into the monopoly area for sale. The Valenciennes Tobacco Factory also served as an import center for Brazilian and Spanish tobacco coming from the Netherlands. In the *grandes* and *petites gabelles* the tobacco store (*entrepôt*) and the *grenier à sel* were nearly always located near to each other and sometimes were in the same building. Frequently the *grenier* receiver served also as the manager (*entreposeur*) of the tobacco store. They had the same bureaucratic rank in the General Farms.

ing market for tobacco. Supply and price responses in the channels of distribution of the *tabacs* were governed, more than in the *gabelles*, by the condition of a supply schedule reflecting market demand. Despite the apparently limitless character of the effective demand for tobacco, the General Farms had no guaranteed market for tobacco in the same sense as it enjoyed a fixed market for salt in the *grandes gabelles*. For, although legally the sale of tobacco was conducted in a closed monopoly market, actually the General Farms faced serious competition in many parts of France. This was due to the prevalence of tobacco smuggling which from at least the mid-eighteenth century mounted in a volume proportionate to the increase in monopoly price due to the imposition of the *sous pour livre* surtaxes.[8]

As a first line of defense against this threat the General Farms depended upon a system of surveillance enforced by the corps of guards which differed in no significant way from the police of the *gabelles*.[9] But such action could do no more than minimize the penetration of illicit tobacco into the market. Therefore, the General Farms offensively entered into the price competition with the smuggler. In areas in which the black-market sale of tobacco was most prevalent (along the borders of

[8] Moreau de Beaumont, *Mémoires concernant les impositions,* IV, 645-647. In the eighteenth century a veritable smuggling population existed along the international frontiers. By mid-century tobacco was the most valuable single item in the smugglers' stock in trade. See Funck-Brentano, *Mandrin,* pp. 43-46.

[9] Moreau de Beaumont, *Mémoires concernant les impositions,* IV, 651-674; *Encyclopédie méthodique: Finances,* II, 365-367, III, 623-627. Brigades of guards patrolled the frontiers; others, based on the tobacco stores, *greniers,* and customs houses, policed the interior. They were armed with arbitrary rights of *visite* and *saisie* similar to those applying to the *gabelles*. Penal codes in the *tabacs* were modeled directly upon the codes in use in the *gabelles*. There were no special *tabacs* courts. In the *grandes* and *petites gabelles* the *jurisdictions des gabelles* heard tobacco cases; in the rest of the country the *juges des traites* had competence over tobacco litigation. But these courts all tended to be superseded by the intendants and by the special tax *commissions.*

Savoy and Spain, the privileged French provinces, and in the vicinity of seaports) the General Farms adjusted retail prices downward in order to frustrate the smuggler and fraudulently inclined retailers and to make less economically attractive the risks which the consumer assumed whenever he purchased the contraband product. In the same manner the Company sold cheap grades of tobacco at extremely low prices in army canteens in order to discourage the troops from entering the black market.[10]

But these particular measures only reflected the general commercial policy of the General Farms in its management of the tobacco monopoly. From 1730 to the end of the old regime the wholesale prices which the General Farms charged the retailers and the retail prices at which the tobacconists were permitted to sell their tobacco to the public were always considerably below the legal maxima allowed by the declaration of 1721. Moreover the Company strenuously objected to any government-enforced increases in the base price and tax rates. It resisted the imposition of the four *sous pour livre* surtax on tobacco ordered by the government in 1758. The Company was apprehensive that a rise in price would curtail consumption of legal tobacco and stimulate the use of smuggled tobacco. The tax-farmers felt that the added cost of combating such fraud would outweigh any possible gain from heightened prices. When the government proved adamant, the Company absorbed one half of the increase itself and attempted to force the tobacconists to absorb the rest without a rise in retail prices. The one *sou pour livre* surtax levied in 1760 and 1763 and the two *sous pour livre* surtax imposed in 1771 were not applied to the *tabacs* mainly because of the objections of the Company of General Farmers. When in 1781 the final two *sous pour livre* surtax was imposed upon the *tabacs* as well as upon all other taxes, the Company again attempted to hold the wholesale and retail

[10] Bonneau, *Les Législations,* pp. 96-98; Moreau de Beaumont, *Mémoires concernant les impositions,* IV, 655-656.

prices down by absorbing part of the increase itself and forcing the tobacconists to accept only a moderate increase in retail prices.[11]

Thus the *tabacs* was the least surtaxed of all *perceptions*, and the Company of General Farmers did not take full advantage of its rights under the law. To take but one example from the late eighteenth-century price list of the Company, the legal maximum price for a pound of common tobacco prepared as snuff was, after 1781, nine livres sixteen sous, all surtaxes included. Yet in the two years prior to 1789 the wholesale price for this grade of tobacco was three livres twelve sous, while the price the Company permitted the tobacconists to charge the consumer was four livres. Under this low price policy consumption mounted and revenue increased. But at the same time, the policy involved the Company in a bitter dispute with the retailers whose profits it curtailed.[12]

The tobacconists were the weakest elements in the General Farms defense against fraud and smuggling. They were the natural allies of the tobacco smugglers. The most common method of defrauding the General Farms was for the retailer to purchase smuggled tobacco at low prices, mix it with the legal article, and sell the adulterated result at monopoly prices. As a matter of policy the General Farms suspected all tobacconists and attempted to counter their chicaneries by enforcing a comprehensive system of shop inspections and by packaging its own tobacco in such a way as to make adulteration difficult for the retailer to accomplish and simple for the guard to detect.

When the General Farmers took over the administration of the tobacco monopoly two sorts of processed tobacco were sold. The first, selling at the rate of about four million pounds a year, was in the form of a large twist, wrapped and interlaced by identifying string in such

[11] Lavoisier, *Oeuvres*, VI, 138, 584-587; Delahante, *Une Famille de finance*, I, 321-322.
[12] Lavoisier, *Oeuvres*, VI, 637.

a manner that the string must be consumed with the tobacco. Such a twist was called a *carotte*, and to use it the consumer must either shred or powder the tobacco himself by means of a pocket rasp or *râpe*. The second sort of tobacco, selling at the rate of only about one million pounds a year, was *tabac râpé*, snuff prepared at the royal tobacco factory of Morlaix. It was obvious that snuff was ideal for the tobacconist bent upon adulterating legal tobacco with the contraband commodity. Moreover, snuff, being prone to suffer considerable loss of weight through dehumidification, was expensive to process and difficult to transport and to store. Consequently, the Company's first act upon coming into possession of the monopoly was to eliminate the preparation and sale of snuff, except for a luxury grade made at Morlaix for sale in Paris and other important cities. It was ruled that only *carottes* would be offered for general sale by the tobacco monopoly.[13] This policy seemed justified by the steady increase in weight of twists sold, the figure reaching thirteen million pounds in 1742, and by the relative ease with which smuggling was brought under control. It became traditional in the General Farms to concur in the proposition that "hors la carotte, hors la ficelle, il n'y avait point de salut." [14]

However, the taste for cheap snuff in the mid-eighteenth century spread among the poorer classes. Increasingly, the customers, finding the bulky *carottes* inconvenient, demanded prepared snuff from the tobacconists. The retailers obliged by setting up grating mills in which they ground up the General Farms *carottes* for sale as snuff. In order to accommodate the trend, the General Farms instituted a licensing system under which the tobacconist, for a nominal fee, was permitted to manufacture snuff from monopoly tobacco and to pass on the service charges in the form of a slight increase in retail price.

[13] *Encyclopédie méthodique: Finances*, III, 629.
[14] Delahante, *Une Famille de finance*, I, 315-318.

No great difficulty was experienced with this system until 1758, when the Company, anxious to offset the effects of the two *sous pour livre* surtax of that year, ordered the tobacconists to accept a 10 percent increase in wholesale prices without corresponding augmentation of retail prices. It was soon noted that, while the number of applications for new snuff-making licenses leaped upward, the amount of wholesale tobacco sold tended to decrease. Concurrently, an increase in smuggling activity was observed. The tobacconists were offsetting the new wholesale price rise by purchasing equivalent supplies on the black market for purposes of adulteration.

The Company of General Farmers then cautiously reversed its policy concerning snuff. The Company commenced manufacture of its own snuff in the tobacco factories and to withdraw twist tobacco from sale. The snuff-making licenses were rescinded, tighter inspection and control techniques were devised for the supervision of the retailers, and General Farms snuff was declared the only legal *tabac râpé* to be sold in France.

This new policy was put into effect gradually in limited areas. The Company needed time to experiment with mass snuff-making and to develop new packaging techniques. Moreover, the Company wished to allow the tobacconists time to liquidate their investments in snuff-making machinery. The Company was aware that the tobacconists, frustrated in a profitable if illegal enterprise, could stir up trouble for the General Farms among the populace and even among the powerful Parlements and *Cours des Aides*. It was not until 1782, a year after the imposition of the final *sous pour livre* surtaxes, the impact of which the Company expected the tobacconists to bear, that the General Farms canceled all surviving snuff-making licenses and made it a nation-wide policy to prepare and to allow the sale of only its own snuff.[15]

The response of the tobacconists to these developments

[15] *Encyclopédie méthodique: Finances,* III, 630-632; Delahante, *Une Famille de finance,* I, 319-348.

was anguished. They obtained injunctions from provincial Parlements and *cours des aides* prohibiting the sale of General Farms prepared snuff and launched a fierce propaganda campaign against the tax-farmers. The Company was accused of adulterating its own tobacco and of selling tobacco of inferior quality. It was charged with perpetrating fraud by introducing excessive moisture into its snuff during manufacture. The retailers contended that they were forced to buy at the warehouses, wet tobacco which lost weight through dehumidification, entailing a loss to them. Furthermore, it was asserted, the excessive moisture set up a fermentation in the snuff that spoiled the flavor and made it unfit for human consumption.[16] In province after province the courts, after 1782, forbade the General Farms to sell its own snuff and granted permission to the retailers to resume snuff-making activities. These judicial acts clearly exceeded the established competences of the courts to deal with General Farms affairs, but the royal government, itself so deeply embroiled with the Parlements on other counts that it could not risk public defense of so unpopular an institution as the General Farms, refused to silence the magistrates. Acrimonious suits followed in which the General Farms was forced to defend itself.

In the courts the Company met the charges head on. It granted that during the American War it had been hard pressed to maintain the quality of its tobacco imports; however, it pointed out that since the termination of hostilities it had adopted the practice of removing all stems and damaged leaves from its raw material before the manufacture of snuff, thus producing a high grade of snuff at considerable loss to itself. The Company conceded that in 1774 two chemists, working under government orders, had found the snuff prepared at the Morlaix tobacco factory to be excessively moist and inferior in quality; however, the Company argued, steps to correct the situation had immediately been taken under the

16 Necker, *De l'administration*, II, 65-66.

direction of the famous scientist Lavoisier [17] and the unfavorable conditions had not existed since 1780. Furthermore, the Company showed that the preparation of snuff
required several extra stages of humidification, with the
result that inevitably the percentage of water was higher
in a pound of snuff than in a pound of twist tobacco. In
recognition of this fact, the Company demonstrated that
since the amount of water added was one seventeenth the
weight of any given quantity of snuff, it charged the tobacconists for only sixteen of every seventeen ounces purchased.[18]   Finally, the Company argued that to permit the
retailers to continue to prepare their own snuff would be
to give judicial sanction to the crime of tobacco smuggling.

Gradually, most of the courts found in the favor of the
General Farms. By 1787 the courts of Grenoble, Metz,
Dijon, Aix, Pau, Bordeaux, Montauban, and Clermont-
Ferrand had dismissed the charges and ordered the tobacconists to obey the regulations issued by the General
Farms. The Parlement of Rouen did not yield so easily.[19]
Within its jurisdiction General Farms snuff was never
fully sanctioned, although in practice the Company went
ahead with its sale without undue interference. But the
Parlement of Rennes, heavily engaged in the closing years
of the old regime with the royal government over many
political and financial issues, proved thoroughly intract-
able. In a series of injunctions the Parlement forbade
the General Farms either to make or to sell snuff in Brittany and offered its protection to any retailer wishing
to prepare his own snuff for sale. The Parlement publicly
accepted the claim that the General Farms snuff was deleterious to human health.

At this juncture the government asserted its authority
and quashed the Parlement's injunctions. The Parlement
retaliated by refusing to recognize the authority of the

[17] McKie, *Antoine Lavoisier,* pp. 387-388.
[18] Lavoisier, *Oeuvres,* VI, 637-641.
[19] *Ibid.,* VI, 644-653. Extracts from the registers of the various
courts concerned are here published.

council in the matter. Throughout Brittany feeling ran high; in the towns mobs rioted in favor of the tobacconists and demonstrated against the tax-farmers. In the face of such truculent opposition the Company retreated. After 1787 the Company advised the government to press the matter no further. Content with its victory elsewhere in France, the General Farms made no further effort to force its prepared snuff upon the Brittany tobacconists but continued to supply them with old-fashioned *carottes*. The Brittany receipts for *tabacs* were allowed to dwindle, while the retailers and the smugglers prospered under the protection of the Parlement of Rennes.[20]

THE COSTS OF OPERATION: *Tabacs*

The costs of operations in the tobacco monopoly were higher than in the salt monopolies. According to the figures of Lavoisier, the cost of selling at wholesale an average annual gross of 37,608,305 livres worth of tobacco during the first four years of the Lease Alaterre (1768-1772) was two and one eleventh sous of each livre, or $10\,^1/_{10}$ percent, not including a prorated share of the tax-farming profits. This percentage is in contrast to the 7⅛ percent for the *grandes gabelles* and the 8½ percent for the *petites gabelles*. The high cost of operations in the *tabacs* relative to the costs of the *gabelles* is somewhat surprising in view of the comparatively simple structure of the tobacco monopoly. However, it seems to have resulted primarily from two factors. First, the cost of purchasing, transporting, and processing tobacco was much greater than analogous costs of the salt supply. During the period in question 5,410,-000 livres a year was spent on raw materials, 866,895 livres on processing (including 599,836 livres in wages to factory workers), and 1,442,402 livres was spent on transporting and handling tobacco within the distribution system inside France. In addition, 71,872 livres was expended for rent of buildings, and 94,111 livres

[20] Delahante, *Une Famille de finance,* I, 355-379.

went for repairs and other smaller items. All of these costs were borne by the king but were advanced before actual receipt by the Company of General Farmers at 5 percent per year, resulting in a further 394,204 livres interest charge considered as a cost of operation. Furthermore, the *tabacs* was prorated with 1,525,325 livres of the general expenses of the General Farms, handled as king's costs. The second factor accounting for the relative high cost of operating the tobacco monopoly was the cost of the prorated share of the *tabacs* for maintaining the corps of guards. During the period in question Lavoisier listed the *frais de régie*, costs assumed directly by the Company, consisting almost entirely of wages and salaries to General Farms personnel, of which the guards were the bulk, as 3,779,868 livres.[21] This was proportionately as high a share as that of the *gabelles*. It is impossible to say whether this accurately reflected the state of tobacco smuggling. It may have been merely a bookkeeping convention to debit the account of the *tabacs* with such a share, whether or not smuggling was as important in the *tabacs* as in the *gabelles*. In view of the Company's attitude toward the snuff question, it might seem that smuggling was as serious, but less publicized, a threat to the *tabacs* as it was to the *gabelles*. If so, then it would appear that the Company's management of the *tabacs* was efficient within the limits possible under old-regime conditions.

THE CUSTOMS DUTIES: *Traites*

In terms of revenue, the French eighteenth-century customs system was the least valuable element of the General Farms. In the Lease Carlier of 1726 the receipt of the *traites* was leased for 9,500,000 livres per year. By 1761 this figure had been raised to only 13,400,000 livres annually for the duration of the Seven Years War (1756-1763) and to 14,032,000 livres a year once peace were

[21] Lavoisier, *Oeuvres*, VI, 151, and table p. 154.

reestablished. Thirteen years later the *traites* had increased to only 16,138,400 livres in the Lease David of 1774.

However, the foregoing figures do not reveal the full fiscal value of the customs duties. Up to 1780 the various duties levied upon commerce between France proper and her overseas colonies, known collectively as the *domaines d'Occident*, was maintained as an accounting category separate from the *traites*. The *domaines d'Occident* did not become a part of the General Farms until 1732 and was not considered as an element of the *traites* for accounting purposes until 1780, although during that period the colonial duties were collected by the administration of the *traites*. In 1732 the *domaines d'Occident* leased for 500,000 livres a year. In 1761 the General Farmers offered 300,000 livres a year for these duties for the duration of the Seven Years War and 1,139,000 livres as soon as peace could be restored. The loss of Canada did not adversely affect the yield of the *domaines d'Occident;* in the Lease David of 1774 it was evaluated at an annual lease price of 3,257,817 livres,[22] a measure principally of the great and growing worth of the commerce between France and her West Indian possessions.

During the reorganization of 1780 the receipt of the *domaines d'Occident* was joined to the *traites*, and when the *traites* were placed in *régie* in 1783, the *domaines d'Occident* were included. In 1784 the *régie* of the *traites* thus constituted yielded the government a gross receipt of 22,000,000 livres subject to high deduction for costs of operation; by 1788, this figure had been raised to 28,400,-000 livres, also subject to high costs entirely borne by the government.[23]

The various kinds of customs duties comprising the *traites* may be grouped roughly into three classifications:

[22] *Ibid.,* VI, 181; Clamageran, *Histoire de l'impôt,* III, 254, 363, 402.

[23] Necker, *De l'administration,* II, 102; Braesch, *Finances et monnaie révolutionnaires,* II, 72.

the primary *traites,* or general, external import-export tariffs by means of which trade between France and foreign countries and between France and her colonies was controlled; the secondary *traites,* or local, internal duties on goods in trade moving from area to area within France; the tertiary *traites,* or incidental, minor river, bridge, and road tolls, largely of medieval origin, and other minor circulation taxes. At the end of the old regime these three elements constituted a maze of trade barriers which to Necker seemed "monstrous to the eyes of reason" and intelligible to "scarcely one or two men in each generation." [24]

THE PRIMARY *Traites*

From the point of view of international commerce, eighteenth-century France was almost a fully matured customs union protected by high tariffs, or primary *traites,* of mercantilist complexion.   The base rates of the general tariffs of 1667 and 1699 remained in force throughout the eighteenth century, except as modified in specific cases or in favor of particular countries through bilateral trade agreements.   General merchandise was subject to a flat 5 percent ad valorem duty; duties on items specified on the enumerated lists ranged from high to prohibitive. The primary *traites* were concerned only with the import-export commerce of France with foreign nations.   They were collected only along the international frontiers.[25]

There were certain exceptions to the uniform applicability of the general tariffs.   The tariffs of 1667 and 1699 did not apply to trade passing between the *provinces à l'instar étranger effectif* [26] and foreign ports.   Nor did they apply to numerous cities designated as free ports.

By the end of the eighteenth century the *provinces étrangers effectifs* were: Alsace, Lorraine, Trois Evechés, the *pays de* Gex, and, in part, Franche Comté.   Trade

---

[24] Necker, *De l'administration,* II, 100-102.
[25] Cole, *French mercantilism, 1683-1700,* pp. 14-18.
[26] See map, facing page 83.

between these provinces and foreign lands was free of all general tariffs; trade between them and the rest of France was subject to the duties of the tariff of 1699, save for a limited number of goods which could be proved to have been fabricated in either Alsace or Lorraine.[27]

By the end of the old regime, the free ports were: Marseilles, Dunquerque, Bayonne (with Saint-Jean de Luz and the *pays de* Labour), and L'Orient, which became a free port in 1784. These ports enjoyed relative degrees of freedom from the general tariffs only; goods entering their harbors were subject to a variety of local customs duties and transit fees. Goods passing between them and the rest of France were subject to the duties of the general tariffs.[28]

Numerous accessory duties and taxes were closely associated with the general tariffs. Chief among these was the *domaines d'Occident,* the most important element of which was a 3½ percent ad valorem duty on all colonial goods imported into France for consumption in the country. This duty was superimposed upon the general and local tariffs. Colonial products which were reexported from France were given privileges of entrepot. Similarly, certain merchandise, important to the life of the colonies exported from France was relieved of general export duties. Among the accessories to the general tariffs were also the *droit de fret,* a tax on all ships of foreign registry entering France or engaged in French trade; the *droits d'indult,* a 5 percent ad valorem duty on goods from the Far Eastern colonies; the *droits d'abord et consommation,* special import duties on fish from foreign fisheries; and other special duties on oil, soap,

---

[27] *Recueil alphabétique des droits de traites uniformes,* I, cxxvi. Franche Comté occupied an ambiguous position; it was considered to be *étranger effectif* for most but not all goods taxable under the tariff of 1699. The *pays de* Labour was actually a dependency of the free port of Bayonne rather than a true *étranger effectif.* See also Moreau de Beaumont, *Mémoires concernant les impositions,* III, 559.

[28] *Recueil alphabétique des droits de traites uniformes,* I, cxxvi; *Encyclopédie méthodique: Finances,* II, 725.

iron, tin, calicoes, and several other articles.   None of these accessory duties was of much fiscal significance.[29] The primary *traites* contributed the greatest share to the fiscal yield of the receipt of the *traites*.   Of the 22,000,000 livres calculated as the gross revenue from the *régie* of the *traites* in 1784, eleven to twelve million derived from the general tariffs and accessories.[30]

THE SECONDARY *Traites*

Although eighteenth-century France faced the external commercial world with a unified system of general tariffs, internally the kingdom was merely an agglomeration of slowly amalgamating separate customs areas.   The various local tariffs which separated one internal French region from another formed the secondary *traites,* which existed in great profusion and confusion.   Fundamental to them was the distinction between the *provinces des cinq grosses fermes* and the *provinces reputées étrangères.*[31] At the end of the eighteenth century the *provinces des cinq grosses fermes* were: Ile de France, Normandy, Orléannais, Touraine, Poitou, L'Aunis, Maine, Beaujolais, Bresses, Dombes, and Boulonnais.   The area which these provinces covered was known as the *Entendue;* its outer limits roughly but not completely coincided with those of the *pays de grandes gabelles*.   Within the confines of the *Entendue* goods in trade circulated unrestrained by secondary or local tariffs.   The *Entendue* was an island of relatively free trade in the center of France from which had been eliminated, in 1664, four import and five export tariffs totaling nineteen different sets of duties. However, all trade between the *Entendue* and the *provinces reputées étrangères* was subject to the duties of the tariff of 1664.   These duties were levied upon practically

---

[29] *Recueil alphabétique des droits de traites uniformes,* I, xxix-xxxv, xlv-liii, lxiv-lxvi; Moreau de Beaumont, *Mémoires concernant les impositions,* II, 572-578.

[30] Necker, *De l'administration,* II, 102.

[31] See map, facing page 83.

all goods in transit and not upon an enumerated list such
as applied in the general tariffs. The base rates of the
tariff of 1664 were modified and permanently fixed by the
ordinance of 1687; they remained stable throughout the
eighteenth century, although subject to the *sous pour
livres* surtaxes.[32]

The designation *provinces reputées étrangères* was
meaningful only to describe the relationship of those
provinces with the *Entendue* of the *cinq grosses fermes*.
Commerce between the *Entendue* and the *provinces
reputées étrangères* (which comprised all of France except
the *cinq grosses fermes* and the *provinces étrangers
effectifs*) as a whole was subject to the duties of the tariff
of 1664; commercial relations within and among the
provinces reputées étrangères [33] were governed by at least
twenty-one separate and distinct local tariffs. Most of
these local tariffs covered small areas, and only two were
of any particular fiscal importance, the *douane de Lyons*
and the *douane de Valence*.

The *douane de Lyons* produced some 120,000 livres
annually by means of a customs system which levied
duties at places far distant from Lyons, the city of its
inception. At the end of the eighteenth century the
customs houses charged with the collection of the *douane
de Lyons* were scattered throughout Lyonnais, Dauphiny,
Provence, Languedoc, Foix, and Avignon. No unified
schedule of rates was ever published; each customs house
collected a slightly different set of duties upon a slightly

32 *Recueil alphabétique des droits de traites uniformes,* I, cxxv.
Beaujolais, Bresses, Dombes, and Boulonnais were eighteenth-century
additions to the original core of the *cinq grosses fermes*. See also
Elzinger, "Le Tarif de Colbert de 1664 et celui de 1667 et leur signifi-
cation," *Economisch-Historisch-Jaarboek,* XV (1929), 237; Moreau
de Beaumont, *Mémoires concernant les impositions,* III, 512-514.
33 *Recueil alphabétique des droits de traites uniformes,* I, cxxvi.
The *provinces reputées étrangères* were: Angoumois, Artois, Au-
vergne, Barre-Navarre, Béarn, Brittany, Cambrésis, Comté de Foix,
Dauphiny, Flanders, Forez, Franche Comté (in part), Gascogne,
Guienne, Hainault, Isles de Rhé et d'Oléron, Languedoc, Rouerque,
Saintonge, and Viverais.

different list of merchandise. In general, French goods in transit through the area paid an average of 2½ percent ad valorem; foreign goods paid 5 percent.[34]

The *douane de Valence* produced 500,000 livres a year gross out of a customs system even more confused than that of the *douane de Lyons*. The *douane de Valence* covered an ill-defined but extensive region having at its center Dauphiny, Forez, and Bresse (in part). Throughout this region, which overlapped the territory of the *douane de Lyons,* a customs schedule unique among old-regime tariffs was applied. General merchandise was arbitrarily classified into nineteen categories, according to estimated value and weight. To take one example from among many, equal weight of cloth of gold and ostrich feathers was deemed to have equal value and was taxed equally; mirrors, carpets, and tapestries were grouped with drugs and dyes.[35]

The ossified secondary *traites* produced low yields at high costs, interminable law suits, and an inordinate amount of petty smuggling. But in the late eighteenth century they were more of an irritant than a positive burden upon internal trade. Their rates remained fixed at levels appropriate to the mid-seventeenth century; even the ten *sous pour livre* surtaxes did not elevate them excessively. Moreover, in the latter part of the eighteenth century the government increasingly relieved specific goods from the duties of the secondary *traites.* Just prior to the Revolution such piecemeal government action had created a practically free internal market for such basic goods as steel, textiles, coffee, paper, soap, and sugar. Thus, in 1784 the entire collection of secondary traites produced a gross yield of not more that 5,000,000 livres.[36]

[34] *Encyclopédie méthodique: Finances,* I, 488, 635, 646, III, 305, 674, 683, 728; *Recueil alphabétique des droits de traites uniformes,* I, xvi-xx.

[35] *Recueil alphabétique des droits de traites uniformes,* I, xxv; *Encyclopédie méthodique: Finances,* III, 749-757.

[36] *Recueil alphabétique des droits de traites uniformes,* I, x-xiii, IV, 240-252, 253-256. Goods relieved of payment of the secondary *traites*

THE TERTIARY *Traites*

Any attempt to define or to describe the content of the tertiary *traites* is foreordained to incompleteness. Important among them were the countless *péages* or bridge, river, and road tolls which still existed to impede commercial traffic. Juridically the royal *péages* belonged to the *domaines,* but most were collected as taxes supplementary to the secondary *traites.* Not all *péages* were royal; hundreds were still possessed by lords, religious communities, and other corporations. Some of these were collected by the General Farms, which paid their owners a part of the yield; some were still collected by the owners themselves. There were no sharp lines drawn between the various kinds of *péages.* Many ambiguous situations existed which were profitable only to the lawyers who argued the endless law suits that resulted from conflicts between the General Farms and the proprietors. In 1724 a royal commission appointed to verify all rights of *péages* reported the existence of at least 3,120 such local transit fees. In 1779 another royal commission was appointed to liquidate all existing *péages;* yet in 1789 at least 1,600 were still being collected, either by the General Farms or by other public and private agencies.[37]

In addition to the *péages,* the tertiary *traites* also contained numerous taxes which juridically were not customs duties but which were collected by the administration of the *traites.* Thus the *droits de convoi* and the *traites de Charente* were circulation taxes on salt entering the *pays rédimés,* but they were accounted for as if they were

---

were placed on what was called the *droits uniformes* list. An item so classified paid special duties in lieu of all secondary *traites* only upon entering or leaving France or only once in its movement across the country. Some estimates made just prior to the revolution indicated that from two fifths to two thirds of all merchandise had been placed on the *droits uniformes* list. See also Marion, *Histoire financière,* I, 30, and Necker, *De l'administration,* II, 102.

[37] *Encyclopédie méthodique: Finances,* III, 311-313; Levasseur, *Histoire du commerce de la France,* I, 449; Marion, *Histoire financière,* I, 29.

traites. Many taxes which were accounted for as if they were *aides* actually were collected as if they were *traites.* The boundaries were never clearly drawn, and for accounting purposes there was always much shuffling and reshuffling of these tertiary *traites* among the various receipts of the General Farms.

ADMINISTRATION OF THE *Traites*

To collect the welter of tariff duties and tolls just described and to guard the revenues of the *traites* from the incessant threat of smuggling and fraud,[38] the General Farms maintained some 1,400 customs houses toward the end of the old regime. Nearly 1,000 of these were concerned with the secondary *traites.*[39] The French international land and sea frontiers (exception being made for the *provinces étrangers effectifs* and the free ports, for here the customs lines ran between one block of French provinces and another) was ringed by one interlocking system of customs houses, while at least twenty-one differ-

---

[38] Smuggling placed a constant pressure upon the customs lines. All kinds of goods figured in the contraband trade with buttons, books, drugs, coffee, hats, suits, dresses, silks, cottons, and woolens bulking large. After 1730 tobacco became extremely important. Obviously no statistics were kept as to the volume of smuggling, but the reasoned guess of C. M. Arnould is indicative of the extent of the illicit business. Arnould estimated that of some 23,000,000 livres worth of English goods annually imported into France around 1784, 10 to 11,000,000 livres entered the country as contraband. The administration of the *traites* shared the use of the corps of guards with the *gabelles* and *tabacs,* employing the brigades to police the borders and to search out contraband in the interior. The rights of search and seizure in the *traites* were almost as arbitrary as in the *gabelles.* Antismuggling laws in the *traites* were as savage as those applying to the salt and tobacco monopolies. Jurisdiction over smuggling in the *traites,* from a judicial point of view, rested with the *juges des traites* as courts of first instance and with the *cours des aides* as courts of appeal. These courts tended to be superseded in the late eighteenth century by the special *commissions.* See Arnould, *De la balance du commerce,* I, 173-174; Levasseur, *Histoire du commerce,* I, 524; Funck-Brentano, *Mandrin,* p. 43; *Recueil alphabétique des droits de traites uniformes,* IV, 206-222, 241-243.

[39] Lavoisier, *Oeuvres,* VI, 161. For example, the *douane de Lyons* required 177 customs houses and the *douane de Valence* needed 147. See also *Encyclopédie méthodique: Finances,* I, 148, 635, III, 749.

ent chains of control points protected the major internal tariff lines. Due to the enormous variety of duties and tolls levied on different localities and on different kinds of goods, there was no possibility of uniformity of tariff rate schedules among the customs houses, even those connected with the primary *traites*. The situation was further complicated by the system of designating certain customs houses as ports of entry or exit for special kinds of merchandise. For example, spices destined for sale in the *Entendue* of the *cinq grosses fermes* could enter France only at La Rochelle, Rouen, and Calais, while similar commodities not destined for the *Entendue* could enter only at Bordeaux, Lyons, and Marseilles. Analogous regulations applied to most goods imported into the country.[40]

However, by the mid-eighteenth century the General Farms had succeeded in developing a considerable degree of coordination in the administration of the *traites*. No attempt was made to manage the several tariff systems individually. Instead the entire country was divided into regions approximately coincident with the royal generalities, each region containing a segment or segments of whatever *traites* were levied within its jurisdiction. In each region was located at least one principal customs house which served as headquarters of several dependent units. The principal customs houses were located in the chief inland market towns and in commercial seaports, and they ranged in size from great institutions at places like Nantes or Bordeaux to small establishments in the interior. Each was in the charge of a receiver who directed operations and centralized receipts. He was assisted by a controller who acted as the accounting control officer. Each principal customs house disposed of the services of a numerous staff, varying in size according to need. The personnel included customs inspectors, clerks, porters, and guards. At least one brigade of guards was stationed at each principal customs house. The harbor

[40] *Bail fait à Forceville*, Art. 395.

and river patrol craft which operated along the coastal and inland waterways were manned by guards attached to the principal customs houses.[41]

Dependent upon the principal customs house were several subordinate customs houses, each headed by a receiver assisted by at least one customs inspector and a number of guards. Along the frontiers most exposed to smuggling there were generally two concentric lines of customs houses; one located at or near the border, the other situated three or four leagues back. Traffic was routed in such a way as to force it to stop at each of these stations for inspection in turn. To many of these customs houses were attached minor control points, which, located off the main stream of commerce, intercepted the flow of petty local trade. Each of these stations required at least a customs inspector and usually one or two guards. In 1774 the administrative structure of the *traites* commanded the services of 997 receivers plus 565 customs inspectors [42] and an unknown number of less important employees, in addition to sharing the use of the corps of guards with the *gabelles* and *tabacs*.

Despite the multiplicity of customs houses and the wide divergence of tariff rates collected by each, the entire administration of the *traites* was operated on the basis of certain uniform procedures which the universality of the General Farms rendered applicable to the entire country.

Juridically, the key to the procedure of the *traites* was the sworn declaration. All goods moving across customs lines had to be declared by the owner or his agent as to place of origin, destination, weight, and measure, quantity, and value. Such declaration was made upon special forms prepared by the General Farms and was recorded in the register of the customs houses. Using the sworn declaration filed by the merchant as a guide, the customs inspector checked the cargoes and issued verification certificates

---

[41] *Encyclopédie méthodique: Finances,* I, 148.
[42] *Ibid.,* I, 147; Lavoisier, *Oeuvres,* VI, 155.

on the basis of which the receiver calculated the duties due.[43]

Upon being presented with the tax bill, the merchant had various options as to his next move. He could pay the duties on the spot, receive a tax acquittal, and proceed on his journey. If the merchant could not or did not choose to pay at the time of the declaration, he could request an *acquit-à-caution,* which signified that his goods had been declared and verified and that he had posted bond in lieu of payment of duties. The bond was redeemable at some other customs house at a future date upon payment of duties. Failure to pay the duties within the specified time entailed forfeiture of the bond and payment of taxes at four times the normal rate, in addition to probable prosecution for fraud. These forms of tax acquittal generally were valid only within a given customs system. Upon entering a different system, a new series of acquittals was required, unless the merchant had availed himself of a *passe-avant* or a *passe-debout.* The former was a certificate that permitted the merchant to continue along a designated itinerary and to pay the duties due for various secondary tariffs crossed enroute after he had reached his destination. The *passe-debout* was a certificate of deposit that indicated that the merchant upon entering a customs area had paid his duties but was entitled to a refund should he exit without disposing of his goods on the way. In all of these cases the merchant was constrained to stop at every customs house enroute for inspection and verification of his clearance papers.[44]

[43] *Recueil alphabétique des droits de traites uniformes,* IV, 74-93. This reference contains all relevant legislation and cites all court rulings affecting declarations for the entire eighteenth century. The tendency of all rulings was to make the law more precise but at the same time to limit the freedom of the merchant. See also *Encyclopédie méthodique: Finances,* III, 193.

[44] *Recueil alphabétique des droits de traites uniformes,* I, 141-142, IV, 99-100, 127-143; *Encyclopédie méthodique: Finances,* I, 6-10, III, 299-304. The use and limits of use of *acquits-à-caution* were subjects of extensive court actions in the eighteenth century. Usage varied

If the initial declaration was found to be false, or in error, the goods in question, along with the ships, wagons, barges, and horses used in their conveyance, were subject to impoundage. The General Farms instituted a civil suit for recovery of duties plus fines and costs, and might initiate criminal proceedings on the grounds of fraud and smuggling. Conversely, the merchant might enter a countersuit for illegal seizure or collection. Cases of this nature were heard in the first instance by the *juges des traites,* with appeal to the *cours des aides.* A judgment against the merchant resulted in the confiscation of the goods and the imposition of civil fines or criminal penalties. Confiscated merchandise was periodically put up at public auction by the General Farms. The proceeds, together with the fines involved, were divided among the personnel of the administration of the *traites.* Often, established merchants and artisan groups resented these public auctions. For example, in 1774 the curriers of Nantes bitterly opposed the sale of 2,300 confiscated tanned hides from Ireland which the General Farms auctioned to the prejudice of the leather trade.[45] Similar protests were perennial throughout the eighteenth century.

In such a chaotic system as the *traites,* the margin for dispute was considerable. The general tariffs had one schedule of rates on one list of goods, the local tariffs imposed entirely different rates on a different list, and the *péages* still a third. Whereas the primary *traites* were

---

from one part of France to another. The General Farms was well disposed toward the *acquits-à-caution* but insisted upon hedging them with precise formalities; merchants tried to loosen these formalities. The use of *passe-debouts* was peculiarly subject to abuse by merchants seeking to evade payment of duties; the loopholes for evasion were widened by the issuance of a writ in 1742; after that date the *passe-debouts* became a chief means of nonpayment of many of the *traites.* In 1772 the General Farms obtained a drastic limitation in their use, but in 1776 merchant clamor was such that the *passe-debouts* were restored to their 1742 status.

[45] *Recueil alphabétique des droits de traites uniformes,* IV, 93-97, 223-232, 169-172; Wybo, *Le Conseil de commerce,* p. 47.

governed by relatively clear-cut rate schedules, the laws of the rest of the customs were most often so obscure as to be capable of wide divergence of interpretation. These difficulties were compounded by the ad valorem character of most of the *traites*. There were no uniformly acceptable formulas for an objective determination of the value of a given quantity of goods. The result was that the merchant, anxious to avoid the duties, tended to declare the value as low as possible; while the customs inspector, anxious for bonuses, tended to overvalue. The customs inspector could challenge any declaration and seize the goods. The merchant was then faced with a lengthy law suit with the General Farms which no matter how settled was time-consuming and expensive.

The government and the Company of General Farmers recognized the need for more precise means of evaluation than that provided by the judgment of a simple customs inspector. While nothing was done to alleviate the difficulty so far as most of the secondary *traites* were concerned, both cooperated to elaborate objective standards of value for the general tariffs and for the tariff of the *cinq grosses fermes*. This was one of the chief functions of the eighteenth-century council of commerce and its various mutations: the *bureaux, chambres,* and *deputées du commerce*. Membership in these bodies always included certain municipal deputies representing the commercial interests and a number of General Farmers representing the interests of the fisc. By the end of the eighteenth century the *deputées du commerce* were routinely negotiating, every six months, standard tables of values to be applied to the chief articles of export and import. Whenever conflict arose between the General Farms and biggest merchants, the council of commerce normally settled it by administrative decree, thus circumventing the tedious and expensive procedures of the ordinary *juges des traites* and *cours des aides.*[46]

46 Wybo, *Le Conseil de commerce,* pp. 45-46, 54-55.

THE COSTS OF COLLECTION: *Traites*

The customs duties, fiscally the least valuable of all the receipts of the General Farms, were the most expensive to collect. According to Lavoisier's data, 15 9/10 percent of an annual average gross yield of 20,199,735 livres for the four years 1768-1772 was absorbed as costs of collecting the *traites,* not including the *domaines d'Occident.* It cost three sous two deniers to collect one livre of customs duty. The costs of collection in the *traites* totaled 4,061,257 livres, of which only 851,265 livres were costs borne by the king (32,000 livres for certain incidental expenditures and 819,265 livres as the prorated share of the general expenses of the General Farms), the remainder being borne by the Company of General Farmers. The primary reasons for the high cost of collection in the *traites,* as Lavoisier himself pointed out, were: first, the existence of the nearly one thousand Customs Houses connected with the internal tariffs, each requiring at least one agent and generally more; and, second, the necessity of using large elements of the corps of guards to patrol the involuted customs frontiers against smuggling. Whatever the efficiency which may have resulted from the uniform procedure of collection introduced by the General Farms into the administration of the *traites,* the fact remained that the old-regime customs system was antiquated beyond repair. That the system was never reformed was due not so much to opposition from the tax-farmers, anxious to cling to their profits (as so often they were depicted), as to the necessity of the treasury to cling even to the small revenues obtained at such great costs from the archaic *traites.*[47]

[47] Lavoisier, *Oeuvres,* VI, 150, 161, and table, p. 154.

6. The Excises and Sales Taxes, the Town Duties, and the Registry Taxes: Aides, Entrees, and Domaines

EXCISES AND SALES TAXES: Aides and Droits y jointes

At the end of the old regime the group of taxes conventionally known as the *aides* was the most valuable of all indirect taxations. Under the Lease Carlier of 1726 the *aides* accounted for 32,000,000 livres of the annual lease price of the General Farms. In 1774 the *aides* contributed only approximately 38,300,000 livres toward the annual price of the Lease David. But in 1788 the budget estimate of the net yield of the General Commission of the *aides* (constituted, as has been seen, in 1780) was 49,000,000 livres. However, to this figure must be added the yield of the *entrées* of Paris (the town duties of the capital), traditionally a part of the *aides* but left within the General Farms when the General Commission of the *aides* was created in 1780. In 1788 the *entrées* was valued at an annual lease price of 30,000,000 livres. Thus all those taxes which in 1726 were considered as *aides* produced a net receipt of approximately 79,000,000 livres in 1788.[1]

[1] Clamageran, *Histoire de l'impôt,* III, 242; Lavoisier, *Oeuvres,* VI, 180; Braesch, *Finances et monnaie révolutionnaires,* II, 72, 85, and

The word *aides* was an administrative rubric used to indicate a complex of taxes, the contents of which was not precisely defined. In 1760 there were in existence some nine to ten thousand separate pieces of legislation, in addition to the ordinance *sur le fait des aydes* of 1680, bearing upon the *aides*. This whole corpus embodied the utmost in diversity as to kinds of taxes, objects taxed, and tax rates.[2] However, it is possible to simplify the subject by classifying the *aides* according to three broad categories.

The three categories were: the true *aides,* sales taxes on wine, and various accessory and supplementary taxes and fees levied on the wine trade; the town duties, or *octrois,* of which the most important was the *entrées de Paris;* the *droits y jointes,* special excises customarily attached to the *aides* since 1663 for administrative purposes. Of these categories the true *aides* were the most valuable. The *entrées de Paris* grew to such stature during the eighteenth century that it must be regarded as a body of taxation distinct from the true *aides*. The *droits y jointes* were of least fiscal significance. There was no fixed number of these *droits* joined to the *aides*. In any lease on the General Farms the receipt of the *aides* might have associated with it a dozen minor excises or only two or three as the government created or suppressed in-

---

tables between pp. 200-201 and 210-211. The figures for the Lease David were arrived at by adding together *aides* and *droits rétablis.* Lavoisier lists them separately, but they were all *aides* under a broader definition.

[2] Lefebvre de la Bellande, *Traité général des droits d'aides,* p. ii. This treatise was the most thorough to appear in the eighteenth century. It was written, under the inspiration of Lamoignon de Malesherbes, first president of the Paris *Cour des Aides,* by a man who for years had worked in the administration of the *aides;* the work was checked for accuracy by the experts of the General Farms. Pagination of this work requires a special note. The work is divided into two parts, the first comprising two books, the second four books. The pages are numbered consecutively in Books I and II, but begin again in Book III. Therefore references, except those to the lengthy Introduction which is numbered in Roman, will cite book as well as page.

cidental levies from year to year. Only the three most permanent of these *droits* joined to the *aides* will be considered here.[3]

THE *Droits y jointes*

The *droits de timbre et formule* were the greatest revenue producers among the *droits* joined to the *aides*. The law required that all legal documents be drawn up on special paper or parchment bearing a royal watermark or stamp. The amount of the *droit de timbre,* or stamp tax, was calculated according to the size and quality of the paper. The stamped paper was manufactured at licensed paper mills under General Farms direction and was sold exclusively in General Farms stores located in the principal cities. The *droit de formule* was a tax levied at varying rates upon the legal formulas printed or written on stamped paper. The rates of the *timbre et formule* were established in 1690 and did not change until 1748, when they were greatly increased. The *timbre et formule* suffered from a peculiar administrative ambiguity. In those parts of France where the true *aides* were collected, the twin taxes were managed by the administration of the *aides;* elsewhere they were under the control of the *domaines.* The receipt, amounting to about 6,000,000 livres a year, was split between the two administrations. In 1780 this duality was terminated and the *timbre et formule* was placed squarely in the new General Administration of the *domaines.*[4]

---

[3] Among the taxes appearing frequently as *droits* joined to the *aides* were: the *droit des cartes,* recreated in 1745 and heavily increased in rates in 1755, the yield being earmarked for the new Ecole Militaire, produced about 130,000 livres annually; the *droits sur l'amidon,* collected at the starch works; the *droits sur huiles and savons,* town duties on oils and soaps; the *droits sur les cuirs,* excises on leather goods; the *marque et contrôle des ouvrages d'or et d'argent,* a tax on jewelry collected from the gold and silversmiths. Most of these taxes were designed to regulate the crafts and trades involved rather than to produce revenue.

[4] Moreau de Beaumont, *Mémoires concernant les impositions,* IV, 541; *Encyclopédie méthodique: Finances,* II, 254-258.

Closely associated with the *timbre et formule* were the *droits sur papier et cartons,* a series of excises levied upon the manufacture of paper, cardboard, and parchment. This tax was applied generally throughout the country. Its last definitive formulation was in 1771, when there was promulgated a detailed schedule of rates which varied with the quality and type of paper. Strict surveillance of the paper mills, with the producers initially bearing the impact of the tax, guaranteed the collection of this excise. In 1787 it yielded about 2,500,000 livres a year.[5]

The *marque des fers,* a light excise on a variety of iron products, was collected by the administration of the *aides* at scattered points within the jurisdictions of the Parlements of Metz, Dijon, Grenoble, and Paris. The tax was collected from the producer, his iron being stamped with a mark when he had acquitted himself of the tax. In the jurisdiction of the Parlements of Toulouse and Rouen, the *marque des fers* took the form of a toll on iron products collected at the gates of leading cities and towns. The *marque des fers* was extremely complicated, supervision of it being shared between the General Farms and the Parlements. It was productive more of litigation than of revenue, and toward the end of the old regime yielded no more than 1,500,000 livres a year.[6]

THE TRUE *Aides:* SALES AND ACCESSORY TAXES ON WINE

For purposes of the *aides,* eighteenth-century France was divided into two parts, the *pays où les aides ont cours,* or more briefly the *pays d'aides,* and the *pays où les aides n'ont pas cours* or *pays d'exempts.* The true *aides* were levied and collected only in the *pays d'aides,* a region, roughly coextensive with the *pays des grandes gabelles,* which embraced the fourteen royal generalities of Alençon, Amiens, Bourges, Caen, Châlons, La Rochelle, Lyons,

---

[5] *Encyclopédie méthodique: Finances,* III, 277, 280-282.
[6] Lefebvre de la Bellande, *Traité général des droits d'aides,* III, 127, 129-130.

Moulins, Orléans, Paris, Poitiers, Rouen, Soissons, and Tours.[7]

The true *aides*, levied exclusively upon the *pays d'aides*, were classified according to their geographical applicability within that region. There were general *aides*, taxes which in theory were levied at uniform rates throughout the *pays d'aides*. There were also local *aides*, taxes levied only upon particular parts or places in the *pays d'aides* at a variety of different rates. The general *aides* were superimposed upon and collected simultaneously with the local *aides* wherever they coincided. Both general and local *aides* were subject to the general *sous pour livre* surtaxes.[8]

The true *aides* were also classified according to their functional characteristics. The local *aides* usually operated in the form of town duties or regional transit fees. They taxed at low rates a variety of consumer goods, among them wine, grain, fish, cattle, wood, and metalware. The local *aides* were of incidental fiscal significance.[9] The principal objects taxed by the general *aides*

[7] *Ibid.*, pp. viii-x. In addition to the generalities listed, five elections of the generalities of Limoges and Dijon were also included in the *pays d'aides*. There were also numerous petty enclaves of the *pays d'aides* in the midst of the *pays d'exempts*. No map was ever drawn of the distribution of the *aides*. A look at the map, facing p. 82, with the following changes in mind might be helpful: Lower Normandy (*quart bouillon*) was not *grandes gabelles* but was *pays d'aides*; Poitou (Poitiers) was *pays d'aides* but only partly *grandes gabelles*; Saintonge (La Rochelle) was *pays d'aides* but not *grandes gabelles*; Burgundy (Dijon) was *grandes gabelles* but only in small part *pays d'aides*; a small part of Limousin (Limoges) was in the *pays d'aides* but none of it was in the *grandes gabelles*.

[8] *Encyclopédie méthodique: Finances*, I, 24-25.

[9] Lefebvre de la Bellande, *Traité général des droits d'aides*, I, 104-106, 272-281; Moreau de Beaumont, *Mémoires concernant les impositions*, II, 314-315, III, 380-388. The complexity of the local *aides* epitomized the old regime's lack of fiscal uniformity. Some were of antique origin, having been created by feudal authorities antedating royal taxation. Some had been created by the king. Although by the eighteenth century most local aides had been absorbed into the rate schedules of municipal *octrois*, some still operated as petty wholesale and retail sales taxes. A few local *aides* embraced areas containing several generalities; all of these were transit fees upon commerce resembling some of the secondary *traites*.

were wine and other alcoholic beverages.   The chief general *aides* were levied in the form of wholesale and retail sales taxes.   But some general *aides* functioned as taxes on the circulation of wine within the *pays d'aides* and between that region and the *pays d'exempts*.   Some others took the form of license fees for the privilege of selling wine; others were fees for certain services which the Genral Farms rendered the wine trade.[10]   The sales taxes on wine [11] were overwhelmingly of greatest fiscal importance.

The *droit de gros* was the basic wholesale tax of the *aides*.   It was an ad valorem 5 percent (base rate) tax upon the sales prices of each muid (Paris measure) of wine sold or resold at wholesale within the confines of the territory subject to the tax.   Each successive sale from original producer to final wholesale merchant was equally subject to the *gros*, the effect of the tax being accumulative in the price of each muid of wine to the last wholesale transaction.   Associated with the *gros* was the *augmentation*, a special surtax of seventeenth-century origin.   It was a specific surtax on quantity of wine sold.   Thus, while the basic wholesale tax, the *gros*, was an ad valorem sales tax, its accessory surtax, the *augmentation*, was a

[10] Originally, in the late fourteenth century, the *aides* had been levied upon the sale of nearly every commodity sold in the *pays d'aides*.   Gradually the list of goods struck was shortened until by 1668 only four categories were left.   These were called *quartes espèces réservées*.   They comprised wine and other alcoholic beverages, sea fish, cloven-hooved animals destined for the butcher's block, and wood.   Of these taxes, those on wine became so emphatically the most important that the remaining three *espèces réservées* tended to be overlooked in discussions of the *aides*.   Yet up to 1791 they continued to exist, collected, however, not as sales taxes but as 5 percent ad valorem duties merged with the various town duties.   By the eighteenth century most large cities had bought freedom from the *espèces réservées*, but Paris remained subject to them.   See Lefebvre de la Bellande, *Traité général des droits d'aides,* I, 61-94; Moreau de Beaumont, *Mémoires concernant les impositions,* III, 352.

[11] The *aides* taxed not only wine but brandy, beer, apple and pear cider, liquors, and other alcoholic beverages.   They also taxed the fruit from which those beverages were made.   For convenience, however, the single word *wine* will be used hereafter to indicate all of these taxation objects, unless otherwise stated.

specific tax of sixteen sous three denier per muid of wine sold, regardless of the sales price.[12]

Although the *gros* and *augmentation* were considered as general *aides*, in actuality they were applied to four out of the fourteen generalities of the *pays d'aides*. These four generalities were called the *pays de gros* and included the generalities of Paris (except after 1719 the city of Paris itself), Amiens, Châlons, and Soissons. In addition, the *gros* only was collected in four elections and numerous cities located in generalities other than those of the *pays de gros*. The city and county of Auxerre, Bar-sur-Seine, Chartres, Issodun, Lyons, Orléans, Poitiers, and Tours were the most important of these places. The city and suburbs of Rouen were subject both to the *gros* and to the *augmentation*, but in this case the *augmentation* was a percentage tax on wholesale price.[13]

Even within the area of the *pays de gros* there were many exemptions and moderations of the wholesale taxes in favor of special cities and social classes. At least forty-five privileged places and nine annual fairs were exempt in whole or in part from the *gros* and *augmentation*. Moreover, a close inspection of even these localities shows that the franchises did not apply evenly to all classes within them. Important to an understanding of this subject was the distinction between *vin d'achat* and *vin de cru:* the former was commercial wine bought and sold in the open market by regular vintners; the latter was wine produced upon the estates of certain privileged groups and consumed or sold by the owners of those estates. In general, the organized *bourgeoisie* of a city was privileged to import its *vin de cru* free in whole or in part of the *gros* and *augmentation*. Such wine presumably was for the personal consumption of a particular *bourgeois*. But ex-

[12] Lefebvre de la Bellande, *Traité générale des droits d'aides*, I, 5, II, 310-317; *Encyclopédie méthodique: Finances*, II, 441; Moreau de Beaumont, *Mémoires concernant les impositions*, III, 343, 407.
[13] Lefebvre de la Bellande, *Traité général des droits d'aides*, II, 318-322, 404.

ceptions existed even in this rule. At Orléans and Lyons the *gros* and *augmentation* was not levied on any wine brought into the city by a *bourgeois,* whether *vin de cru* or *vin d'achat:* in these places the *bourgeoisie* sold its own wine free of the wholesale taxes. The *bourgeoisie* of Sens, Montreau, Troyes, Vincennes, Montrenil, and other places paid the *augmentation* but not the *gros.* City after city enjoyed similar exemptions in favor of the organized and moneyed groups. Yet nowhere was there a clear definition of what constituted the *bourgeoisie.* Therefore, litigation and dispute was great. The General Farms attempted to restrict the legal membership of the *bourgeoisie*; individuals tried to claim the right to be regarded as *bourgeois.* Fraud on the part of the General Farms employees and tax evasion on the part of the merchants was inevitable.[14]

But the *bourgeoisie* (however defined) was not the only group to enjoy special status in regard to the wholesale sales taxes. The clergy and nobility, as estates, were exempt from payment of those taxes on wine produced on their own properties located within the *pays de gros.* Nobles could sell at wholesale any wine produced in their own wineries free of the *gros,* while wholesale wine produced in ecclesiastical vineyards was free both of the *gros* and of the *augmentation.* The privilege applied only to the first wholesale transaction made directly between the noble or cleric and the wine merchant. Even though limited in scope, in the course of the eighteenth century, by increasingly stringent regulations, the privilege was an important one. It gave the nobility and the clergy of the *pays de gros* an immediate price advantage over their peasant competitors in the market of wholesale wine.[15]

The basic retail sales taxes on wine levied in the *pays d'aides* were the *quatrième* and the *huitième.* The *quatrième* was collected only within the jurisdiction of the

[14] *Ibid.,* II, 382-399, 401-403; *Encyclopédie méthodique: Finances,* II, 448-449.
[15] *Encyclopédie méthodique: Finances,* II, 446.

Rouen *Cour des Aides*, that is, within the generalities of Alençon, Caen, Rouen, and in large but not contiguous parts of the generality of Amiens. It was also collected in the cities and elections of Bar-sur-Seine and Pontoise and in the lower suburb (*bas-fauxbourg*) of Aumône. The *quatrième* was an ad valorem tax upon the sales price of all retail sales of wine. Its rate, however, was a fourth, 25 percent, of the sales price only in the case of brandy and beer. In the case of wine and cider, it was in practice reduced to a fifth, or 20 percent.[16] Both rates were, of course, subject to the *sous pour livre* surtaxes.

The *huitième* was collected within the jurisdiction of the Paris *Cour des Aides*—that is, in the generalities of Amiens (except those parts subject to the *quatrième*), Bourges, Châlons, La Rochelle, Lyons, Moulins, Orléans, Paris (except after 1719, the city of Paris itself), Poitiers, Soissons, and Tours. It was also collected outside that jurisdiction in numerous cities, several elections, and in two dependencies of the generality of Limoges, Angoûleme, and Bourganeuf. Despite the implication of its name, the *huitième* was not an ad valorem tax of an eighth of the retail sales price of wine. Since 1663 the *huitième* was a specific tax on the quantity of beverages sold, regardless of their price.[17]

A distinction between wine sold *à pot*, or in places offering no other fare than drink, and wine sold *à assiette*, or in establishments offering food as well as liquors, was basis for a calculation of the rate of the *huitième*. The proprietor of a retail establishment selling wine *à pot* paid a fixed *huitième* of five livres eight sous per muid

16 *Ibid.*, III, 433, 453; Lefebvre de la Bellande, *Traité général des droits d'aides*, III, 62-67; Moreau de Beaumont, *Mémoires concernant les impositions*, III, 331. The original retail tax of 1360 had been a *treizième*, a thirteenth of the retail sales price. In the course of three hundred years this was raised to a *quatrième* which in due course was reduced to a *huitième* everywhere in the *pays d'aides* except for the jurisdiction of the Rouen *Cour des Aides.*.

17 Lefebvre de la Bellande, *Traité général des droits d'aides*, III, 2, 4-5; Moreau de Beaumont, *Mémoires concernant les impositions*, III, 130; *Encyclopédie méthodique: Finances*, II, 516.

sold; proprietors of places selling *à assiette* paid a fixed *huitième* of six livres fifteen sous. These rates were subject to the general *sous pour livre* surtaxes. The effort to maintain these distinctions led to endless litigation between the proprietors and the General Farms. The former tried always to prove that the *à pot* rate was applicable to their establishments; the latter endeavored to prove just the opposite. The fine distinctions among the *cabaretiers* (who were deemed to sell *à pot*) and the *hôteliers and taverniers* (who were deemed to sell *à assiette*), and among the numerous grades that lay between, were not only difficult to draw in law, but difficult to recognize in practice. In any case, the *huitième*, like the *quatrième*, was initially borne by the seller. It was officially recognized that he would shift the impact to the consumer upon whom it was presumed the incidence of the retail sales taxes rested.[18]

The *quatrième-huitième* retail sales taxes nearly everywhere in the *pays d'aides* had associated with them their own special surtax, known as the *subvention à détail*. This surtax was collected at the fixed rate of twenty-seven sous per muid of wine sold at retail.[19] Like its base taxes, the *subvention à détail* itself was also subject to the general *sous pour livres* surtaxes.

The *quatrième-huitième-subvention à détail* were, theoretically, general *aides* bearing on all retail transactions throughout the *pays d'aides*. In practice, only the *subvention à détail* could lay claim to universality; it was

[18] Lefebvre de la Bellande, *Traité général des droits d'aides,* III, 2-3. The presumption was that inns and restaurants serving food as well as drink also provided their guests with tables and chairs, charging them therefore higher prices than simple dram-shops and pot-houses, which were equipped more crudely. The difference in rates, a higher rate imposed upon sales made in a place presumed to charge higher prices, was reminiscent of the earlier times when the *huitième* actually was a percentage of sales price. See also Moreau de Beaumont, *Mémoires concernant les impositions,* III, 407.

[19] Lefebvre de la Bellande, *Traité général des droits d'aides,* III, 69-70; *Encyclopédie méthodique: Finances,* II, 515.

collected even in localities which were exempt from the *quatrième* or the *huitième*.   The base rate of the *huitième* was merely a standard against which to judge particular variations.   Within the jurisdiction of the Paris *Cour des Aides,* the *huitième* was rarely collected at full rate, especially in the larger cities.   Everywhere the *bourgeois* was permitted to sell *vin de cru* from his own domicile at retail free of some part of the *huitième*.   The opportunities for fraud were endless.   Precisely what was *vin de cru,* exactly what was a domicile, were matters which the courts for centuries had not been able to determine. As in the case of the *gros,* the General Farms and the *bourgeoisie* were at perpetual loggerheads.   In the three generalities of the Rouen *Cour des Aides* where the *quatrième* was levied, the pattern of privilege was even more complete.   Some Norman cities (Boulogne, Calais, Ardes, Cherbourg, Dieppe) enjoyed outright exemption from the *quatrième;* in all Norman cities the tax was drastically reduced in favor of the *bourgeoisie*.   Such privileges were jealously defended by the Rouen *Cour des Aides,* which, in fact, not only attempted to guard the franchises against the encroachment of the General Farms, but tried to extend them.   In Normandy only the politically and economically impotent were exposed to the full weight of the *aides;* the peasant countryside and the villages alone bore the *quatrième* without reduction.[20]

In order to facilitate the collection of the wholesale and retail sales taxes as well as to regulate the commerce in wine in the public interest, the monarchy licensed the wine sellers to engage in their trade.   Wine-selling licenses were called *annuels*.   They were obtained from the local agents of the General Farms at annual fees that ranged from eight livres in the cities to six livres ten sous in the countryside.   A separate *annuel* was required for each category of merchandising, wholesale or retail, and for each kind of beverage dealt in.   Thus a vintner selling

[20] *Encyclopédie méthodique: Finances,* II, 516-517, III, 433-434.

both at wholesale and at retail was required to have paid fees for two different *annuels* for each kind of beverage handled.[21]

In addition to the sales taxes and the *annuel*, among the general *aides* were numerous taxes, or transit fees, on the commercial movement of wine. These circulation taxes had originally been designed to equalize the disparity of tax rates among the various subdivisions of the *pays d'aides* and between the *pays d'aides* and the *pays d'exempts*, by taxing wine as it moved from place to place seeking a market. In this purpose the circulation taxes failed, but they did offer the General Farms the means of supervising the wine trade the better to protect the retail and wholesale taxes. Thus all wines entering or leaving the *pays d'aides* were subject to the *subvention par doublement* collected at the borders like an import-export customs duty. Similarly, wine entering, leaving, or merely passing through the *pays de gros* was subject to the *gros à l'arrivé, sortie, et au passage* while the three Norman generalities of the jurisdiction of the Rouen *Cour des Aides* were guarded by an import duty, the *subvention à l'entrée*. In the eighteenth century the *subvention par doublement* was collected like a secondary *traite* by the customs houses of the *cinq grosses fermes*, the receipt being credited to the account of the *aides*. The *gros à l'arrivé* and the *subvention à l'entrée* were collected at the gates of cities located along the principal trade routes and hence tended to merge with the town duties and local *aides* also collected at those points.[22]

In eighteenth-century France at least fifty-nine different systems of liquid measure were in use. From among these, the Paris muid was selected as the standard for taxation purposes in the *pays d'aides*. But the Paris muid was not aliquot to any other measure. Only trained

---

21 *Ibid.,* I, 46; Moreau de Beaumont, *Mémoires concernant les impositions,* III, 339-340.

22 Lefebvre de la Bellande, *Traité général des droits d'aides,* I, 230-231, II, 364-365, III, 69-70.

experts could manage the complicated formulas by means of which the quantity of wine contained in a non-Parisian measure could be converted mathematically into the standard Paris muid without actually pouring the wine from cask to cask. The monarchy seized upon this situation to create venal offices, the proprietors of which weighed and measured wine whenever that commodity was halted in its commercial movement to pay the *aides*. Special fees, the *droits de jauge et courtage*, were created to pay the *gages* of the venal offices. At the end of the reign of Louis XIV these venal offices were liquidated and their functions became part of the duties of the employees of the General Farms, but the *droits de jauge et courtage* were not suppressed. They continued to be collected to the end of the old regime at the rate of fifteen sous per muid of wine measured. These measuring fees were payable wherever the *gros* was applied, or in conjunction with the *quatrième-huitième* wherever the *gros* did not apply. In the case of circulation taxes, each time wine crossed a border at which such taxes were due the measuring fees were collected whether or not any actual measurement took place.[23]

From this discussion of the general *aides* it may be observed that it was, and is, literally impossible to calculate any standard tax rate on any item subject to those taxes. Theoretically general *aides* were levied upon every market transaction in the entire *pays d'aides*; in practice they were collected in full, in part or not at all according to the degree of moderation or complete franchise which each province, city, even each parish had been able to persuade the monarchy to grant. Every small place was a separate case and the whole *pays d'aides* was a maze of exceptions. When this irregularity of the general *aides* was superimposed upon the total diversity of the local *aides* and the whole was surcharged by the *sous*

[23] *Ibid.*, I, 157-159, II, 412-417, III, 73; *Encyclopédie méthodique: Finances*, II, 663-665; Moreau de Beaumont, *Mémoires concernant les impositions*, III, 356-357.

pour livre, only a detailed knowledge of the entire production and commercial history of a given quantity of wine could have revealed the full overt tax burden to which that wine was subject. When the Company of General Farmers leased the tax rights of the *aides* as part of the General Farms, it assumed the obligation to manage a fiscal system so complex as to be almost incoherent. As a result the administration of the *aides* was the most intricate of any in the General Farms.

THE ADMINISTRATION OF THE TRUE *Aides*

The essential principle both of the wholesale *gros* and of the retail *huitième* (or *quatrième*) was that they were levied on each and every successive sale of wine from producer to consumer. In each case it was the seller from whom the General Farms actively collected the taxes. Yet it was manifestly impossible in eighteenth-century France for the General Farms to provide for the physical presence of a tax collector at every sale of wine consummated throughout the *pays d'aides.* Instead, the General Farms employed a running inventory technique, reinforced by an elaborate system of transit controls, as the primary instrument of collection. It was the object of the General Farms to be able to follow each cask of wine from the time it was laid down in a winery to the time it was decanted and sold, by bottle or glass, *à pot* or *à assiette,* in the last retailer's shop, tavern, or pot house.[24]

The basic mechanism of the inventory as a tax-collecting device was simple, although as applied to particular situations it was susceptible of great refinements in detail. A General Farms agent, a *commis des aides,*[25] inventoried a given stock of wine upon a certain date. After an interval a second inventory was run. The difference

---

[24] *Encyclopédie méthodique: Finances,* I, 29.

[25] The title *commis* as applied to the agents of the General Farms requires some explanation. In general, all regular employees were called *commis des fermes.* But in the *gabelles, tabacs,* and *traites* the expression guards was most often used. In the *aides* and *domaines* the agents were called *commis des aides,* or *commis des domaines.*

in the amount of wine in stock was presumed to be the amount of wine sold, and the taxes were collected on the basis of that difference. To guarantee the thoroughness of the inventory, all retailers, and all wholesale vintners throughout the *pays d'aides* without exception as to status or personal exemption from any element of the *aides*, were required to submit their vineyards, cellars, stocks, and stores to the inventory process.

The annual inventory of wine in the *pays d'aides* began at the close of the grape harvest season. In the country-side among the wine producers, the inventory was directed by a General Farms controller who was in charge of a district usually comprising two or three parishes. The controller headed a small staff of field agents known as *commis à cheval,* each one assigned to cover a part of a parish. The *commis à cheval* systematically traveled from vineyard to vineyard inventorying for each producer in his territory the amount and quality of the grapes harvested, the quantities sent to the wine presses, the casks of new wine laid down, and the stock of old wine still left in the cellars. Simultaneously with this production inventory, a similar inventory was run of the stocks of wine in the possession of wholesale and retail merchants in the towns and cities. This inventory was, in each town or city, directed by a controller attached to a local *bureau des aides.* This official supervised agents called *commis à pieds* in their work of inventorying the commercial stocks of wine in the urban places.[26]

These inventories were conducted with great care and formality. The General Farms prepared printed forms and issued to the *commis* special handbooks in which the proper steps were outlined; all the tricks of cheating to which the proprietor might resort were exposed in the handbooks, and every contingency peculiar to the immediate locality was accounted for.[27] The inventory was con-

[26] *Encyclopédie méthodique: Finances,* III, 645.
[27] Lefebvre de la Bellande, *Traité général des droits d'aides,* II, 346-348. Lefebvre prints sample inventory forms.

ducted in the presence of the *commis* and the proprietor, and the parish syndic or church warden was required as a witness. Each paragraph was signed by the *commis* and the proprietor; each page by the syndic or warden.[28] When completed the inventory was drawn up in duplicate and sworn to by the proprietor and the officiating *commis*. At the same time all new casks of wine were sealed and marked by identifying symbols. The second copy of the inventory was given to the proprietor for his records, the original was deposited at the local *bureau des aides*, with the responsible receivers who headed the *bureaux* in towns and cities or with the *buralistes* who collected the *aides* in rural communities.[29] The information contained in the individual inventories was compiled in registers at various levels of the administration of the *aides* until, within a few months of the grape harvest, the central headquarters of the General Farms in Paris was in possession of a complete record of all old wines remaining, all new wines laid down by producers, and all wines in the possession of the vintners and retailers throughout the *pays d'aides*.[30]

Once the inventories were completed, the business of collecting the wholesale and retail sales taxes began. Basic to the entire procedure was the obligation of the producer, the wholesaler, or retailer to report all movement or to declare all sales of wine to the *bureau des aides* in the district. In the case of a producer making a sale to a

---

[28] Brunet de Grandmaison, *Dictionnaire des aydes,* I, 262-269. This work was one of the handbooks issued by the General Farms for the instruction of its employees.

[29] Large *bureaux des aides* (of which there were 146 in 1763) in the cities were headed by receivers assisted by the *contrôleurs sédentaires* and a large staff of employees. In small rural districts the *bureau des aides* consisted of one man, the *buraliste,* who was not a regular employee but a part time worker who received not a wage but a percentage of taxes collected. Often the *buraliste* of the *aides* served also as a salt vendor and tobacconist. In the 1780s there were some three to four thousand *buralistes* in the administration of the *aides*. See *Encyclopédie méthodique: Finances,* I, 29, 146; Necker, *De l'administration,* I, 107; *Dictionnaire géographique,* I, 34-35.

[30] *Encyclopédie méthodique: Finances,* II, 26, 645-646.

merchant, each party to the transaction was required to go to the nearest *buraliste* to settle accounts. The *buraliste* made notation of the transaction on his copy of the registered inventory and, if in the *pays de gros*, collected the range of wholesale *gros* and *augmentation* and local *aides* due. He then issued a tax acquittal to the seller and proper transit permits to the buyer, who was then free to move the wine. If an owner moved his wine with intent to sell, or even if he merely wished to transfer it from one storage place to another, he had first to obtain a transit permit. At the market in the *pays de gros* he had to declare his wine at the *bureau des aides* and pay his taxes either on the basis of an anticipated sales price or after the sale on the basis of certified bills of sale. In the case of the retailers subject to either the *huitième* or the *quatrième*, the merchant was required to maintain a daybook of all sales. Once a month this daybook was cleared by a *commis à pied* who compared it to the inventory and at that time collected taxes on the difference in quantity indicated.[31]

Periodically additional inventories were conducted as spot checks. In the case of the retailers these were conducted regularly every six months. In the case of the producers and wholesalers, these special inventories were on a surprise basis. Every muid of the difference between wine listed in the original inventory and that noted in the subsequent inventory had to be accounted for by tax acquittals, transit permits, and certified bills of sale, or, in the case of the retailers, by proper entries in the daybook. Any part of the difference not accounted for was presumed to have been sold in tax evasion.[32]

The General Farms recognized that a wine producer was entitled to consume a certain amount of his own vintage tax free and further that a certain proportion of the vintage inevitably spoiled and hence could not be sold.

[31] *Ibid.*, II, 27-35.
[32] Lefebvre de la Bellande, *Traité général des droits d'aides*, II, 350-362.

Elaborate quotas of personal and household consumption and of spoilage were developed in the course of the eighteenth century to apply to different regions, economic conditions, and social stations. These quotas were generally ample to provide for the normal needs of the producer, his family, and household. The amount indicated by the producer's quota was always deducted as tax free from the amount recorded in the first inventory before the second inventory was taken. However, should a producer attempt to declare a greater amount of personal consumption or spoilage than allowed under his quota it was presumed that he had sold the wine without payment of taxes. He was then charged with the *gros-manquant* or missing *gros* at a rate equivalent to the *gros* at a sales price determined by the General Farms plus high fines and costs. The *gros-manquant* was popularly called the *trop bu*; it was the object of bitter denunciation on the part of certain publicists antagonistic to the General Farms. But in actuality the *trop bu* yielded only a trifling sum. Either there was great laxity in its collection or more likely the inventory system was such an efficient way of managing the wholesale taxes that few attempted to evade.[33] Similar quotas for personal consumption were applied to the wholesalers and retailers.

Supplementary to the use of production and wholesale inventories, the administration of the *aides* maintained check points strategically located at the gates of the cities and towns to intercept the movement of the wine commerce. Circulation taxes, local *aides* in the form of town duties, and measuring taxes were collected at these stations. All wine in transit had to be declared and be accompanied by proper tax acquittals and transit permits before it was allowed to proceed upon its way.[34]

The maintenance of the inventory system and allied

---

[33] *Ibid.,* II, 349; *Encyclopédie méthodique: Finances,* I, 516. In 1759 the *trop bu* yielded but 13,000 livres.

[34] Lefebvre de la Bellande, *Traité général des droits d'aides,* II, 324-333.

forms of surveillance depended upon an enforced round of inspections, house-to-house and shop-to-shop searches, and traffic controls. Like the guards of the *gabelles, tabacs,* and *traites,* the *commis des aides* were uniformed, armed, and invested with powerful police rights of arbitrary domiciliary search without court warrants. During the period of the regular annual inventory the *commis des aides* were granted almost unlimited entry into houses, cellars, barns, shops, stores, churches, monasteries, convents, noble chateaux, and royal fortresses. Outside of the inventory period the *commis des aides* were granted unlimited right of search over all persons subject to the *gros* and *huitième* (or *quatrième*). The premises of persons not so subject could be searched only with written warrant of the courts. As a matter of routine the *commis des aides* were deployed to make periodic inspections in search of illegal sales and movement of wine and for evidence of other forms of tax evasion. On the basis of such evidence, drawn up in the form of *procès-verbaux,* legal action was taken by the General Farms.[35]

Litigation in the *aides* was extraordinarily complicated, slow, and expensive. On the one hand, the system of courts dealing with the *aides* (courts of the *élus* for the general *aides,* municipal and provincial courts for the local *aides,* with appeals running either to the Paris or the Rouen *Cour des Aides*) was a jumble of jurisdictional tangles. On the other hand the laws of the *aides* were imprecise, contradictory, and in part unintelligible. As has been seen they were also riddled with exceptions pertaining to imperfectly defined persons, classes, and places. In consequence the late eighteenth-century General Farms, faced with the task of collecting the heavily surcharged sales taxes from a population notorious for its intransigence towards the fisc, avoided formal litigation except for test cases designed to tighten or clarify the royal law or its own regulations. Usually the General Farms was agreeable to settlement out of court by negotiation and

---

[35] *Encyclopédie méthodique: Finances,* II, 444-445, 791-792.

compromise. Where this was not possible, the General Farms applied with increasing frequency to the royal council for *arrêts d'évocation,* removing *aides* cases from the jurisdiction of the ordinary courts into that of the royal intendants and of the council itself.[36]

Unlike the *gabelles, tabacs,* and *traites,* the *aides* were not threatened by overt and direct smuggling. What few attempts were made to smuggle wine into and out of the *pays d'aides* or *de gros* were of a petty and local nature. In consequence, cases in the *aides* tended to be of a civil rather than a criminal nature, revolving around suits for unpaid taxes. Penalties for evading the *aides* normally were confined to fines, seizures of goods, and enforced payment at increased rates. The most common and troublesome offense was selling wine *á muchepot*—that is, of retailing without license, inventory, or declaration and hence without payment of the *huitième* or *quatrième.* All classes in the population indulged in *muchepot*; tavern keepers sold wine under the counter, peasants sold wine without licenses, the *bourgeois* imported wine alleged to be *vin de cru* and sold it clandestinely at retail, nobles and even ecclesiastics were not unfamiliar with the practice. Yet the penalty consisted merely of payment of one hundred livres fine and confiscation of the wine in question. Evasions of the *gros* were similarly penalized. The savage brutality of corporal punishment characteristic of the codes of the *gabelles, tabacs* and *traites* had few counterparts in the *aides.*[37]

THE COSTS OF COLLECTION : *Aides*

The excises of the *droits y jointes* and the complex of general and local *aides* operating amid countless confusions and contradictions were inherently expensive to collect. Although by 1780 the General Farms' inventory

---

[36] *Ibid.,* II, 40-41; Stroum, *Les Finances,* I, 336-337; Perrot, *Inventoire des arrêts du conseil du roi, passim.*
[37] *Encyclopédie méthodique: Finances,* III, 184.

system was functioning smoothly and effectively, it was a costly technique of tax collection. The principal cost was in the great number of employees required to run it. The administration of the *aides* had the largest personnel roster of any element of the General Farms, exclusive of the auxiliary corps of the guards of the *gabelles, tabacs,* and *traites.* In 1774 Lavoisier estimated that the administration of the *aides* (excluding the *entrées de Paris*) employed a total of 2,400 regular, permanently employed *commis des aides,* not counting the three to four thousand *buralistes,* who were considered as casual, part-time agents.[38]

The maintenance of this regiment of tax collectors cost, on an annual average of the years 1768 to 1772, close to 4,964,115 livres. This expense was borne entirely by the Company of General Farmers. In contrast, costs assumed by the king in the administration of the *aides* were only 1,962,112 livres of which 1,553,055 livres represented the *aides* prorated share of the General Farms general expenses. Thirteen percent of the gross yield of an annual average of the years 1768 to 1772 was absorbed as costs of collecting the *aides,* the second most expensive tax in the General Farms to manage (the first being the *traites*).[39]

By the end of the old regime the administration of the *aides* was noted for its "spirit of order . . . method and sound accountability,"[40] and in fact many of its basic procedures survived the Revolution and were incorporated into the nineteenth-century administration of the *impôt sur boissons.*[41] But so long as the taxes themselves remained unreformed in all their incoherent diversity, the *aides* could never be collected efficiently, if costs of collection are taken as a measure of efficiency.

[38] Lavoisier, *Oeuvres,* VI, 155.
[39] *Ibid.,* VI, table on p. 154.
[40] *Archives parlementaires,* IX, 270 (Oct. 21, 1789).
[41] Stroum, *Les Finances,* I, 336.

THE TOWN DUTIES: *Entrées de Paris*

In origin the town duties, or municipal *octrois*, were specific mechanisms of city finance antedating royal taxation. The *octrois* had been established at various times according to the different commercial and industrial circumstances of the chartered towns. They differed in objects struck, in mode of collection and in name. In certain places *octrois* were collected as wholesale and retail sales taxes within the towns themselves; more frequently they were levied as tolls upon goods entering the city gates.[42]

Municipal autonomy disappeared with the development of Bourbon absolutism. One certain sign of this loss of independence was the edict of 1647 which converted all municipal *octrois* into royal *octrois* and appropriated their yields to the benefit of the king's treasury. At the same time, however, the municipalities were permitted to double the rates of the existing *octrois* and to retain for themselves the second half of the increased receipts. There remained but one *octroi* for each city so far as the taxpayer was concerned, but its receipt was divided between the royal treasury and the municipality. That part of the receipt which was accredited to the king was called the royal *octroi*; that part accredited to the city was called the municipal *octroi*. By and large the cities of the *pays d'aides* were the only ones subject to the royal *octrois*. Cities elsewhere were either totally exempt or annually compounded the royal *octrois* by paying lump sums into the General Receipts.[43]

It has been observed that many general and local *aides* were circulation taxes upon the commercial movement of alcoholic beverages and that for administrative reasons these taxes tended to be collected at specific points, generally at the gates of cities through which the liquors

---

[42] Lefebvre de la Bellande, *Traité général des droits d'aides,* I, 281-282.

[43] *Encyclopédie méthodique: Finances,* III, 240-243.

passed. In 1663, in order to reduce the costs of duplicate services, the royal *octrois* were included in the lease on the *ferme-générale des droits d'aides*. From that date onward the same agents collected both orders of taxes at the same place. Ordinarily, the tax-farmers of the *ferme-générale des droits d'aides* also contracted separately with each city for the collection rights over its share of the *octroi*.[44] The royal and municipal *octrois* and the general and local *aides* tended to be collected jointly wherever they coincided. From the point of view of the taxpayer they soon lost their real identity. By the eighteenth century most of the larger cities (such as Paris, Rouen, Orléans, or Tours) supported combined schedules or tariffs of *octrois* and *aides*, such tariffs being called *entrées*. In total the *entrées*, all collected by the General Farms, represented a huge fiscal revenue. In 1789 they yielded some seventy millions of livres, of which forty-six millions were reserved for the monarchy. Of this latter figure, the *entrées de Paris* alone accounted for between twenty-eight and thirty million livres.[45]

The city of Paris bore a greater burden of indirect taxation than any other place in old-regime France. The municipal and royal *octrois* struck at nearly all commodities imported into the city. To these town duties were added a range of royal domainal *péages* levied on an equally comprehensive list of goods. On these tolls, the monarchy piled further duties (called after 1745 *les droits rétablis*) on the same list of goods, the yield of which, about 5,500,000 livres a year, was earmarked to pay the *gages* of a host of venal offices connected with the financial service. In addition, the city of Paris owed numerous special excises, some among the *droits* joined to the *aides*. Others were administered by minor tax-farms or *régies*, on selected items from the list taxed by the *octrois*. It was on top of this formidable accumulation of taxation that the general and local *aides* were heaped.

---

[44] Lefebvre de la Bellande, *Traité général des droits d'aides*, I, 284.
[45] Marion, *Histoire financière*, I, 25-26.

Paris bore three distinct local *aides* in the form of tolls and five general *aides*, the *gros-augmentation*, the *huitième*, the *subvention à détail*, the *droits de jauge et courtage*, and the *annuel*. All indirect taxation levied on Paris was also subject to the general *sous pour livre* surtaxes.[46]

Prior to 1719 the *octrois*, domainal *péages*, special excises (converted into tolls), and the local *aides* were organized as a single *entrées* tariff and collected once at the city gates. But the general *aides* (the sales taxes) were still collected by the General Farms from the wine merchants by inventory. As the city grew in the early eighteenth century, the overhead costs of the inventory system applied to the teeming capital became excessive. Therefore, in 1719 John Law joined the general *aides* to the existing town-duties tariff to produce the final form of the *entrées de Paris*. In the process, the character and function of the *gros* and *huitième*, as those taxes were applied to the greatest single market in France, was completely altered. After 1719 in the city of Paris the *gros* and the *huitième* were no longer wholesale and retail sales taxes. They were now specific tolls on quantity of wine passing through the city gates, functionally indistinguishable from the other town duties.[47]

The development of a single entry toll in place of a

---

[46] Saint-Julien and Bienaymé, *Histoire des droits d'entrée*, pp. 87-88, and table on pp. 141-142; *Encyclopédie méthodique: Finances*, I, 24-25; Lefebvre de la Bellande, *Traité général des droits d'aides*, I, 116-123. Lefebvre presents a list running for six quarto pages of the articles taxed to support useless venal offices. These offices dated principally from 1689. They were periodically suppressed but the taxes created to support them, while moderated, remained. In 1730 the offices were revived and collectively called "les communautés d'officiers." At that date there were 3,196 offices. In 1745 the taxes needed to support them were consolidated and called *les droits rétablis*. They were leased to the Company of General Farmers as part of the *aides* collected with the Paris *entrées*. Despite the fact that in 1776 all the venal offices were suppressed once again, the *droits rétablis* remained to the Revolution. See also *Encyclopédie méthodique: Finances*, II, 50-51. It should be observed that the city of Paris was also one of the few places left in the eighteenth century in which the original *aides* on fish, animals, and wood were still collected.

[47] *Encyclopédie méthodique: Finances*, II, 47.

dozen or more individual taxes did not mean any great alleviation of the disparities in rates and erratic exemptions which characterized the *aides* and *octrois* as a whole. Those institutions and persons which had claims to exemptions under the *aides* still enjoyed the same privileges under the *entrées*. Thus in the city of Paris, some sixty-five religious and eleemosynary institutions (*les hôpitaux*) and at least ten civil establishments (such as the *Ecole Militaire*) enjoyed specific exemptions from the *entrées* on wine and other comestibles coming from estates belonging to such establishments or brought in for their consumption. In general, normal quotas were calculated; when the institution exceeded the limit, it paid the full range of taxes although at reduced rates. The *bourgeoisie de Paris* (members of the dominant guilds, officials in local government, and other notables of similar status) were permitted to import *vin de cru* at reduced rates. The swarms of venal officers connected with the judiciary and financial services were generally privileged in regard to the *entrées* as were members of the royal households and other kinds of functionaries.[48]

Thus in 1760 a muid of wine consigned to a *bourgeois* of Paris and arriving at the city gates by land paid thirty-five livres for the *entrées,* including the current four *sous pour livre.* If the same muid were brought into the city by river barge, the rate was increased by a little over three livres due to additional tolls on the Seine. Again, if the same muid were consigned to a wine merchant, it was charged with forty-six livres if arriving by land and forty-eight livres eight sous if arriving by river. This sum was divided between the king and the municipality. Of the thirty-five livres paid on a muid of wine consigned to a *bourgeois* and arriving by land, twenty livres represented the local and general *aides* and the four *sous pour livre* current in 1760. These sums were credited to the account of the king. The *octrois* (and incidental levies)

[48] Lefebvre de la Bellande, *Traité général des droits d'aides,* III, 57-60, 383-390.

accounted for thirteen livres, of which eight were credited to the account of the king for the royal *octrois* and the remainder was divided about evenly between the municipality and the *hôpitaux*. The General Farms collected all of these tolls at one time as the goods entered the city gates. But for accounting purposes each of the several individual items comprising the *entrées* schedule were kept separate and distinct on the books.[49]

The development of the single *entrées* tariff in 1719 greatly simplified the administrative problems of the General Farms. At that time the city was divided into segments, jurisdiction over each of which was confided to a *bureau des entrées*. In 1774 there were twenty-nine such offices, each headed by a receiver. Part of the function of the *bureaux des entrées* was to police the capital's markets and shops. But more important was the management of several of the city's *entrées* gates. These toll gates lay athwart all roads leading into the capital. They were specialized as to the kinds of goods which might pass them; some were exclusively reserved for animals headed for the butcher's block, others for wood and building materials, others for garden truck, still others for textiles and metals. Only eighteen were designated as the legal entrances for wines, brandies, beers, and other beverages. Each barrier was in the charge of a controller who was assisted by several toll-gate guards who actually manned the portal, inspected incoming and outgoing vehicles, levied and collected the taxes due. In 1774 the administration of the *entrées* employed 756 agents, of which 453 were directly stationed at the toll gates.[50]

Smuggling was the chief problem facing the administration of the *entrées*. Much of it was petty, some was on a grand scale; combined it was a formidable threat to the revenues of the *entrées*. All levels of the population en-

[49] *Ibid.*, I, 11-18; Lefebvre prints comprehensive tables of rates for all *entrées* for 1760 for Rouen as well as Paris.

[50] Lavoisier, *Oeuvres*, VI, 155; *Encyclopédie méthodique: Finances*, I, 92.

gaged in the practice; every conceivable trick was used to infiltrate goods past the toll-gate guards. With each addition of a *sou pour livre* surtax the volume of smuggling increased despite successive edicts giving the toll-gate guards greater and greater powers of inspection over incoming traffic. In 1777 it was ruled that even royal carriages of the queen and princes of the blood would be stopped and searched. In the early 1780s the population of Paris was consuming at least a fifth more taxable goods of all kinds than the revenue receipts of the *entrées* reported as entering the city. It was estimated that the annual revenue loss was in the vicinity of 6,000,000 livres.[51] When revenue loss reached these proportions, the government as well as the General Farms became alarmed. General Farmer Lavoisier, who for years had been engaged in statistical studies of the Paris population, was directed to turn his analytical talents to the problem and to suggest a solution.

Lavoisier discerned two major faults in the administration of the *entrées* to which the high degree of fraudulent activity might be attributed. The first, but less important, stemmed from the flagrant abuses to which the privileges of the religious, charitable, and state institutions located in Paris were subject. The purveyors and commissary agents of these places annually imported far greater quantities of goods than the establishments could consume. It was obvious that the excess was being sold at contraband prices throughout the city. In this matter the legitimate merchants were as much exercised as the General Farmers. As a solution Lavoisier suggested that the privileges of the offending institutions be annulled and replaced by guaranteed annual incomes paid by the treasury. The proposal was adopted and quickly implemented.[52]

The second and more important reason for the inability

[51] Mercier, *Tableau de Paris,* I, 139-140, II, 33-35; *Encyclopédie méthodique: Finances,* I, 81, 84, III, 792.
[52] Mollien, *Mémoires d'un ministre,* I, 81.

of the administration of the *entrées* to control smuggling was related, according to Lavoisier, to the physical growth of the city in the late eighteenth century. The expansion of the capital was such that the arrangement of the toll gates as established in 1719 was no longer capable of halting the illegal traffic. Originally the toll gates had been placed on the outskirts of the city, in some cases amid open fields so as to command an unobstructed view on all sides. They were physically unconnected, ramshackle wooden structures.[53] No wall ran between them and they were linked only by a single communications path. Theoretically this path was patrolled day and night by the General Farms. But in the course of the eighteenth century dense suburbs had grown up between the toll gates, and the communications path was obstructed by walls and gardens, houses and outbuildings, all interconnected by alleys, gates, and passageways. Much of this new suburban area was supplied by goods which never passed the toll gates at all; even more serious, the suburbs served as the channels through which goods could easily be smuggled into the city proper. In view of these facts, Lavoisier suggested that the entire city of Paris be physically enclosed by a continuous wall, broken only by new toll gates. The proposal was submitted to the government and was soon approved. The Company of General Farmers was to supervise and finance the construction of the wall, but the royal treasury was ultimately to pay for it as a capital investment in the General Farms.[54]

Construction on the wall began in 1783 under the guidance of the General Farmer de Saint-Cristeau according to plans drawn up by the architect Ledoux. Gradually the seventh wall of Paris (the *enceinte des fermiers-généraux*) took shape. As finally approved by the government, the plans of the wall and its gates were grandiose. It was built of heavy masonry higher than a man's head, pierced by sixty-six archways containing the

53 Pessard, *Nouveau dictionnaire historique de Paris*, p. 108.
54 Mollien, *Mémoires d'un ministre*, I, 81, 82-84, 86.

toll gates. The gates themselves were of wood, but the archways were of stone embellished by rich sculpture and grille work. Around the inside circumference a new communications road, or *ronde,* was laid out, the construction of which necessitated the removal of numerous private dwellings. Around the outside circumference a broad boulevard completely encircling the city was planned, also involving the destruction of parts of the new suburbs.[55] The cost of the wall was considerable. By 1787, 2,853,000 livres had been expended, while in 1788 an additional 3,600,000 livres were earmarked for the completion of the project.[56] By 1789 fifty-eight of the planned sixty-six handsome new gates had been installed and the wall was almost finished.[57]

However much the wall may have curtailed smuggling activity, its construction was, in terms of popular opinion, a disaster to the General Farmers, to the government, and to Lavoisier personally. It was taken as a symbol of the "tyranny" of the tax-farmers; the expenditure of such great sums on ornamenting an instrument of "fiscal oppression" during a time when the poor of Paris were suffering economic distress was regarded as offensive; the General Farmers were accused of trying to imprison the city; it was seriously argued that the wall shut out such amounts of sunlight and fresh air as to render the capital unfit for human habitation. As one wit put it: "La mur murant Paris, rend Paris murmurant." [58]

On July 12, 1789, two days before the taking of the Bastille, restless mobs fell upon the structure and demolished and burned several of the ornate gateways and barriers. At the same time the administration of the *entrées de Paris* ceased to function.[59]

[55] *Ibid.,* I, 94-97; Pessard, *Nouveau dictionnaire historique de Paris,* p. 831.
[56] *Collection de comptes rendus,* p. 208; Braesch, *Finances et monnaie révolutionnaires,* II, 79.
[57] Pessard, *Nouveau dictionnaire historique de Paris,* pp. 108-110.
[58] *Ibid.,* p. 521; Monin, *Etat de Paris en 1789,* pp. 604-606.
[59] Saint Julien and Bienaymé, *Historie des droits d'entrées,* p. 113.

THE REGISTRY TAXES: Domaines

In the eighteenth century the receipt of the *domaines* was the third most valuable element of the General Farms. Under the Lease Carlier of 1726 the *domaines* was evaluated at 11,500,000 livres out of an annual lease price of 80,000,000 livres. For about thirty-five years after 1726 the net yield of the *domaines* remained relatively stable, but by 1774 it had risen to 20,244,473 livres in the Lease David of that year. In 1781 the yield of the newly organized royal General Administration of the *domaines* was budgeted at about 42,000,000 livres, less operating costs; in 1788 the administration yielded a gross receipt of about 50,837,000 livres and a net receipt of approximately 43,715,754 livres. The post-1780 General Administration, however, contained several elements which had not been included under the receipt of the *domaines* of the period of 1726 to 1780. The chief of these was the *eaux, bois et forêts,* which in 1788 yielded a gross receipt of about 7,000,000 livres and a net receipt of about 4,533,000 livres. The *droit de timbre et formule,* which in 1784 yielded about 6,000,000 livres, less a very low operating cost, was fully included in the *domaines* only in 1780. Prior to that date its yield had been divided between the receipts of the *aides* and the *domaines,* the greater part going to the former.[60] After deducting these items from the schedule of taxes comprising the General Administration of the *domaines*, it may be said that approximately the same range of taxes which in 1726 produced a net receipt of about 11,500,000 livres while a part of the General Farms as the receipt of the *domaines* yielded a net receipt of about 31,000,000 livres in 1788 while a part of the General Administration.[61]

---

[60] Lavoisier, *Oeuvres*, VI, 181; Necker, *Compte rendu*, p. 106; Marion, *Histoire financière*, I, 32; Braesch, *Finances et monnaie révolutionnaires*, II, 86-87; Clamageran, *Histoire de l'impôt*, III, 242.

[61] This figure can only be a very rough approximation. The accounting difference between the General Farms and the General Administration, the presence or absence of various items between the

The eighteenth-century receipt of the *domaines* comprised two major sources of revenue: the *domaines* proper, representing all that remained of the ancient patrimonial and feudal *finances ordinaires,* and the *droits domaniaux,* or those relatively modern taxations concerned with the public registration and authentication of certain legal acts and instruments. The boundary between the two was, however, often obscure, while within both areas there was great complexity and much uncertainty. Both dealt primarily with juridical rather than with economic matters; both consequently were embroiled in the tangle of old-regime jurisprudence.

Of the two sources of revenue available to the receipt of the *domaines* in the eighteenth century, the *domaines* proper were of least fiscal importance. Centuries of alienation, usurpation, and inefficiency had reduced the *finances ordinaires* to obsolescence. The king's seignorial rights (*cens et rentes, péages, passages*) and profits from the direct exploitation of real property (the *domaines corporals*) produced only some 600,000 livres per year. The rights of feudal suzerainty (*lods et ventes, quints, requints, treizièmes, reliefs, rachats, sous-rachats,* and many others) due on changes of tenure within the royal domain yielded at best a million to a million and a half livres per year. Of only slightly more fiscal importance than these revenues were the remnants of medieval taxations dealing with cases of *mainmorte, aubaine, bâtardise, déshérance, confiscation,* and *franc-fief.* The *franc-fief* alone of these levies achieved even a modicum of financial significance. Under the *franc-fief* each common possessor of noble land was required to pay every twenty years the value of one year's revenue from the land to the king; one year's revenue was also due upon every purchase of noble land by a commoner. Large legal loopholes for tax evasion, coupled perhaps with the relative scarcity of this

---

two periods and the lack of accurate statistical break-downs make impossible more than a gross comparison. This is more particularly true of the *domaines* than any other category.

kind of transaction, accounted for the poverty of the yield of the *franc-fief.* Toward the end of the old regime it amounted to only 1,600,000 livres per year.[62] The most important taxes of the receipt of the *domaines* were the *droits domaniaux.* These levies, of which there were more than a score, centered around the series of taxes collected at the time of the compulsory registration of all legal instruments in public record-books. There were three such registry taxes: the *contrôle,* the *insinuation,* and the *centième denier.*

Laws requiring the registration of private legal documents, such as deeds, titles, testaments, and contracts, with competent public authority, were much older than the attempt of the monarchy to exploit the procedure as a source of taxation. Legal documents in which the public at large might have an interest or which might form the basis for a settlement of civil disputes needed to be authenticated and registered in the public record. In this sense the formality of *contrôle* and *insinuation,* two variants of the procedure of registration, were both products of the sixteenth century. But until the end of the seventeenth century the laws were not strictly enforced, nor were they applied to all legal documents. Moreover, the fees charged for the service of *contrôle* and *insinuation* were until 1693 almost purely nominal.

In 1693 an edict of Louis XIV extended the scope of the formality of *contrôle:* it was now mandatory that all legal instruments (with only limited exceptions) drawn up by public notaries, scriveners, clerks of court, and bailiffs be subject to *contrôle,* or registration in extract, in the public records. The act of registration was accompanied by the payment of a tax. This was the *droit de contrôle des actes des notaires.* Without payment of the *droit de contrôle* the formality of registration was invalid.

---

[62] Bosquet, *Dictionnaire raisonné des domaines,* II, 450; *Encyclopédie méthodique: Finances,* I, 217; Moreau de Beaumont, *Mémoires concernant les impositions,* IV, 371; Marion, *Histoire financière,* I, 32-34.

In 1705 the formality of *contrôle* was extended to require registration of all instruments drawn up personally without the aid of public notaries. This was the *contrôle des actes sous seing privé*. The only exception to the *contrôle des actes sous seing privé* were commercial contracts, such as letters of exchange, bills of sale, and personal notes drawn between merchants actively engaged in business. The *contrôle des actes sous seing privé* was purely restrictive in purpose. It was designed to force persons with legal business to employ the services of the notaries and hence to pay the *contrôle* tax. At the same time, the issuance by the courts of writs and injunctions in favor of private persons for purposes of certain kinds of civil actions was subject to the *contrôle des exploits*. A *droit de contrôle des exploits* accompanied the registration of such documents. Up to 1722 the rates of the *contrôle* taxes were moderate; in that year they were drastically increased. The base rate became ten sous per one hundred livres for documents involving values in excess of ten thousand livres. An elaborate tariff of rates applying to special circumstances was built upon these base rates. In 1781 the *contrôles* yielded the General Administration of the *domaines* a net receipt of 15,000,000 livres.[63]

Fundamentally, the eighteenth-century *insinuation* tax and *centième denier* acted as surtaxes on the registration of special kinds of legal documents already subject to the *contrôle* taxes. In 1703 all legal instruments bearing on conveyances of property, claims to property, or liens on income from property arising from gifts, sales, or exchanges between living persons and those arising out of rights of inheritance were subjected to the formality of *insinuation*, a special form of registration. At the same time, they were subjected to a specially created *insinuation* tax. Only gifts from parents to children, marriage

[63] Bosquet, *Dictionnaire raisonné des domaines,* I, 28, 544-568; *Encyclopédie méthodique: Finances,* I, 373-376; Moreau de Beaumont, *Mémoires concernant les impositions,* IV, 505; Besson, *Un Chapitre de notre histoire financière,* p. 21; Stroum, *Les Finances,* I, 394-396.

contracts, direct inheritances, and certain kinds of entails were exempted from the *insinuation* tax. Whereas the *contrôle* taxes were levied upon the registration of all kinds of legal instruments, the *insinuation* tax was levied only upon those connected with property transfers. In general, gifts, sales, and legacies were taxed at the rate of twenty deniers per livre of the declared value of the property involved. A maximum limit of fifty livres was set for any single payment of the tax. The *centième denier* was created in 1703 at the same time as the *insinuation* tax. This was a one percent levy upon the value of property devised by one person to another and paid at the time of the registration of the legal papers involved in the transaction. The distinction between the *insinuation* tax and the *centième denier* was extremely difficult to draw. In general, the *insinuation* tax was applied to *biens meubles*, such as *rentes*, annuities, and commercial and financial investments, while the *centième denier* was applied only to *biens immeubles*, real property, and the rents and usufruct thereof. However, in eighteenth-century jurisprudence real property as a legal term included such medieval forms of "property" as seignorial rights, the benefits of lordships and justices, feudal dues and fines, and manorial claims against land and persons, as well as the private ownership of land, houses, and other material objects. The relative importance of real property so defined in the economic and legal life of France in the eighteenth century may, in part, be judged from the fact that, whereas the *insinuation* tax yielded only about 2,000,000 livres annually, the *centième denier* yielded an annual net receipt of 8,000,000 livres.[64]

The formality of registration, of *contrôle* and *insinuation*, was mandatory throughout the lands of the French monarchy. No province was exempt. The *droits de contrôle, insinuation*, and *centième denier* as taxes levied

[64] Bosquet, *Dictionnaire raisonné des domaines,* I, 389-391, II, 544-568; Moreau de Beaumont, *Mémoires concernant les impositions,* IV, 533-535; *Encyclopédie méthodique: Finances,* I, 217, II, 608.

upon that formality were also applied generally throughout France. To a greater degree than any other group of indirect taxes, save for those connected with the tobacco monopoly, the *domaines* covered nearly the whole of France. Nonetheless, certain exempted regions existed. Flanders, Hainault, Artois, and Cambrésis were conspicuous in having compounded all three of the registry taxes. These provinces paid, in lieu of the taxes, an annual indemnity. Alsace, however, was exempt without the necessity of paying an indemnity. In addition, several cities enjoyed degrees of moderation in the rates of the registry taxes. None, however, was so peculiarly favored as the city of Paris. In 1694, in return for a million livres loan which the Paris notaries made to Louis XIV, all legal documents drawn up and registered by the Paris notaries were freed of the *droit de contrôle des actes*. When in 1772 the new tariff of augmented rates for the *contrôle* was promulgated, the Paris notaries again were exempted on condition that the legal paper and parchment employed by them be subjected to a relatively steep *droit de timbre et formule*. The added stamp taxes did not offset the advantage derived from the exemption from the *contrôle* tax. The result was extremely profitable to the Paris notaries. Legal business from all over France was attracted to the capital because of the comparatively low rate of the registry taxes prevailing there.[65]

In addition to the three main registry taxes, the *droits domaniaux* of the eighteenth-century receipt of the *domaines* included several other minor levies associated with special kinds of property or with the administration of civil justice. Mortgages were subject to special taxation under the *droits d'hypothèques*, which yielded some 160,-

[65] Bosquet, *Dictionnaire raisonné des domaines,* II, 412-416, III, 109-112; Moreau de Beaumont, *Mémoires concernant les impositions,* IV, 499; Marion, *Histoire financière,* I, 32. The eighteenth-century notaries were extremely important elements in the French judicial-economic system. They served as counselors at law, as business agents, as real estate brokers, and often as a species of investment trustees.

000 livres per year. The *droits de greffes*, levied in bewildering variety upon a complex of legal procedures, yielded in 1785 only 120,000 livres. The necessity of having a facsimile of the royal privy seal apposed to all legal papers occasioned the payment of the *droit de petit scel*. This tax yielded a net receipt of six to seven hundred thousand livres at the end of the old regime. The ingenuity with which the monarchy exploited the intricacies of the French legal system was not exhausted by these taxations. Seventeenth- and early eighteenth-century fiscality had created a series of venal offices, the ostensible functions of whose proprietors was to control the expenditures and to supervise the accounts of the law courts. These offices were suppressed and liquidated in 1716, but the taxes which had been imposed upon diverse functions of the courts to provide for their *gages* were continued. In 1727 all these taxes were given the name *droits reservés* and leased as a group to the General Farms as part of the receipt of the *domaines*. The *droits reservés* were of no great fiscal importance, yet they served further to complicate and make expensive the already cumbersome system of civil law.[66]

THE ADMINISTRATION OF THE *Domaines*

Initially the administration of the *domaines* under the General Farms suffered from several ambiguities which were not eliminated until late in the eighteenth century. The greatest difficulty lay in the management of the antique *domaines corporals* (royal seignorial rents, profits of exploitation of royal real property, fees from use of the resources of the king's forests, fisheries, mines, and quarries). On the books of the royal treasury these incomes

---

[66] Bosquet, *Dictionnaire raisonné des domaines,* II, 350, 353, 354; *Encyclopédie méthodique: Finances,* I, 675, II, 524, 547; Moreau de Beaumont, *Mémoires concernant les impositions,* IV, 563. The *droits de greffe* were joined to the receipt of the *domaines* only in 1718; the *droits de petit scel* in 1719. The *droits d'hypothèques* were always leased as an individual farm separate from the General Farms. They were joined to the General Administration of the *domaines* in 1780.

were called the *revenus casuels*, of which only a part (largely confined to the generalities of Tours, Poitiers, and Amiens) was leased as an element of the General Farms receipt of the *domaines*. The remainder was customarily entrusted to the management of a horde of venal officers, totally unconnected with the General Farms, the chiefs of which were the *receveurs généraux* and *receveurs des domaines et bois*. The difficulty was that it was never clear in any given locality which part of the *revenus casuels* pertained to the General Farms and which part to the venal *receveurs*. The situation was further complicated by the fact that both the *receveurs* and the General Farmers leased (or subleased in the case of the latter) the rights of the *revenus casuels* to small revenue-farmers. The entire situation was so tenuous and confused that it was impossible to prevent the revenue-farms from overlapping and duplicating each other. The result was an administrative jungle in the shadows of which only the revenue-farmers profited.[67]

Various half-hearted attempts were made to correct the situation. But it was not until 1771 that the Abbé Terray, then royal controller-general, detached the *revenus casuels* from the lease on the General Farms.[68] The administration of the *domaines*, now occupied principally with the *droits domaniaux*, was considerably simplified.

When the *droits de contrôle, insinuation*, and *centième denier* were first levied, the guardianship of the public registers was confided to venal officers called *contrôleurs des actes* who collected the registry taxes as *gages* of their offices. In 1713-1714 the venal offices of the *contrôleurs des actes* were suppressed, and the formalities of *contrôle*

---

[67] Bosquet, *Dictionnaire raisonné des domaines*, II, 367; *Encyclopédie méthodique: Finances*, I, 207-209, III, 444-445.

[68] Lavoisier, *Oeuvres*, VI, 175. Terray placed all *revenus casuels* out on lease in small revenue-farms. In 1774 Turgot converted these into a *régie*. In 1777 the venal offices of the *receveurs* were suppressed. In 1780 the entire range of *revenus casuels* was placed in the General Administration of the *domaines*. See Turgot, *Oeuvres*, IV, 173-177.

and *insinuation* were entrusted to the public notaries in the cities and the scriveners in the country villages who drew up the legal documents and collected from their clients the taxes due. Rights to recover from the notaries and scriveners in various localities were then placed in several small tax-farms which were leased to individual tax-farming companies. In 1719 these individual tax-farms were joined together to form the *ferme-générale des contrôles, actes, et exploits* which, amalgamated with the existing *ferme-générale des domaines*, became, in 1726, the receipt of the *domaines* of the General Farms.[69]

For several years after 1726 the General Farms continued the practice under which the notaries and scriveners maintained the public registers and initially collected the registry taxes from their clients. But this method was inefficient from the point of view of the General Farms and irksome to the notaries and scriveners. The latter received only a small percentage of the tax yield as their remuneration and tended to interpret the laws of the *contrôles* and *insinuations* in the favor of their clients. Therefore, the General Farms sought to tighten the lax management of the *droits domaniaux*. By a gradual process which was not fully completed until 1774 the maintenance of the public registers and the duties of tax collection were taken away from the notaries and scriveners and confided to General Farms agents. In the larger cities and towns these agents were called controllers of legal acts, and in the smaller rural villages they were called *buralistes*. The difference between the two, aside from the greater volume of business handled by the former, was that the controllers were regular, wage-earning professionally trained employees of the General Farms, while the *buralistes* were only casually employed, being paid a percentage rather than a wage. As this system was extended throughout France, the General Farms centralized

[69] Bosquet, *Dictionnaire raisonné des domaines,* I, 548.

control in large *bureaux de contrôle* to whose chiefs the controllers and *buralistes* remitted revenue collected and submitted their accounts for audit and their registers for inspection.[70]

The process of collecting the registry taxes was mechanically simple. Since no legal document was valid at law without registration in the public registers, and since the controllers and *buralistes* had possession of these books, outright tax evasion was practically impossible. But once presented with a tax bill, the taxpayer had great opportunity to contest the General Farms claims and turn his protest into legal action. By their very nature, the registry taxes were the most litigious in the General Farms. Such suits, entirely civil in nature, were argued in a variety of courts, the chief being the court of the *bureaux des finances* and the court of the royal intendants, with appeals running to the Parlements, the *cour des aides,* and even the *chambres des comptes. Domaines* cases were generally extremely complicated and expensive to all parties concerned. Consequently, the General Farmers, on the one hand, strove to maintain a high level of competence among its *commis des domaines* so as to prevent errors and, on the other, to give to its reading of the basic law of 1722 a precision uniformly applicable throughout France. During the course of the eighteenth century the General Farmers refined and codified the law and issued detailed instructions on all possible contingencies to the employees in the form of dictionaries, handbooks, and special bulletins. Through a rigid system of inspections, the Company tried to eliminate capricious action on the part of the controllers and *buralistes* at the same time as it meticulously scrutinized each legal document to obviate fraud on the part of the taxpayer. To individuals possessed of no knowledge of the law, the actions of the General Farms often seemed arbitrary and unjust; but the

[70] Poujaud, *Plan général de régie, ferme des domaines,* pp. 2-8, 89-103.

basic fault lay not with the General Farms but with the obscurities of the old-regime jurisprudence.[71] Even the irascible Marquis d'Argenson admitted, in 1749, that the administration of the *domaines* was a model of order and regularity with intelligent, well-trained men in charge.[72] The fundamental procedures of the eighteenth-century General Farms in regard to the registry taxes were sound to the extent that when, in 1790, the Revolutionary Assembly created the modern French *enregistrement* tax, the administration of that levy was modeled after that created by the General Farmers.[73]

THE COSTS OF COLLECTION : *Domaines*

The *droits domaniaux* of the receipt of the *domaines* were the least expensive to collect of all elements in the General Farms. According to the statistics of Lavoisier, only 4½ percent of the annual average gross yield of 24,225,384 livres for the years 1768-1772 was absorbed as costs of collection. It would seem that this low percentage was largely a reflection of the fact that, of all receipts, the *domaines* required the least number of regular employees. In 1774, according to Lavoisier, there were only 884 regularly employed agents in the *domaines*, not including two to three thousand casually attached *buralistes*.[74]

---

[71] Bosquet, *Dictionnaire raisonné des domaines,* II, 367.
[72] D'Argenson, *Journal et mémoires,* V, 109.
[73] Stroum, *Les Finances,* I, 394-398.
[74] Lavoisier, *Oeuvres,* VI, 151-155, table on p. 154.

7. The Bureaucracy
of the General Farms

The bureaucracy of the General Farms was one of the most highly organized segments of civil administration in eighteenth-century France. In structure it was a series of administrative levels each depending upon the one above for direction. Action occurred only on the basis of standing rules and regulations or upon written orders from higher authority. The General Farms moved by bureaucratic inertia rather than by individual initiative. The permanently employed agents of the General Farms, the *commis des fermes*,[1] were professional functionaries dependent upon the organization for livelihood and status. Unlike other branches of the royal fiscal service, within

[1] A fairly clear distinction was drawn between the *commis des fermes* and casually employed workers. A *commis* was a commissioned royal officer and not, technically, an employee of the Company. Juridically it was only by virtue of his commission that the *commis* had any authority to enforce royal tax rights. That authority, upon which rested the entire tax-collecting enterprise was leased by the Company as part of the General Farms. All administrative officers, actual tax gatherers and guards were *commis des fermes*. Many clerks, workers in such places as the tobacco factories were casual noncommissioned employees. However, the *buralistes*, while casual, were commissioned and hence were *commis des fermes*. By law the *commis* had to be twenty-one, Catholic, and of good character. He was forbidden to have private business activity while in the service. He was forbidden to have a financial interest in the Company of General Farmers. See *Répertoire universel de jurisprudence*, IV, 80-85; *Encyclopédie méthodique: Finances*, I, 333-334, III, 701-702.

the General Farms venal proprietorship of office did not exist . The General Farms was probably more responsive to centralized control than most other comparable parts of the administration of the kingdom.

The bureaucracy of the General Farms, however, contained many peculiarities and ambiguities. Originally, the General Farms had been an amalgamation of individual tax-farms joined together in a piecemeal fashion. In the course of the eighteenth century other units, such as the registry taxes and the tobacco monopoly, had been added. Most often the additions were effected by dovetailing the new with the old. Resultant organizational stresses and strains were never entirely eliminated. Like the government of which it was a part, the General Farms contained many administrative disjunctures, both at its center and in its provincial branches.

PROVINCIAL ADMINISTRATION : THE
PROVINCIAL DIRECTIONS

The Provincial Direction was the key division of the General Farms.[2] Essentially a grouping of functional local units, such as *greniers,* tobacco stores, customs houses, *bureaux des aides* and *domaines* and of service units, such as divisions of guards, primary warehouses, and *caisses* for the centralization of receipts,[3] the Provincial Direction was equipped with the administrative and legal machinery of actual tax collecting.

In geographic distribution, the Provincial Directions were modeled after the royal generalities. As a rule there was approximately one Provincial Direction for each royal generality and for each receipt of the General Farms applicable to the area. For example, the generality of Orléans contained five Provincial Directions, one each for *gabelles, tabacs, traites, aides,* and *domaines.* But in the

---

[2] See Appendix pp. 286, 289-292.

[3] The *caisses* referred to are those of the general provincial receivers shown in Appendix p. 287. They are not to be confused with the General Receivers of the royal *taille.*

generality of Bordeaux there were only three Provincial Directions, one each for the *traites, tabacs,* and *domaines.* Thus, while in 1763 there were but 33 royal generalities, there were 123 Provincial Directions (or equivalents).[4]

In the *gabelles, tabacs,* and *traites* there was considerable interchange of functions and personnel among the Provincial Directions. Wherever a Provincial Direction of *gabelles* coincided with one for *traites,* or *tabacs* (after 1730), one individual Provincial Director headed all sections simultaneously. The controllers-general, who, as deputies of the Provincial Director, supervised the *greniers,* tobacco stores, and customs houses in the districts into which the Provincial Direction was subdivided, also were charged with management of the three sorts of taxes simultaneously. It has already been shown that the corps of guards policed the country in the service of the *gabelles, tabacs,* and *traites* indiscriminately. The tendency to treat the salt and tobacco monopolies as one administrative body on the provincial level was so far advanced in the late eighteenth century that the common heading *gabelles et tabacs* was frequently used. However, Provincial Directions concerned with the *aides* and *domaines* always remained separate and distinct one from the other and from those of the *gabelles et tabacs* and *traites.*[5]

---

[4] Typically the area of a Provincial Direction was somewhat less than that of a royal generality, especially in the *aides* where many were no bigger than a royal election. There were several Provincial Directions, especially in the *traites* which were not located in areas coterminous with a generality. However, in the majority of cases the Provincial Direction headquarters was located in the same city in which the intendant was seated. Like the generality, the Provincial Direction derived its name from that city. The equivalents mentioned are certain units, especially in *gabelles, aides,* and *domaines,* which were administered in a manner different from that described. They concerned the atypical case of Paris. Also included as equivalents were certain administrative units of the *droits* joined to the *aides* atypical of the Provincial Directions as a whole. See *Dictionnaire géographique,* III, 102-103.

[5] See Appendix pp. 289-290. *Dictionnaire géographique,* III, 103-104; Moreau de Beaumont, *Mémoires concernant les impositions,* IV, 641; Lavoisier, *Oeuvres,* VI, 155; *Encyclopédie méthodique: Finances,* I, 33, 376. In the *gabelles, tabacs,* and *traites* the Provincial Director's

The Provincial Director, holding the highest bureaucratic rank in the service of the General Farms, was the active, responsible, executive head of the Provincial Direction. He was the prime mover of the administrative machinery, the tax collector-in-chief, the head of the accounting system, the chief of personnel in his Provincial Direction. Moreover, he was invested with power of attorney to act, in the name of the Company of General Farmers, in all legal matters affecting his jurisdiction. The Provincial Director was to the regimen of the General Farms what the intendant was to the royal government—the direct representative of central authority in the provinces and the mainspring of local administration. But unlike the commission issued to the intendant, which contained only a broad description of duties and provided for personal initiative, the commission of the Provincial Director was detailed and rigid. Expected to be familiar with the minutiae of bureaucratic procedure, the Provincial Director was often overburdened with work, especially when he was in charge of a Provincial Direction combining *gabelles et tabacs* with *traites*. The quantity of reports and statistical data which he was required to submit to General Farms headquarters in Paris was formidable. Generally he was inadequately provided with clerks; those whom he had, he hired himself and housed in his own home as part of his family. Too much of his time was taken up prosecuting cases in the courts or defending General Farms personnel before local tribunals. In the *gabelles et tabacs*, particularly in areas bordering the *pays rédimés* or *francs*, he was forced to act as a kind of commander of the financial militia in a ceaseless campaign against the smugglers. Furthermore, the Provincial Director was given little leeway to exercise discretionary authority. Initiative tended to be discouraged,

---

deputies were called controllers-general, but in the *domaines* they were, in the north, *vérificateurs*, and in the south, *inspecteurs*. Provincial Directors of the *aides* had no deputies.

and a premium was placed upon an exhaustive knowledge of laws, rules, and regulations. Above all, vigilance over the accounts was regarded as the mark of a successful Provincial Director. The result was a provincial administration which, while efficient and precise, was overly dedicated to routine. The impulse to improve the quality of service normally came to the Provincial Directors only from higher authority.[6]

CENTRAL ADMINISTRATION : THE *Hôtel des Fermes*

One of the peculiarities of administration in the General Farms was the fact that the Provincial Directions were not organized in monocratic departments, each representing one of the five major receipts of *gabelles, tabacs, traites, aides,* or *domaines* and each headed by a single executive officer or office. The *régie de l'Hôtel des Fermes*,[7] to give the central Paris headquarters its proper title, comprised two sections. The first consisted of five special units, one each for General Receipts (treasury),

[6] *Répertoire universel de jurisprudence,* IV, 89-90; *Encyclopédie méthodique: Finances,* I, 562-567 (the complete commission and procuration of a late eighteenth-century Provincial Director is printed here with comments by Rousselot de Surgy) ; Brunet de Grandmaison, *Dictionnaire des aydes,* I, 170; Poujaud, *Plan de régie, ferme des domaines,* pp. 185-200; Delahante, *Une Famille de finance,* II, 29-46, presents a description of the life of a mid-eighteenth-century Provincial Director.

[7] The *régie de l'Hôtel des Fermes* was usually referred to simply as the *Hôtel des Fermes,* after the principal building which housed it. But actually, in a physical sense, the central headquarters was distributed among four separate structures. The center of affairs was the *Hôtel des Fermes,* a sumptuous establishment, once occupied by the French Academy, which had been acquired by the Company at the end of the seventeenth century. In its elegant chambers sat the Assemblies of the Company of General Farmers; in its offices functioned the main central agencies of the General Farms. Annexes to the *Hôtel des Fermes* were the *Hôtel de Bretonvilliers* which housed the offices of the *entrées de Paris,* the *Hôtel de Longueville* from which the tobacco monopoly was administered since the time of John Law, and the handsome *grenier à sel* built by Louis XIV which served as the headquarters of the salt monopolies. See Pessard, *Nouveau dictionnaire historique de Paris,* p. 577; Grimaux, *Lavoisier,* p. 65; Funck-Brentano, *Mandrin,* p. 5.

General Accounts, Personnel, Legal Affairs and General Secretariat. These sections, handling affairs common to the entire General Farms on a nation-wide basis were recognizable functional departments. But the second section of the *Hôtel des Fermes*, called the General Direction, was only a series of *bureaux de correspondance*, the ostensible function of which was merely to facilitate communication between the Company of General Farmers and the Provincial Directions.[8] Each bureau was in constant communication with several Provincial Directions, but there was no one bureau for *gabelles et tabacs, traites, aides,* or *domaines.* Moreover, in certain cases, integration of administration on the provincial level was not carried through on the central level; for example, Provincial Directions combining *gabelles et tabacs* with *traites* under one Provincial Director reported to at least two distinct *bureaux de correspondance.*

The *bureau de correspondance* [9] was headed by a Director, but this official was not an executive chief over the Provincial Directions assigned to his office. In bureaucratic dignity he ranked below the Provincial Directors with whom he corresponded. Further, he was only an administrative assistant, albeit a permanent and highly skilled one, to his superior, the Correspondent General Farmer, a tax-farmer delegated to serve for a short term as supervisor of the bureau. While it is true that, as will be shown presently, the Directors of the several *bureaux de correspondance* actually exercised the kind of authority common to a permanent undersecretariat, offi-

[8] See Appendix pp. 289-292. In terms of personnel, the *régie de l'Hôtel des Fermes* was very large. In 1774 Lavoisier gave 591 as the total number of *commis* laboring in the central headquarters. See Lavoisier, *Oeuvres,* VI, 157; *Dictionnaire géographique,* III, 106.

[9] In 1773 the *bureau de correspondance* communicating with the Provincial Directions of Angers, Tours, Orléans, Bourges, and Moulins for *gabelles et tabacs,* consisted of the director, one *chef,* and one *sou-chef de bureau,* two chief clerks, and several supernumeraries, besides the Correspondent General Farmer. See Delahante, *Une Famille de finance,* II, 99.

cially they were only superior clerks in a complex message center for the transmission of instructions and reports to and from the Provincial Directors and the ultimate authority in the General Farms, the Company of General Farmers.

THE COMPANY OF GENERAL FARMERS: THE ADMINISTRATIVE ROLE

The discretionary authority exercised by the Company of General Farmers over the bureaucracy of the General Farms was rooted in the related fictions of the unity of the Company, and of its universal competence to decide and to execute policy throughout the entire organization. After 1756 the Company of General Farmers was a multiple partnership of sixty members.[10] Unlimited liability and collective responsibility were the essential principles of this partnership. Each General Farmer contributed an

[10] Up to 1756 the Company comprised forty General Farmers. However, during the period 1726 to 1756, the Company customarily subfarmed the *aides* (except *entrées de Paris*) and the *domaines* to some twenty-seven regularly established *compagnies des sous-fermiers-généraux*. These subfarming companies supplied part of the capital for the total tax-farming enterprise and assumed managerial responsibility over their *sous-fermes-générales,* most of which were organized into Provincial Directions according to the standard adopted throughout the General Farms. The existence of the subfarms had little effect upon the bureaucratic structure of the whole since they were administered under the supervision of the Company of General Farmers according to procedures laid down by it. At the highest echelon of administration, that of the Company itself, the subfarming companies simply met as supplementary bodies to the Company's own administrative assemblies. In 1756 subfarming was suppressed and the Company of General Farmers assumed direct responsibility for the *aides* and *domaines,* As a consequence, the membership of the Company of General Farmers was raised to sixty. It remained at that figure until 1780, when the *aides* were detached to form the new General Commission of the *aides* and the *domaines* were detached to form the new General Administration of the *domaines.* At that time the membership of the Company of General Farmers dropped back to forty, to be increased again to forty four, for certain financial reasons, in 1787. The period selected for study is *circa* 1763, a date for which considerable data are available. See Lefebvre de la Bellande, *Traité général des droits d'aides,* VI, 170-171, and Lavoisier, *Oeuvres,* VI, 137.

equal share of the capital funds of the Company. Each enjoyed formal equality of voice in all financial and administrative decisions. Consequently, the Company of General Farmers did not delegate its authority to a single board of directors, nor did it have an elected or appointed president, treasurer, or secretary. Officially everything connected with the General Farms was done by the Company acting as a collective body. Ultimate responsibility was thus diffused throughout the membership of the entire Company. No one General Farmer had the right to assume responsibility or to act as an individual for any part of the General Farms.[11]

This conception of unity and equality entailed a "collegiate" form of administration. The Company governed the General Farms by means of a series of collective boards called Assemblies,[12] one at the head of each major segment of the bureaucracy. The Assembly was conceived of as both a legislative and an executive body. It represented the ongoing authority of the Company of General Farmers to formulate policy or to undertake basic alterations in procedure within that part of the bureaucracy submitted to its jurisdiction. It verified accounts and served as a board of review for all activities. But the Assembly also, theoretically, directed the execution of the policies it made. It received reports and requests for instructions from the Provincial Directors on matters of detail affecting even the most obscure parts of the General Farms. Ostensibly nothing of even a routine nature was done without sanction of the Assembly; nothing in the order of new action was undertaken without its approval. A constant stream of directives and instructions flowed from the Assembly dealing with all matters great and small. Each of these bureaucratic orders was regarded as the expression of the Assembly as a whole, speaking in the name of the Company. For validity all

---

[11] Delahante, *Une Famille de finance,* I, 202.

[12] *Encyclopédie méthodique: Finances,* I, 58, 321. After 1780 the Assemblies were called Committees.

orders bore the signatures of at least six General Farmers.[13]

In 1763 there were sixteen Assemblies, averaging about twelve General Farmers each, for a total membership of two hundred and two.[14] Every General Farmer customarily sat on four or five Assemblies simultaneously and was rotated among the Assemblies at least every two years, thus affording him the chance to participate in the deliberations of a majority of the Assemblies in the course of a six-year lease. Each Assembly was chaired by a president, but this position was also rotated annually among the membership. Thus membership was largely interchangeable among all Assemblies and among certain of them it was identical.[15]

Appointment to the Assemblies, as to all administrative positions in the General Farms, was subject to the approval of the royal controller-general, who each year issued an *arrêt des départements des messieurs les fermiers-généraux* in which the composition, time, and place

---

[13] Orders in the General Farms took various forms. The most formal was the *délibération,* an official pronouncement of the Company of General Farmers on a matter of fundamental policy signed by a majority of the partners. A *délibération* required the countersignature of the royal controller-general and was registered with the Paris *Cour des Aides,* thereby becoming can act of royal legislation. It was phrased in language reminiscent of a royal edict always concluding with the formula, "Fait et délibéré à l'Hôtel des Fermes du Roi, à Paris, le . . . [date]." An *ordre* generally dealt with some interpretation of royal law rendered by the Assembly. It was countersigned by the royal controller-general and was posted and published for public inspection. *Lettres-circulaires* were similar to *ordres* except that they were designed to be read only by General Farms personnel. Directives on purely routine matters of administration were handled by the less formal *mémoires* and *instructions.* These were not countersigned by the royal controller-general but did require the signature of at least six General Farmers. Increasingly in the eighteenth century *ordres* and *lettres-circulaires* came to resemble special forms of *arrêts* issued by the *conseil de finances.* Sometimes they were printed by the *imprimeur des fermes,* sometimes by the *imprimeur du roi.* See *Encyclopédie méthodique: Finances,* I, 415.

[14] See Appendix p. 286.

[15] *Dictionnaire géographique,* III, 102; Delahante, *Une famille de finance,* I, 202-203.

of meeting of the Assemblies was officially announced.[16] The Assemblies were in session five and a half days a week every week in the year. Although the conduct of business was often more formal than actual, they met according to a rigid schedule arranged in such a manner that each Assembly was in session at least once a week. Various aspects of the administrative business of the Company of General Farmers were thus conducted in orderly sequence, each General Farmer being given the opportunity formally to voice his opinion on at least a majority of issues during the term of a lease.

There were two categories of Assemblies in 1763. The first (called the *assemblées de la ferme-générale*), a series of six interlocking Assemblies with a total membership of about forty-eight General Farmers, represented the Company meeting to consider affairs affecting the General Farms as a whole. These Assemblies were placed over the five special departments of the *Hôtel des Fermes* for administration of the General Receipts (treasury), General Accounts, Personnel, Legal Affairs, and General Secretariat. The second category of Assemblies (called the *assemblées des régies des fermes*), with a total mem-

---

[16] The *arrêt des départements des messieurs les fermiers-généraux* was registered in the Paris *Cour des Aides* and was thus a part of royal law. It was also published in the *Almanach Royal*. During the eighteenth century the *départements* grew increasingly rich in details. In 1703 it occupied barely a page in the *Almanach Royal* and consisted merely of a list of the General Farmers and their addresses. In 1749 it contained names, addresses, and administrative posts of all General Farmers and subfarmers, lists of the Assemblies with time of meeting, list of all Provincial Directors and General Provincial Receivers, together with the names and functions of the Directors of the *Hôtel des Fermes*. In 1785 the *départements* occupied eighteen pages in the *Almanach Royal*. It contained a comprehensive breakdown of all administrative posts in the General Farms from the General Farmers and their Assemblies (Committees), through the *Hôtel des Fermes* and the Provincial Directions down to the level of the most prominent Receivers of the *bureaux des fermes*. This development indicates not so much a progressively more articulated bureaucracy as an exposure to public view of administrative details once kept secret by the Company and the royal government. See *Almanachs Royals*, (1703) p. 54, (1749) pp. 350-358, (1785) pp. 553-571, and the entire series *passim: Encyclopédie méthodique: Finances*, I, 489-491.

bership of 154, represented the Company meeting to consider affairs directly affecting each of the five major receipts of *gabelles, tabacs, traites, aides* (and *entrées*), and *domaines.* These received reports from and issued instructions to the Provincial Directors through the intermediary *bureaux de correspondance* of the General Direction of the *Hôtel des Fermes.*[17]

Among the Assemblies none was given formal precedence over the rest, but one, the *Assemblée des caisses,* enjoyed a special preeminence. Unlike other Assemblies, membership in the *caisses* was not rotated systematically among the General Farmers. In practice only the most wealthy and experienced partners were admitted to its meetings, and appointment to its membership was regarded as a life tenure. Although Lavoisier entered the General Farms in 1768, it was not until 1783 that he was called to the *caisses.*[18] The *caisses* dealt mostly with affairs external to the routine administration of the General Farms. It was the only legal intermediary between the government and the Company as a whole. It alone negotiated the terms of the leases. It alone controlled the amount of government indebtedness which the Company would hold. In internal affairs, the *caisses* was at the head of no single section of the General Farms, although it was the final authority in all matters concerning finances, receipts, and accounts. Nevertheless, the *assemblée des caisses* by reason of the wealth and seniority of its members and of its unique connection with the government, exercised a kind of *de facto* leadership among the other Assemblies. By persuasion, rather than by command, the *caisse* intervened in disputes, influenced the appointment of General Farmers to the Assemblies, and in general indirectly guided the Company.[19]

17 See Appendix p. 286.

18 Grimaux, *Lavoisier,* p. 77. The *comité d'administration* to which Lavoisier was appointed in 1783 was the name commonly used for the *assemblée des caisses* after 1780.

19 *Dictionnaire géographique,* III, 102; Delahante, *Une Famille de finance,* I, 204. Delahante says of the *assemblée des caisses* that it

The same need of positive leadership, which created for the *assemblée des caisses* an informal suzerainty over the other Assemblies, also tended to reduce the omnipotence of the Assemblies over the Provincial Directions. It was difficult to manage quickly the detailed affairs of the Provincial Directions through the medium of slow-moving, collective boards adapted more to debating than to making decisions. In consequence, the Correspondent General Farmers (of whom there were thirty-three in 1763) [20] and the permanent bureaucratic Directors of the *bureaux de correspondance* were of considerable practical importance.

Officially the Correspondent General Farmer had no discretionary authority; he was only a temporary executive secretary nominated by his Assembly to supervise the activities of a *bureau de correspondance*. His formal function was simply to follow the "contentieux et police" of the Provincial Directions served by the bureau, to submit reports and recommendations to his Assembly and to transmit to the Provincial Directors the decisions and instructions of the Assembly.[21] Actually the position of the Correspondent General Farmer was such that an energetic, intelligent man could easily take initiative away from the Assembly. Often he assumed active leadership of the Provincial Directions assigned to his bureau. Occasionally he acted as the unofficial head of an entire grouping of bureaus handling the affairs of a whole branch of the General Farms.

The Correspondent General Farmer alone had the power to decide what to report to his Assembly and in what order. Moreover, he alone interpreted the instructions of the Assembly. Institutionally there were only two

was "without title, without apparent dignity . . . fundamentally the senate, or better, the council of ten of the oligarchic republic" of finance.

[20] *Dictionnaire géographique*, III, 103-104.
[21] *Encyclopédie méthodique: Finances*, I, 58.

checks upon the actions of the Correspondent General Farmer. All bureaucratic orders had to be signed by at least six General Farmers of the Assembly in whose name they were made out. But since the membership of the Assemblies was interchangeable, practically any six signatures were sufficient. The Correspondent General Farmer had no difficulty securing the necessary names to a document which he might draw up and dispatch to the Provincial Directions solely upon his own initiative. The second institutional check was equally weak. Correspondent General Farmers were rotated among the bureaus on an annual basis, leaving little time for familiarization with the routine before being removed. But the rotation was always from one bureau to another within the same branch of the service during a six-year lease. It was a simple matter for the Correspondent General Farmer of one bureau to issue orders affecting another bureau. An industrious Correspondent could easily exercise predominating influence over his colleagues and emerge as a kind of chief among them.[22]

It would seem that much of the business of the General Farms was actually conducted in this informal but effective manner.[23] The *assemblées des régies des fermes* were often reduced to the position of approving decisions executed weeks earlier. Thus the young E. M. Delahante, Correspondent General Farmer for the second *bureau de correspondance, petites gabelles,* in the late 1770's, entirely on his own initiative, negotiated directly with the Estates of Viverais for the settlement of a vexing dispute involving a shift in the boundaries of the *gabelles de Languedoc.* He sought the approval of the *assemblée des petites gabelles* only after he had completed the transaction. The Assembly routinely accepted his action without question. In 1786 he performed a similar feat in the elimination of certain customs houses in Rous-

22 Delahante, *Une Famille de finance,* I, 205.
23 *Ibid.,* I, 98-99.

sillon; the *assemblée des traites* sanctioned his action after it had already been accomplished.[24]   The Assemblies were important as repositories of collective responsibility but not as executive instruments.   Moreover, the Assemblies tended to be dominated by the more cautious of the General Farmers.   Admirably suited to a patient, exhaustive consideration of basic policy, the Assemblies were slow to react to new conditions.   Nearly always it was the Correspondent General Farmer who initiated changes. While the Assemblies debated, exchanged memoires, and recommended investigations, policies were often being changed through the efforts of small groups of Correspondent General Farmers working through the bureaus of the *Hôtel des Fermes*.   It took fourteen years for the *assemblée des tabacs* officially to arrive at the decision to exclude the tobacconists from the snuff-making business and to prepare snuff in the royal tobacco factories.   Yet during that time in Provincial Direction after Provincial Direction the change was being effected by independent action of the Correspondent General Farmers.   In 1782 the *assemblée des tabacs* merely sanctioned a reversal of policy which for all practical purposes had been long since accomplished throughout most of the General Farms.

A certain unevenness of administration resulted from the assumption of initiative by individual Correspondents, an unevenness aggravated by the lack of monocratically designed departments for each of the five major receipts. Not all General Farmers, most likely not even a majority, were men dedicated to efficiency and hard labor in the *bureaux de correspondance*.   An uninterested or indolent General Farmer placed in a bureau tended to defer to more industrious colleagues or, in the absence of such personalities, tended to leave the real management of affairs to the professional Director, a bureaucratic official wedded to routine.   In such a situation the wheels of the tax-collecting engine, moving in well-worn grooves, required little guidance.   The basic procedures, embodied in standing

[24] *Ibid.,* pp. 108-116.

rules and regulations meticulously observed by a trained but uninspired personnel, were so well and minutely formulated that the Provincial Directors could continue indefinitely along accustomed paths without loss of revenue. Thus while one set of Provincial Directions in, for example, the *gabelles*, might be spurred into unusual activity by an assiduous Correspondent, another set might be working in an entirely routine manner. On the whole, the bureaucracy was inherently conservative and content to function within the narrow limits of a lethargic compliance with existing regulations. Unless constantly prodded from the top, it moved sluggishly.

It was recognition of the fact that the sprawling bureaucracy of the General Farms required a measure of direct supervision not possible for the Assemblies and Correspondent General Farmers seated in Paris to accomplish that led the Company to forge its most useful administrative tool. This was the *tournée* or regular inspection. Each year from six to eight General Farmers were placed on detached service from their Assemblies as *tourneurs*. The *tourneur* was often the most crucial figure in the Company management of the General Farms. His authority to inspect, verify, and correct on the scene was virtually unlimited. Through him the Company exerted direct control over the most remote branches of the service.

A *tournée* was not a casual meandering through the provinces but a rigidly scheduled tour of inspection consuming months of travel far from the comforts of Paris. For example, in the years 1745 and 1746 the General Farmer de Caze made two *tournées*, each of eight months' duration, in the Provincial Directions of Dijon and Châlons-sur-Saone for *gabelles et tabacs* and *traites* in the Burgundy-Franche Comté area. Much of this time he spent in the saddle from dawn to dusk; at nights he penned reports on his findings which were sent by special messenger to the *assemblée du personnel* for ultimate distribution to all interested Assemblies and Correspon-

dent General Farmers.   In the course of his inspection
de Caze visited thirty-two *greniers à sel*, running special
audits on the books of each.   He inspected thirty-five
customs houses, settled disputes among local officials,
ordered the creation of new customs houses, interviewed
employees, advanced some in rank, dismissed others.   He
scrutinized the accounts and operations of two general
tobacco offices and twenty tobacco stores.   He visited the
posts of the corps of guards, organized a more efficient de-
ployment of forces, commended a few captains-general
for their meritorious service, criticized others for laxity.
He audited the books of the General Provincial Receiver
for Dijon and found them lacking.   His weekly reports
on each of these local units were filled with technical
knowledge of the operations he was observing and revealed
a serious mind intent upon improving the service.[25]

While de Caze was in Burgundy, at least five other
General Farmers were making similar tours in other parts
of France.   During the course of Antoine Lavoisier's
career in the General Farms, the financier-chemist went
on three *tournées*.   During these trips he traversed the
whole of northern and central France inspecting primarily
the tobacco factories and stores.   Sometimes several *tourneurs* joined forces on a trip.   In 1770 Lavoisier was one
of four General Farmers inspecting the operation of the
whole General Farms in northern France.   When the snuff
problem became acute in the 1760's the General Farmers
Delahante, Lavoisier, and Parseval made repeated *tournées* to the tobacco factories and stores in Brittany, Clermentois, Trois Evechés and Lorraine to gather information on technical processes.[26]

The General Farmer on *tournée* represented the wealth
and power of the Company of General Farmers: he
traveled with a suitable train of assistants and squires.
In 1764 the General Farmer de Parseval on *tournée* in

[25] Pitre, *La Ferme-générale en Bourgogne, passim.*
[26] Grimaux, *Lavoisier,* pp. 32-34; Delahante, *Une Famille de
finance,* I, 325.

the Provincial Direction of Coustance for *gabelles et tabacs* and *traites* was accompanied by a cavalcade of fifteen to eighteen men uniformed in the semimilitary garb of the General Farms.[27] Often special agents from the Department of General Accounts journeyed with the *tourneur*, riding in advance to the outlying *bureaux des fermes* for preliminary surprise inspections. The *tournée* was a grueling physical experience; occasionally it was emotionally upsetting. The philosopher-financier General Farmer Helvétius while on *tournée* in the Provincial Direction of Bordeaux for *aides* was appalled at the severity of certain General Farms procedures and offered to lead the local citizenry in an attack upon the local *bureau des aides*.[28] In any case, the *tournée* was one of the most important devices of the Company of General Farmers. Vigorously conducted, it kept open the channels of communication between the Company in Paris and the Provincial Directors. Periodically it energized the provincial bureaucratic machinery.

However, the greatest administrative difficulties in the General Farms were to be found in the General Direction of the *Hôtel des Fermes* and in the Company of General Farmers itself. As the data on costs of collection in each of the five receipts have shown, provincial administration was reasonably efficient within the limit set by the involuted character of the taxes themselves. But central administration was uneven and top-heavy with General Farmers, most of whom rendered only nominal service. The elaborate organization of the Assemblies carefully preserved the fiction that sixty General Farmers were required to legislate for the General Farms. The system of rotating the Correspondents through the *bureaux de correspondance* perpetuated the illusion that thirty-three General Farmers were needed each year to execute policy. In reality the system only complicated the General Direction of the *Hôtel des Fermes,* creating duplicate offices

---

27 Delahante, *Une Famille de finance,* II, 34.
28 Thirion, *La Vie privée des financiers,* p. 205.

wasteful of personnel and effort. The existence of the
Assemblies and rotating Correspondents disguised the fact
that the majority of General Farmers made only token
contributions to the management of the General Farms
and some not even that.

Informed observers of the General Farms were always
aware of this state of affairs. In 1719 John Law entrusted the General Farms to thirty directors and planned
rapidly to reduce the figure. In 1753 the Marquis
d'Argenson, with customary acerbity, declared that of
forty General Farmers only six or seven ever did any
work; in 1756 he complained that, of the twenty new
General Farmers appointed that year, only three would
be managerial assets to the General Farms. Eighteen
years later Turgot insisted that ten tax commissioners
could have managed the General Farms more efficiently
than the sixty General Farmers. In 1784 Necker openly
admitted that twenty administrators carefully chosen from
among the ranks of the Company could have administered
the entire range of indirect taxation.[29]

In the latter half of the eighteenth century it was clear
that there were two kinds of General Farmers. The first,
a large majority, approached their duties passively. These
were not necessarily amateurs or dissolute court favorites,
although some were such, especially in the reign of Louis
XV. Most were professionals fully acquainted with the
General Farms.[30] But they were possessed of a rentier
mentality. Regarding their places in the Company as
gilt-edged investments, they realized that with minimum
effort the returns on those investments were secure and
considerable. These passive General Farmers were not
indifferent to General Farms affairs, but they tended to
be tolerant of abuses sanctioned by custom. So long as

[29] D'Argenson, *Journal et mémoires,* VII, 424, IX, 278; Turgot,
Oeuvres, IV, 151; Necker, *De l'administration,* I, 135.

[30] Mouffle d'Angerville, *Vie Privée de Louis XV,* I, 261-317.
Mouffle's short biographies reveal the mid-century General Farmers
to have been, for the most part, sober professionals with long years of
experience in the General Farms.

their own rate of profit was not impaired, they were not unduly impressed by evidences of waste in the bureaucracy. Above all, the rentier-minded financiers were content to leave the real management of affairs to a small inner core of colleagues who, for whatever personal reasons, actually ran the fiscal engine. It was this minority of experienced, skillful financiers who assumed leadership, initiated policy, and saw to its execution. In the late eighteenth century the active minority (composed of such men as Delahante, Paulze, Lavoisier, de la Borde, Parseval) was affected by the general spirit of renovation and enlightenment which pervaded even the government of the Bourbon monarchy. By hard work as Correspondent General Farmers, and by domination of the *assemblée de caisses,* they did much, in a piecemeal fashion, to ameliorate conditions within the General Farms. It was this minority which assisted Necker in his reorganization of 1780.

THE ROLE OF GOVERNMENT IN THE ADMINISTRATION OF THE GENERAL FARMS

Emphasis has been laid upon the fact that the bureaucracy of the General Farms was a royal agency leased to the quasiprivate Company of General Farmers. Once the lease was signed, the government was excluded from direct participation in the administration of the General Farms. Even in the last decade of the old regime most General Farmers "were scrupulous guardians of the old traditions, believing that each renewal of a lease made them alienees of the taxes for six years . . . during which the government could make no changes." [31] For most of the eighteenth century, the General Farms was regarded as an autonomous province, in the internal affairs of which the monarchy could not intervene except on invitation. The relation of government to the Company of General Farmers, unlike the relation of the Company to the General Farms itself, was contractual rather than bureaucratic.

[31] Mollien, *Mémoires d'un ministre,* I, 79.

There were, of course, numerous lines of contact between the royal controller-general and the Company during the course of a lease. His countersignature was required on all important Company decisions concerning the physical inventory or personnel of the bureaucracy. He issued the *départements des messieurs* which assigned General Farmers to their administrative posts. But none of these constituted a regular institutional mechanism binding the Company to the civil administration.[32]

In the absence of structural controls, the personal characteristics of the royal controller-general were important. Ostensibly he had great authority; but it rested with him whether or not he used it. The degree of government participation in the internal affairs of the General Farms depended upon his personal knowledge, upon the firmness of his footing in the quagmire of court politics, and upon his private influence with individual General Farmers. A powerful minister such as Colbert could dominate the Company and run the General Farms as an integral branch of the government. But most finance ministers in the reigns of Louis XV and Louis XVI were ephemeral figures.[33] Moreover, to the time of Turgot (1774-1776), all of them were personally indebted to the Company for an annual income of at least 50,000 livres.[34] Under such conditions the royal controller-general rarely exerted himself to interfere in the administration of the General Farms. Usually he countersigned what was presented to him without much question.

[32] The fact that *délibérations, lettres-circulaires,* and *ordres* were countersigned by the royal controller-general does not indicate institutional control; more often than not such signatures were purely formal. The same may be said of the *Département des messieurs.*

[33] Pietre, *La Réforme de l'état,* p. 7.

[34] Upon signature of a lease, the Company awarded the royal controller-general 300,000 livres *pot de vin* payable in six installments, 50,000 livres each. If he left office before expiration of the lease, his successor received the income. Turgot was the first to refuse this largess for his personal use; he donated it to charity. Necker abolished the practice in 1780. See Dakin, *Turgot,* pp. 160-161 and *Encyclopédie méthodique: Finances,* III, 357.

But these conditions changed in the last fifteen years of the old regime. Turgot, in his brief tenure as royal controller-general, used his power of countersignature negatively to influence the conduct of management. Necker (1777-1781) went even further. He positively intervened in administration, ordered chosen Correspondents to remain at strategic posts, altered the composition of Assemblies and took an active part in affairs. In 1778 he placed, for the first time since Colbert, agents of the finance ministry in the *Hôtel des Fermes*. After 1778 an *intendant de finance* regularly met with the *assemblée des caisses*. In 1780 four *premiers commis* were given wide powers of audit and inspection over the four receipts (*gabelles, tabacs, traites,* and *entrées*) remaining in the General Farms after that year.[35] By the time of the Revolution the General Farms had ceased to be an autonomous province; it was recognized to be in fact what it had always been in law, a part of the royal fiscal service.

SPECIAL DEPARTMENTS: SECRETARIAT, LEGAL AFFAIRS, PERSONNEL, RECEIPTS AND ACCOUNTS

In addition to the *bureaux de correspondance* which received primary consideration in the discussion of the central bureaucratic administration of the General Farms, the *Hôtel des Fermes* contained five functional departments rendering specialized services to the organization as a whole.

THE GENERAL SECRETARIAT [36]

The General Secretariat operated under the direct supervision of the smallest body in the Company of General Farmers, the *assemblée des archives*. Headed by the General Secretary and staffed by a battalion of clerks, copyists, and printers, this compact department maintained

---

[35] Mollien, *Mémoires d'un ministre,* I, 99; Delahante, *Une Famille de finance,* I, 325-329, II, 196.
[36] See Appendix p. 288.

the General Farms central files, rendered general secretarial services to the Company of General Farmers, and performed housekeeping duties in the *Hôtel des Fermes*.[37]

LEGAL AFFAIRS: THE *Conseil de Ferme*[38]

A system of taxation so complicated as that managed by the General Farms produced an enormous amount of litigation. Responsibility for such litigation fell to the permanent *conseil de ferme* which regularly met with the *assemblée de contentieux*.

The *conseil de ferme* consisted of a retained body of attorneys who advised the Company of General Farmers on legal matters and prosecuted or defended General Farms interests before the various high courts of the realm. The *conseil* also provided legal advice and assistance to the Provincial Directors and the innumerable lawyers handling General Farms cases in the lower courts. In 1763 the *conseil de ferme* consisted of fourteen legal experts, six of whom were *avocats* pleading before the Parlement of Paris and two of whom were in constant attendance upon the royal council of finances, by whose administrative rulings many of the cases in which the General Farms was interested were settled. The *conseil de ferme* also included five *procureurs* and six *agents* concerned with suits brought before the Paris and Rouen *Cours des Aides* and the criminal court of the Châtelet. Supplementary to the *conseil de ferme,* the administration of the *aides* maintained a special *bureau de contentieux*. In 1763 an additional *bureau de contentieux* was established for prosecution of cases falling within the special judicial system of Lorraine.[39]

PERSONNEL

There was no unified department of personnel in the *Hôtel des Fermes*. Instead there were, after 1768, two offices dealing with problems of employment in the

---

[37] Lavoisier, *Oeuvres,* VI, 156; *Dictionnaire géographique,* III, 106.
[38] See Appendix p. 288.
[39] Lavoisier, *Oeuvres,* VI, 157; *Dictionnaire géographique,* III, 105.

General Farms on the level of central administration. These were: the *bureau de cautionnement et commissions* (reporting to the *assemblées du personnel* and *cautionnements*) and the *bureau des retraites* (reporting to an *assemblée des retraites*).[40]

In number of employees, the bureaucracy of the General Farms dwarfed all other branches of the royal civil government. Except for the military services, it was the largest employer and organizer of manpower in eighteenth-century France. However, exact data on the number employed were never made public. Antagonistic public opinion tended to exaggerate the size of the General Farms fantastically. Critics listed the tax collectors in the hundreds of thousands and spoke of "hordes" and "armies" of *commis des fermes*.[41] But the best available figures, those of Lavoisier, indicate some 29,500 regular *commis des fermes* working in the bureaucracy in 1774, not including the *buralistes* of the *aides* and *domaines,* who although commissioned, were considered as casual rather than as regular employees. Six years later Mollien placed the number of *commis* at a total of 30,000, also exclusive of the *buralistes*.[42]

This great body of *commis des fermes* was distributed among the five major tax-collecting branches, the corps

---

[40] See Appendix p. 288.

[41] For examples of popularized exaggeration, see Goudar, *Les Intérêts de la France malentendus,* I, 214-221, who believed that an alleged shortage of agricultural labor could be attributed to the fact that the General Farms drew off thousands of hands into its "sterile" occupation. Also Rouillé d'Orfeuil, *L'Ami des français,* p. 208, who repetitiously referred to " cette multitude innombrable" of tax collectors, and Darigrand, *L'Anti-financier,* p. 61, who insisted that eighty thousand *commis* were assigned to collect the *trop bu* of the *aides* alone.

[42] Lavoisier, *Oeuvres,* VI, 155-157; Mollien, *Mémoires d'un ministre,* I, 66. Compare Necker, *De l'administration,* I, 107-108, who estimated the total number of *commis des fermes* at 50,000 in 1784, and Sénac de Meilhan, *Le Gouvernement, les moeurs et les conditions en France avant la révolution,* pp. 115-116, who speaks of the *commis des fermes* as being the majority of some 50,000 total tax collectors in France just prior to the Revolution. If the *buralistes* are added to Lavoisier's figure, some 35,000 to 36,000 results.

of guards, and the *Hôtel des Fermes* in hierarchically organized systems of grades, the details of which varied with the particular part of the service. Theoretically, advancement on merit was possible from the bottom to the top of the administrative ladder. Practically, however, there was a dividing line between high and low ranks. Above the line stood the relatively small body of *préposés* or executive and supervisory personnel such as the directors, controllers, and receivers and their office staffs. Below the line was a mass of *commis simples* or ordinary tax collectors and guards. As the eighteenth century advanced, the line was drawn with greater clarity and became increasingly difficult for the *commis simples* to cross.

There was no standard system of recruitment for service in the General Farms. On the higher levels the Company, operating through the *assemblée du personnel* and the *bureau de cautionnements et commissions,* directly appointed the *préposés.* On the lower levels the *commis simples* and guards were hired by provincial and local office chiefs with final approval being given routinely by the *assemblée du personnel.* Although much progress was made, particularly after 1780, on the systematic accumulation of personnel records, efficiency reports, and related data,[43] no objective method of selecting applicants was developed. Hiring techniques were haphazard and nepotism and favoritism played important roles in General Farms personnel management.

As a group, the *préposés* and the more important office personnel of the *Hôtel des Fermes* tended to be drawn from the financial and legal classes, segments of the population generally well schooled and often highly cultivated. Most of this type of personnel received a thorough training in the bureaucracy, often working for years in the

[43] After 1780 the Provincial Directors were required to submit an efficiency report in which data concerning his subordinates were compiled: the *commis'* age, name, physical description, marital and parental status, amounts of wages and bonuses earned, his conduct, aptitude, and capacity for the work. See *Encyclopédie méthodique: Finances,* I, 562-567.

lower ranks before being called to responsible positions. Many *préposés* came from the families of high functionaries already in office or had connections with the ruling General Farmers. Often sons, nephews, or clients of a General Farmer received an apprenticeship in lowly positions preparatory to assuming important posts reserved for them. Etienne-Marie Delahante entered the General Farms under the wing of his uncle General Farmer Jacques Delahante who had already placed two other relatives in the service. One of these was Provincial Director of Coustance when Etienne-Marie began his career as a copyist in the *Hôtel des Fermes*. On two occasions Etienne-Marie was advanced in rank when openings in the bureaucracy occurred due to the departure of Directors for predestined places in the Company of General Farmers.[44]

Thus much of the upper echelon appears to have been drawn from a fairly restricted circle in which service in the Farms was regarded as traditional by the end of the old regime. This method of recruitment did not necessarily corrupt working discipline. On the contrary, it provided a legitimate way of training a professionally minded corps bound to the organization by ties of loyalty. However, it did tend to reinforce the conservative attitudes already seen as predominant among the General Farmers. Bureaucratic reorganizations aimed at cutting down excess office personnel and overhead might meet with solid resistance when the posts of relatives and clients were threatened.

The General Farms, of course, was not immune to the venal characteristics of the age in which it flourished. With recruitment of its higher functionaries exposed to the dangers of nepotism, the enlistment of personnel in subaltern positions was even more vulnerable to the effects of favoritism and sheer influence peddling. Those who were close to the centers of authority in the *Hôtel des Fermes* attracted clients for whom they sought advantage-

[44] Delahante, *Une Famille de finance*, II, 15-16.

ous places for a price. Goudar exaggerated when he insisted that "the whole department of personnel . . . [is] the province of the women. Highest grade commissions are disposed of at the Opera, the lowest by the street walkers." [45] But even Turgot, a more temperate and better-informed observer, was convinced that "cupidity, which sells as it buys all, has filled the places with unworthy subjects" who, in order to regain what it cost them to obtain their positions, "rob the king, the public, and the Farmer." [46] Excessive personnel, swollen payrolls, and faltering bureaucratic discipline were inevitable concomitants of patronage. Equally important was the effect upon ambitious but unknown men in the lower ranks who hoped for promotion on merit alone. As the clients of the high administrators in Paris more and more dominated the upper echelons, the opportunities for advancement of a *commis simple* without powerful friends grew slimmer. In consequence, the split between high and low employees, already great on grounds of social background, grew more impassable.

Moreover, by 1758 advancement into the grade of *préposé* was impossible without evidence of solid financial worth. Like any large-scale financial enterprise the General Farms required surety bonds of its employees as guarantees against possible embezzlement or mismanagement of funds. But up to 1758 the bonding requirement was moderate and was demanded only of a limited group of the highest functionaries. In 1758 the government, then deep in the financial crisis of the Seven Years War, ordered a revision of the system which extended the bonding requirement to lower levels of the bureaucracy, increased the amounts required, and sequestered the total of money obtained from the surety bonds to the benefit of

[45] Goudar, *Les Intérêts de la France malentendus*, II, 220.
[46] Turgot, *Oeuvres*, IV, 152. See also D'Argenson, *Journal et mémoires*, VII, 425, who complained bitterly of the "insolent ones, the rascals" who buy their commissions and "rob the Farms."

the royal treasury. The government promised to pay 5 percent annual interest to the employees for the use of their bonds, the promise being underwritten by the Company, which deducted the interest payments as charges from the annual lease prices. In 1761 the government insisted on supplements to existing bonds, and many employees, finding it impossible to comply with the demand, were forced into retirement. In 1779 the government ordered further changes of such extent that for the first time all *commis des fermes* were required to post bonds of at least nominal value, while the value of bonds required of the *préposés* was drastically increased. Again a large group of employees, unable to raise the money, was forced into retirement.[47] To the government, this manipulation of the General Farms bonding system was essentially a means of tapping additional sources of credit.[48] From the

[47] *Encyclopédie méthodique: Finances,* I, 210-213; *Répertoire universel de jurisprudence,* II, 783. Prior to 1758 most surety bonds were *cautionnements immobiliaires,* that is, legal instruments deposited with the Company entitling it to order the sale of specific real property owned by the employee and to enjoy a first lien on the proceeds of the sale, should the employee be convicted of malversation or negligence. The 1758 ruling ordered that all bonds be converted into *cautionnements mobiliaires,* that is, money or negotiable securities. Employees already bonded had great difficulty converting, while employees bonded for the first time experienced difficulty obtaining mortgages on property to raise the money. Gradually compromises were reached in which the surety bond consisted of mixtures of the two basic kinds. Thus, according to the 1779 ruling, all accountable officials handling tax receipts in excess of six hundred livres a year must post *cautionnements mobiliaires;* officials handling less, posted bonds containing a proportion of real and liquid property which varied according to average amounts of tax receipts; finallly, all *commis* and guards, even those not handling receipts directly, posted *cautionnements immobiliaires* of token value.

[48] The employee bonds were a rich financial resource bearing an interest rate lower than was current for most government obligations. In 1758 the government had hoped to obtain 18,500,000 livres. This objective was at first frustrated by legal and economic difficulties, but the total of employee bondsmoney deposited in the royal treasury steadily mounted. In 1788 the surety bonds of the *commis* of the attenuated General Farms alone amounted to 27,142,000 livres while those of the General Commission of the *aides'* employees amounted to

point of view of the Company of General Farmers, it was an excellent means of insuring its revenues at a minimum of cost. But to the employees, the new bonding requirements constituted both a forced loan (albeit at a reasonable rate of guaranteed interest) and a further impediment to advancement in the organization. While the fact that all employees had to post surety bonds of at least token value implied that a measure of financial responsibility had become one of the minimum requirements of employment, actually the value of the bonds required of *commis simples* and guards was negligible. But the higher the employee mounted in the hierarchy, the greater became the amount demanded. For example, between 1758 and 1779 the surety bonds of controllers, one of the lower grades of *préposé*, amounted to ten thousand livres in money or negotiable securities; after 1779 the figure was raised to fourteen thousand livres. Provincial Directors posted bonds of from twenty-five to thirty thousand livres. This meant that only persons already fairly well-to-do or persons already supported by wealthy patrons could hope for admittance into the higher and more desirable echelons of administration.

The late eighteenth-century bonding requirement created an almost insurmountable barrier between the high and low ranks of General Farms personnel. An ordinary tax collector might conceivably rise unassisted to the grade of receiver in charge of a small bureau or customs house, but beyond that point he could hardly move without influence and patronage. However, at the same time, the high bonding requirement tended to act as a screen against those who sought sinecures in the bureaucracy. Thus the bonding system was a means of selecting personnel and of controlling movement within the General Farms.

3,354,500 livres and those of the General Administration of the *domaines'* employees amounted to 6,562,900 livres. The combined total was 37,059,000 livres, on which the monarchy paid 1,672,418 livres in interest for 1788. See Braesch, *Finances et monnaie révolutionnaires,* II, 73, 85, 87.

The spread between the upper and lower ranks of the bureaucracy was further widened by the wage policies of the Company of General Farmers. The disparity between the salaried incomes of the small group of high-ranking officials and the wages [49] of the mass of ordinary tax collectors and guards was glaring. Such functionaries as the Provincial Directors were amply paid. In 1781 these executives received twelve to fifteen thousand livres a year. Such incomes, free of all direct taxation except the *capitation*, enabled the Provincial Directors to move in the highest circles of provincial bourgeois society.[50] Controllers-general, controllers, receivers, and others in comparable posts were also well remunerated. But below these ranks the prevailing wage rates fell off precipitously. Important officials like the inspectors in the *domaines* earned only two thousand to two thousand four hundred livres a year, while the bulk of the tax collectors received far less. At the bottom of the personnel hierarchy, among the guards, wages were extremely low. Captains-general were paid at best one thousand two hundred livres a year, while ordinary guards received only three hundred a year maximum.[51]

[49] The basic money wage of the *commis des fermes* was the *appointement fixe* which was guaranteed by law. The *commis* could not be deprived of his *appointement* except by court order, which meant that he could not be dismissed arbitrarily from service. Furthermore, his wages could neither be garnished by personal creditors nor attached by court order; these measures protected the *commis* from reprisal of irate taxpayers who might sue on grounds of false collection and injury. See *Répertoire universel de jurisprudence,* I, 506.

[50] *Encyclopédie méthodique: Finances,* I, 560. Out of his salary the Provincial Director paid for his own clerical help, although at the end of the old regime he was provided with an expense account partly to pay for such outlays. See also Sée, *La Vie économique et les classes sociales,* pp. 185-187.

[51] *Encyclopédie méthodique: Finances,* II, 352; Delahante, *Une Famille de finance,* II, 96. Some captains-general received as low as six hundred livres. At about the same time (1781), to take one example, hod carriers in Paris earned thirty to forty sous a day and in the provinces fifteen to twenty. But they would have to work each day of a year to equal the pay of a guard. See Sagnac, *La Formation de la société française moderne,* II, 237, and Labrousse, *Esquisse du mouvement des prix,* II, 456-465.

To some extent, these low wages were offset by tax immunities. All *commis* were privileged in the *impositions.* They paid neither the *taille* nor the *vingtième* and were subject to only light *capitation.* Furthermore, they were automatically *franc salé* in the *gabelles.*[52] These privileges represented important supplements to pay among the lower grades, but even so were poor compensation for the responsibilities and risks which the tax collector assumed.

The depressed wage rates of the General Farms had a deleterious effect upon the quality of its personnel and the efficiency of its service.[53] The competence and honesty of the inferior *commis simples* and guards was more than questionable. In the opinion of contemporary observers, the fundamental reason was that the level of wages was not sufficient to attract desirable men, while slow promotions created much instability among those already employed. In consequence, the thousands of guards and underling *commis* tended to be drawn from the "last class of the people," from the least reliable and literate elements of the population. Many were commissioned without regard to moral or intellectual qualifications, and there was much time-serving by them. Some sought an obscure post merely for its tax privileges, a motive hardly indicative of zeal for the service.[54] There was also much ignorance. Because of widespread illiteracy in the ranks, in 1778 it was necessary for the royal council of finances to rule that *procés-verbaux* sworn out by *commis* who could neither read nor write were still to be considered valid in the courts. As late as 1781 the Company was satisfied if one guard out of a brigade of five or six could write. This one drew up and signed the *procès-verbaux*

---

[52] *Encyclopédie méthodique: Finance,* I, 330.

[53] Mollien, *Mémoires d'un ministre,* I, 105.

[54] *Encyclopédie méthodique: Finances,* I, 366, II, 532; *Recueil alphabétique des droits de traites uniformes,* IV, 236. *Commis* could receive commissions "sans information de vie et moeurs," according to special rulings of the council. See also Bigo, *Bases historiques,* pp. 5-6.

of his unlettered comrades, a "vicious practice which . . . [gives] birth to many abuses." [55]

Moreover, ignorance and low pay often entailed callousness and dishonesty. Eighteenth-century literature portrayed General Farms employees as brutes and "odious . . . scoundrels" [56] bent upon pillaging the citizenry more to fill their own pockets than to benefit the organization which employed them.[57] Voltaire described the tax collectors as "subaltern brigands . . . the General Farms does not draw profit from their daily rapines; everything goes to the *commis;* they are authorized to rob and they exercise their right to the full." [58] It was the solemn opinion of the Paris *Cour des Aides* in 1774 that one of the greatest hardships borne by the common people was to be obliged "daily to suffer the caprices, the arrogance, even the insults of these *suppôts de la ferme,*" [59] while phrases such as "vermin that gnaws in the marrow of the bones" [60] to allude to the *commis* were commonplaces in the *cahiers de doléance* of 1789. No doubt the picture thus drawn was a caricature; yet it limned the truth partially. The enormous contraband trade of the eighteenth century, for example, could not have been possible without the connivance of the customs officials. With the smugglers offering attractive bribes, "how to hope that they [the guards] . . . could resist the appetite to gain in a single day a whole year's pay?" [61] M. de Châteaubrun, harassed Provincial Director of Laval for *gabelles et tabacs* in 1781, bitterly complained to the *Hôtel des Fermes* that "the employees are, for the most part, salt smugglers, pillagers, thieves; one cashiered rascal is almost always replaced by

---

[55] *Encyclopédie méthodique: Finances,* II, 352, III, 382-384.
[56] Rouillé d'Orfeuil, *L'Ami des français,* p. 184.
[57] Darigrand, *L'Anti-financier,* pp. 44-45.
[58] Cited in Turgot, *Oeuvres,* V, 101.
[59] *Recueil de la Cour des Aides,* p. 631.
[60] "Cahiers de doléance du baillage de Blois," *Collection de documents inédits sur l'histoire économique de la révolution française,* I, 555.
[61] *Encyclopédie méthodique: Finance,* I, 365-366.

another or some miserable abortion without courage or talent." [62]   But malfeasance was not confined to the lower ranks; with good reason the General Farms suspected even its higher officials.   During a single *tournée* in Dijon and Châlons-sur-Saone General Farmer de Caze detected two receivers of *gabelles* in acts of open malversation and suspected fourteen others out of a total of thirty-one investigated.[63]   One old employee, reminiscing years after the Revolution, remarked, "I do not believe that the General Farmers were thieves; but what I do believe is that they were always robbed unconscionably" by their own employees.[64]

The Company of General Farmers was aware of the apathy and instability of its personnel.   It never appreciably raised wages, but it offered monetary inducements, in the form of rewards and prizes, to industrious tax collectors and guards to spur them to their duty.   Sliding scale bonuses paid to the *commis simples* proportionately to amounts of tax money collected, were used judiciously to stimulate collections in specific areas in which recovery was lagging.   The guards were offered bounty money for the capture of smugglers.   Goods confiscated by the General Farms were sold, and the money so obtained was split among the personnel.   Similarly fines collected from persons convicted of tax evasion were divided among the personnel instrumental in the case.[65]   Finally in 1768, in order to raise the morale of the guards, the Company established in the General Farms the first formally organized retirement and pension fund ever to be introduced into the French civil service.[66]

[62] Calléry, "La fraude des gabelles sous l'ancien régime," *France judicataire,* Part one (1881-1882), p. 386.

[63] Pitre, *La Ferme-générale en Bourgogne,* p. 47.

[64] Delahante, *Une Famille de finance,* I, 209.

[65] *Encyclopédie méthodique: Finances,* I, 49, II, 401-402.   Such supplemental income was called *emoluments casuels.*   Frequently bonuses and prizes might be worth more to a guard than his fixed wages.   The *emoluments,* however, were uncertain and erratically paid.

[66] Marion, *Dictionnaire des institutions,* p. 235.

On February 21, 1768, the Company issued, with the approval of the government, a *délibération* establishing the *caisse des retraites,* as the pension fund was called, an action which, according to the tax-farmers, conformed admirably "to the laws of humanity and justice as well as to the good of the service." The pension fund was conducted on the basis of compulsory contributions deducted in advance from the wages and bonuses of all personnel in the *gabelles et tabacs* and *traites.* A regular schedule of contributions was developed for all grades and ranks. Directors and receivers paid three deniers of each livre of annual wages and bonuses; the various subordinate ranks paid one denier of each livre. Each year the Company, out of its own capital, matched the total of all employee contributions, a matter of 260,000 livres in 1774. All employees of the *gabelles, tabacs,* and *traites* shared equally in the benefits. After twenty years of uninterrupted and honorable service a guard could retire on an annual life pension the amount of which was calculated in accordance with his rank and seniority upon retirement. Individuals injured while in the General Farms service received benefits prorated according to the years of employment to date of incapacitation. Shortly after 1768 the Pension Fund was extended to cover personnel in the *entrées de Paris,* but it was never applied to the *aides* or *domaines.*[67]

THE DEPARTMENT OF GENERAL ACCOUNTS [68]

The accounts of the General Farms were centralized in the Department of General Accounts whose chief, the Controller-General of the Farms, reported directly to the *assemblée administrative* and through that body ultimately

[67] Lavoisier, *Oeuvres,* VI, 152; *Encyclopédie méthodique: Finances,* II, 495-496. Prior to the establishment of the Pension Fund by the Company, various groups of personnel in the *gabelles* had for years sponsored private, voluntary mutual aid societies. The Company entered the picture to standardize practices and to end the many squabbles which characterized the life of the private societies.

[68] See Appendix p. 287.

to the *assemblée des caisses*. The department consisted, in 1774, of twelve specialized *bureaux des comptes* functioning under a *bureau-général* supplemented by a *bureau des états au vrai*.

The General Farms accounting system was rudimentary in principle, although highly complicated in practice. Double-entry bookkeeping was not used, and the system rested upon the accumulation of simple income-outgo items entered chronologically in a series of records extending from the daybook of the *commis simple* to the ledgers of the *bureaux des comptes* and the final balance sheets of the *bureau des états au vrai*. The objective was to record the amount of taxation collected for all parts of the General Farms and the whole collectively for a given accounting period and to balance that amount by a record of expenditures incurred in operation. By the end of the eighteenth century the General Farms accounts enjoyed a reputation for detailed exactitude [69] unrivaled by any other branch of the royal fiscal service. But its precision was purchased at the expense of simplicity, ease, and speed of determining a final verified statement for a given accounting period. In part this was due to the use of single-entry bookkeeping to account for taxes so diverse as those collected by the General Farms. In part it was due to the rigid system of accounting controls and counter-controls, requiring checks and cross-checks of the books on every level of the organization, which the General Farms applied in an effort to protect its revenues from malversation. The sheer amount of clerical work involved was enormous. The amount of time consumed to prepare final balances was formidable.[70]

In 1738 it was legally recognized that the final, verified

[69] Mollien, *Mémoires d'un ministre,* I, 100-101. With the failure of Pâris-Duverney to establish double-entry bookkeeping during the *régie* Cordier, that system was never tried again.

[70] *Encyclopédie méthodique: Finances,* I, 564; Lavoisier, *Oeuvres,* VI, 133-134.

statement of accounts of operation for a given fiscal year could not be presented to the royal council until two years after the expiration of the year in question.[71] By 1780 the multiplication of accounting control formulas was so great that it was admitted that "the General Farms could know . . . only in the course of the fourth year of a lease the result of divers recoveries made during the first." [72] The General Farms accounting system, while meticulous and accurate, could not prepare a final statement of gross yields and total costs that was not at least four years out of date.

THE DEPARTMENT OF GENERAL RECEIPTS [73]

The General Farms treasury department consisted, in 1763, of 181 provincial subtreasuries centralized in the *caisse de Paris,* the main treasury of the General Farms. The *caisse de Paris* was divided into two sections, the *bureau de dépense* and the *bureau de recette.* It was directed by the highest accountable official in the General Farms, the General Receiver of the Farms, who reported directly to the *assemblée administrative.* Each provincial subtreasury was in the charge of a General Provincial Receiver. The distribution of subtreasuries followed roughly but not exactly the distribution of the Provincial Directions.[74] Under the General Provincial Receivers were grouped the *caisses* of the local receivers in charge of the *greniers à sel,* tobacco stores, customs houses, and *bureaux des aides, entrées,* and *domaines.* Tax money gathered by the ultimate tax collectors (parish collectors,

---

[71] *Bail fait à Forceville,* Art. 60.

[72] Mollien, *Mémoires d'un ministre,* I, 101. Even at this rate the General Farms was speedier than the royal *chambres des comptes* which was at times twelve years behind in certifying the accounts of the General Farms. The controller-general, of course, relied upon the General Farms' accounts. See Turgot, *Oeuvres,* IV, 122.

[73] See Appendix p. 287.

[74] There was normally at least one subtreasury for each provincial direction, but many had two or three depending upon volume of business. See *Dictionnaire géographique,* III, 105.

salt and tobacco retailers, *buralistes,* customs inspectors, excise men, registry tax controllers) was remitted upward through these treasury department channels until it was finally received in the central *caisse de Paris.*

The prime characteristic of this treasury system was that its agencies for receipt functioned simultaneously and without differentiation also as agencies for disbursement. In order to reduce the actual movement of specie to a minimum, the General Farms employed a technique of decentralized payments. At every level in the organization the General Farms incurred financial obligations; it endeavored whenever practicable to discharge these obligations at the level on which they were incurred.

Thus, to take one example, the parish collector for *gabelles* was authorized to deduct his remuneration from his last remittance to the *grenier* receiver; in consequence part of the remittance which the receiver made to the General Provincial Receiver consisted of vouchers to this effect. At the *grenier* the receiver, on orders of the Provincial Director, paid wages and other locally incurred expenses of operation out of current tax income. The actual cash remittance which he made to the General Provincial Receiver was, therefore, always less than the amount received in taxes. The difference was accounted for by vouchers, orders of payment, and signed receipts. The same situation existed in all *bureaux des fermes.* On the level of the provincial subtreasuries the same technique of decentralized payments was employed on a larger and more complicated scale. The General Farms had many and diverse expenditures to make in the Provincial Directions. Some of these were government charges ordering local discharge of royal obligations.[75] Some were expenses of the General Farms itself; payments for wages and bonuses, supplies and services, the expenses of law suits, and so on. Such payments were authorized by means of a order of payment, called a *rescription* which, signed by the General Receiver, directed the General

[75] *Ibid.,* III, 44, 69,

Provincial Receiver to deduct the sum in question from his monthly remittance to the *caisse de Paris*.[76]

The Company invited the general public to avail itself of the financial mechanism of the Department of General Receipts for the transfer of private funds. Any person could purchase for a smal fee a *rescription* from the General Receiver; a special office was open in the *bureau de recette* in Paris for this purpose. The *rescription* directed a designated General Provincial Receiver to pay the bearer the face value of the order upon its presentation at his *caisse* within a stipulated length of time. The General Provincial Receiver would honor the *rescription* and deduct the amount from his remittance to the *caisse de Paris*. Conversely, a merchant in the provinces could purchase from a General Provincial Receiver an order to pay drawn on Paris or upon another General Provincial Receiver.[77]

As a result of this system of decentralized disbursements the Department of General Receipts transferred funds as much as possible through bookkeeping clearances rather than by actual movement of specie or by purchase of commercial bills of exchange. Furthermore, the General Provincial Receivers functioned more as financial agents than as bureaucratic officials. They were paid only small salaries, yet their posts were the most lucrative in the General Farms. The reason lay in the fact that often, for short periods, the amount of disbursements which they paid out exceeded the amount of incoming tax receipts. In this circumstance they were authorized to advance the requisite sums for remittance to Paris from personal funds or money borrowed on the local money markets. The General Provincial Receivers were paid 4 percent interest for these services, the principal and interest being deductible from future remittances. Conversely, funds in a provincial subtreasury frequently exceeded the amounts re-

[76] Necker, *De l'administration*, I, 38; *Encyclopédie méthodique: Finances*, III, 447.
[77] For example, see *Almanach Royal* (1749), pp. 358-359.

quired for remittance according to the schedule of payments set up by the General Receiver in Paris. In this case the General Provincial Receiver could place General Farms funds out on short-term loan, profiting from interest charges. This was an illegal but extremely prevalent practice. As a result of this financial activity, the office of General Provincial Receiver was highly prized. During prosperous times General Provincial Receivers in such large commercial centers as Bordeaux, Lyons, Marseilles, Rouen, and Nantes were reputed to have had no difficulty in clearing thirty to eighty thousand livres a year.[78]

The methods of the internal treasury system of the General Farms were strikingly similar to those employed by the royal fiscal service as a whole. Relations between the General Provincial Receiver and the *caisse de Paris* were analogous to the relations between the General Farms and the royal treasury. The use of centralized receiving treasuries as decentralized disbursement agencies was characteristic of the entire fiscal system of the old-regime state. The assumption of a financial role by agents primarily concerned with purely fiscal technicalities was common to both the General Farms and the state fiscal mechanism. It was indicative of the rudimentary nature of the eighteenth-century French banking system.

THE GENERAL FARMS AND THE ROYAL TREASURY

Any consideration of the eighteenth-century General Farms must take account of the fact that it was an autonomous branch of the royal treasury for disbursement of government expenditures as well as for collection and remittance of taxation. The General Farms was a royal subtreasury which regularly acquitted a great range of public expenditures in the name of the king directly out of receipts.

At the beginning of each new lease on the General Farms a running debtor-creditor account was established

---

[78] *Encyclopédie méthodique: Finances,* I, 563.

between the General Farms *caisse de Paris* and the royal treasury. Upon signature of the lease the royal account was credited with the amount of the bondsmoney and with the first monthly installment on annual lease price. On the basis of this credit, the royal treasury drew up an *état de distribution* which listed the government expenditures, or charges, which the General Farms was to pay during the monthly period. The General Receiver of the Farms arranged for the disbursement either directly from the *caisse de Paris* or by issuing *rescriptions* upon the *caisses* of appropriate General Provincial Receivers. The difference between the amount of annual lease price credited to the royal treasury and the amount of the charges paid by the General Farms was the *parti du roi,* the amount of actual cash transferred physically to the royal treasury. Throughout the post-1726 period the *parti du roi* was always small, often it was negligible, sometimes it was nonexistent.[79]

The range of charges on the General Farms was, in the late eighteenth century, extraordinarily complex. However, four kinds may be distinguished. These were: debt service charges, or charges connected with servicing parts of the regular state debt; fiscal charges, or costs of collection borne by the king; nonfiscal charges, or current expenditures of government on civil administration; financial charges, or expenditures resulting from the state indebtedness to the Company of General Farmers.

The debt service charges were the largest in amount among the expenditures of government handled directly by the General Farms. The bulk of the money went to service the *rentes,* standing orders to pay which were included in every eighteenth-century lease.[80] In 1774 this item (*rentes* and other more minor state debts) absorbed

---

[79] Lavoisier, *Oeuvres,* VI, 599-600.
[80] *Bail fait à Forceville,* Art. 591. Included in the term service was the principal and interest of the *rentes* themselves, the *gages et épices* of the venal *payeurs et contrôleurs des rentes.* See *Collection des comptes rendus,* p. 93, and Marion, *Dictionnaire des institutions,* p. 435.

at least 65,800,000 livres of the 132,000,000 livres annual lease price of the Lease Alaterre. In 1788 the figure was budgeted for at least 101,240,000 livres out of an annual lease price of 150,000,000 livres.[81] Thus severely was the *parti du roi* pruned.

Fiscal charges were next in importance. These items included two sorts of expenditures. The first were direct expenditures by the government on the administration of the General Farms, such as purchase of tobacco or capital investments such as the wall for the *entrées de Paris*. In 1788 these charges were expected to result in about a 9,223,800 livres deduction from annual lease price (including 3,600,000 livres for the extraordinary expense of the Paris wall).[82] The second sort of expenditure handled as fiscal charges were more tenuous in nature, often involving not actual disbursements but *non-jouissances* (indemnities for taxes detached or moderated in rate after a lease was signed). Conspicuous also in the last decade of the old regime were costs of liquidating remnants of the feudal dispersion of rights of taxation on resumption of royal domain, most of which were acquitted through deductible fiscal charges on the General Farms. In 1788 these kinds of fiscal charges amounted to about 5,605,000 livres. The total of all fiscal charges in that year was budgeted at about 15,428,000 livres, a deduction from annual lease price which when added to that already de-

---

[81] *Collection des comptes rendus,* p. 93; Braesch, *Finances et monnaie révolutionnaires,* II, 72, 75-78, 85, 140, 200-202. All figures used in this section are in the round.

[82] Braesch, *Finances et monnaie révolutionnaires,* II, table between pp. 200-201. Direct expenditures of government on the administration of the General Farms amounted in 1788 either to 6,233,750 livres or 9,233,850 livres according to Braesch's reconstruction of the state budget for that year and depending upon whether the wall of the *entrées de Paris,* started by the General Farms in 1784 and paid for by the king over several years by means of deduction from the lease prices is considered an expense of tax collection or a civic improvement. This writer, in company with much irate contemporary opinion, inclines to regard it as in the former category.

ducted for debt service charges further limited the amount of the *parti du roi*.[83]

The third type of charges, consisting of a wide variety of nonfiscal government disbursements, was only slightly less important than the fiscal charges. Custom and convenience limited these expenditures to the internal civil administration of the country. In 1788 salaries, honoraria, and pensions of state functionaries figured in this category, as well as expenditures for civil improvements such as paving the streets of Paris or for support of the economy through commercial subsidies. Certain elements of governmental eleemosynary expenditures also appeared as nonfiscal charges on the General Farms. Nonfiscal charges were never written into the leases. They were ordered by *assignations* usually drawn up by the finance ministry, often without first passing through the royal treasury. In 1788 these nonfiscal charges were budgeted at about 11,603,000 livres.[84]

Any attempt at strict comparison of the total fiscal and nonfiscal charges from lease to lease is not feasible. The charges varied too widely. However, it appears that these types of charges increased in the late eighteenth century. In 1759 Silhouette estimated that the fiscal and nonfiscal charges on the General Farms amounted to a 14,467,265 livres deduction from the 110,000,000 livres

[83] Braesch, *Finances et monnaie révolutionnaires,* II, 75, 77, 79, 85, 87, 110-111, 120-121 and table between pp. 210-211, Compare *Collection des comptes rendus,* pp. 93, 152, 215. See also, Lavoisier, *Oeuvres,* VI, 607-610 and *Encyclopédie méthodique: Finances,* I, 505, II, 432. Indemnities were paid for a variety of changes in the taxes; if an individual were made *franc-salé* the king paid the Company an indemnity; if an article of merchandise were put on the *droits uniformes* list, the Company was indemnified. Liquidations were important in the 1780s. For example, in 1784 the Prince de Condé ceded his right to collect taxes in his *apanage* to the king for 7,600,000 livres cash and 600,000 livres in *rentes.* The bulk of the transaction, still in progress in 1788 was handled by the Company which paid the prince and deducted the sums as fiscal charges from annual lease price.

[84] Braesch, *Finances et monnaie révolutionnaires,* II, 75, 77, 79, 87. Cf. *Collection des comptes rendus,* pp. 92-93, 208.

annual lease price of the Lease Henriet.[85]   In the *compte rendu* of 1788 they were expected to come to a total of about 27,032,700 livres in advance deductions from an annual lease price of 150,000,000 livres.   Expenditure of government for civic improvement and commerce bulk larger in 1788 than in 1759, while the extraordinary costs of reforming the tax structure through liquidation of antique vestiges were especially conspicuous just prior to the Revolution.   There may have been a tendency to increase the amount of government contribution to the direct cost of administration in the General Farms in this last year before the revolution.   In any case, if the sum of 27,032,700 livres (approximate) for fiscal and nonfiscal charges is added to the (approximate) 101,240,000 livres for debt service charges in 1788, a sum of about 128,272,700 livres results.   All of this sum was to be deducted in advance of payment of the annual lease price of 150,000,000 livres before the financial charges were in turn deducted.

The financial charges which constituted the fourth type of government expenditure were interest payments on loans and advances borrowed from the Company of General Farmers and General Farms employees.   In 1788 interest on bondsmoney and other types of government indebtedness held by the Company came to about 3,748,000 livres.   In the same year interest on employee surety bonds figured at about 1,277,000 livres.   The total was about 4,926,000 livres to be deducted from annual lease price.   Adding this to the debt service, fiscal and nonfiscal charges, and deducting the whole from a budgeted receipt of 150,000,000 livres from the General Farms, it may be seen that the anticipated *parti du roi* for 1788 was only about 17,800,000 livres.[86]   Thus the General Farms, functioning as a royal disbursement subtreasury, was budgeted to expend about 131,198,000

[85] *Collection des comptes rendus,* p. 47.
[86] Braesch, *Finances et monnaie révolutionnaires,* II, 73, 79.

livres in 1788, a sum by no means extraordinary at the end of the old regime.

The 17,800,000 livres *parti du roi* for 1788 was only the amount of net cash revenue budgeted for that year, not what was actually received by the royal treasury. For in reality the royal treasury, since at least 1759, normally overdrew its account with the General Farms to an amount between 5,000,000 to 10,000,000 livres a year. In years of financial crisis, such as 1788, the overdraft was much greater. To use the language of the fiscal service, the General Farms was, at the end of the old regime, perpetually in advance of the royal treasury.[87] This meant that the Company of General Farmers was sustaining the government on credit. For an understanding of this circumstance, a classic one in tax-farming, it is now necessary to consider the Company of General Farmers in its distinctive role of financial middleman to the Bourbon monarchy.

[87] Lavoisier, *Oeuvres,* VI, 143.

8. The Organization and Financial Role of the Company of General Farmers

For sixty-three years, from 1726 to 1789, the Company of General Farmers was in continuous possession of the General Farms. This happened, not because of the value of its services in administering the tax-collecting bureaucracy, but because of the value of the financial service which it rendered the endemically bankrupt monarchy. The Company of General Farmers was essentially a financial institution whose primary function was to enable the state to borrow its tax revenues in advance of their collection. Yet to the end of the eighteenth century the Company was restricted in membership to that limited class of financiers which since the late sixteenth century had been in control of the fiscal-financial machinery of the monarchy. In consequence, the Company was incapable of drawing upon the resources of new capitalist wealth and of using newer capitalist techniques of financing large enterprises. Resurrected after John Law failed to float the state upon the tide of modern commercial expansion, the Company dominated *les finances* during the reign of Louis XV. But in the late reign of Louis XVI its resources, drawn principally from the old and narrow financial corps of intermarried families of General Farmers and General Receivers, was strained to the utmost. The technique of mortgaging state loans against specific taxa-

tion, with the holder of the mortgage in physical possession of the tax-collecting machinery, was outmoded. In
1774 the state, for the first time since the late sixteenth
century, went to the international money market to borrow capital funds. By the late 1780s the monopoly of the
antique financial aristocracy over the royal debt was
broken. When the Revolution dissolved the Company of
General Farmers, the business of financing the state was
already beginning to pass into the hands of the new international banking houses, the new stock-jobbing companies,
the new *haute finance* of commercial and industrial
capitalism.[1]

THE PARTNERSHIP: FINANCIAL ARRANGEMENTS

The Company of General Farmers was a multiple
partnership constituted by private agreement, or *acte de
société*,[2] among its members, as a *société-générale,* the
most common type of business organization in the old

[1] Harbulot, "Etudes sur les finances de l'ancienne France," *Révue
des sciences politiques,* LVII, 528-529. See also Bouchary, *Les
Manieurs d'argent à la fin du XVIIIe siècle,* I, *passim.*

[2] The "Acte de société des intéressés du bail David du 29 janvier
1774" may be found in Lavoisier, *Oeuvres,* VI, 629-631. It was a
paradox of old-regime jurisprudence that so far as public law was
concerned the Company of General Farmers did not exist. Unlike the
lease, which as the constitutive act of the General Farms was a part
of the corpus of public law, the *acte de société* was simply a contract
in private law. In the eyes of public law there was for each lease but
one General Farmer, the *adjudicataire-général,* who alone signed the
lease. The General Farmers were in law only the *cautions de l'adjudicataire-général.* Since a new *adjudicataire* was required for each
new lease, a new set of *cautions* was also necessary. Thus legally
there was no single, continuous Company of General Farmers. There
were, instead, twelve separate "Companies," one for each lease from
1726 to 1786. Each had its own distinct capital and books. Consequently, the Company's internal history was punctuated by periods of
liquidation and reformation of capital every six years. During such
periods the General Farmers dissolved their current "Company" on
one set of books and reconstituted it on another. This procedure was,
of course, a bookkeeping fiction. But it was of practical convenience
as a means of distinguishing the assets and liabilities of one lease from
another. See *Bail fait à Forceville,* Art. 551; Lavoisier, *Oeuvres,* VI,
162-163; Bosquet, *Dictionnaire raisonné des domaines,* II, 336.

regime.[3] Legally the number of places in the Company was limited, although its membership was larger than was usual for this form of organization. The number was determined by royal will and could not be increased by act of the Company itself. Thus, from 1726 to 1756 the Company comprised forty places; from 1756 to 1780, sixty places. In 1780 the figure was set at forty but raised again to forty-two in 1786 and to forty-four in 1787.[4] Only persons appointed by the king, through the device of obtaining a *brevet du roi*,[5] could accept a place in the Company and bear the title and dignity of General Farmer.

Like all *sociétés-générales,* the Company of General Farmers was founded on the principle of unlimited liability.[6] The same fiction of the equality of all partners

[3] Lévy-Bruhl, "Les Différentes espèces de sociétés de commerce en France au XVIIe et XVIIIe siècles," *Révue historique de droit français et étranger,* Fourth Series (1937), pp. 299, 323. Save for one brief and entirely exceptional moment in 1719, when the financiers used the General Farms as a weapon against John Law's System, the Company was never organized as a joint-stock company. a *société en commandite par actions.*

[4] *Répertoire universel de jurisprudence,* VI, 330-340; *Encyclopédie méthodique: Finances,* I, 74.

[5] A *brevet du roi* was a title of royal grace and hence carried the privileges of freedom from the *taille, vingtièmes* as well as the status of *franc-salé.* These financial advantages were more than offset by the cost of obtaining the *brevet.* For example, it cost the General Farmer Lallémont de Betz 200,000 livres in gifts to obtain a *brevet* for his son Lallémont de Montouillet. De la Garde paid 300,000 livre for a *brevet* for his son. In 1763 Jacques Delahante, seeking a *brevet* for himself, paid the king 150,000 livres. Similar informal levies were laid upon all aspirant General Farmers. In addition the *brevet* itself was subject to the tax of *marc d'or* (collected by the General Farms as part of the *domaines*). The rate of this tax increased drastically in the eighteenth century, reaching a peak in 1770 when the *marc d'or* amounted to a fortieth of the capital share of a place in the Company, a matter of 39,000 livres payable upon issuance of the *brevet* and upon each renewal of lease participated in by the General Farmer. See Thirion, *La Vie privée,* p. 210; Delahante, *Une Famille de finance,* I, 294-295; Grimaux, *Lavoisier,* p. 66; *Encyclopédie méthodique: Finances,* III, 68; *Répertoire universel de jurisprudence,* III, 543

[6] Lévy-Bruhl, "Les Différentes espèces de sociétés de commerce en France au XVIIe et XVIIIe siècles," *Révue historique de droit*

which determined the formal administrative organization of the Company also determined the character of its internal financial arrangements. The capital fund of the Company was divided into forty or sixty equal portions, one assigned against each place. This was the amount of the capital contribution which each titular General Farmer was required to make; thus each partner was equal to all others in the amount of his investment in the enterprise. Funds for salaries and emoluments, interest on invested capital, and profits were also divided into forty or sixty equal shares; thus each General Farmer received an equal portion of the pecuniary rewards of the enterprise. Conversely, although the point was academic in the post-1726 period, loss was sustained equally by all places.[7]

In the course of the period from the Lease Carlier of 1726 to the Lease Mager of 1786, the capital fund of the Company of General Farmers almost tripled in size; the capital share of each place in the Company increased correspondingly. However, the bulk of this increase was concentrated in the years between 1756 and 1767. The capital fund used to finance the Lease Bocquillon of 1751, a contract typical of those in force from 1726 to 1756, amounted to a total of 33,883,000 livres of which 26,000,000 livres was supplied directly by the Company of General Farmers and 7,883,000 livres was contributed by the twenty-seven subfarming companies (comprising a total membership of two hundred and fifteen subfarmers) of the *aides* and *domaines*. Thus the capital contribution of each place on the Company of General Farmers, during the thirty years prior to 1756, was 622,000 livres. But in 1756, under pressure of the government for increased bondsmoney and loans, the

---

français et étranger, Fourth Series (1937), p. 295. The terms of the lease held the Company collectively responsible for the financial obligations of each member. See *Bail fait à Forceville,* Art. 533.

[7] Lavoisier, *Oeuvres,* VI, 630-631. See especially Arts. 6, 8, 16, and 19 of the "Acte de société du bail David" printed here.

capital fund of the Company was raised to sixty million livres, while the subfarmers were eliminated from the picture. This entailed increasing the places in the Company from forty to sixty, each place assigned a capital contribution of 1,000,000 livres. In order to finance operations of the Lease Alaterre of 1767, the Company's capital fund was raised to 93,000,000 livres, requiring a capital contribution of 1,560,000 livres per place.[8] The share assigned each place remained at this figure to the end of the old regime. Decreases in the capital fund in 1780 or increases in 1786 were accomplished by reducing or adding to the number of places rather than by diminishing or augmenting the contribution of each place. In 1780 the capital fund of the Company stood at 62,400,000 livres with each of the forty places contributing 1,560,000 livres. In 1786 the capital fund was raised to 65,520,000 livres with each of forty-two places contributing 1,560,000 livres.[9] In 1787 financial pressures on the Company were so great that the unprecedented step of creating new places in the middle of a lease was taken. The number of places was raised to forty-four, and the total capital fund was increased to 68,840,000 livres.[10]

The fiction that each partner in the Company was equal was maintained, in a juridical sense, throughout the period 1726 to 1786 by the device of assigning each place an equal share of the capital fund and by legally limiting the number of places. But, in fact, the General Farmers were by no means equal in personal fortune. This became most apparent when the capital contributions demanded of each place leaped from about 600,000 livres to 1,560,000 livres in eleven years and remained at the high figure to the end of the old regime. A few General Farmers, such as Jean-Joseph de Laborde or Michel Bouret, could afford to "buy" and maintain a place on the basis of their own pri-

---

[8] *Ibid.,* VI, 135-136.
[9] *Encyclopédie méthodique: Finances,* I, 74; Mollien, *Mémoires d'un ministre,* I, 106-107.
[10] Braesch, *Finances et monnaie révolutionnaires,* II, 72.

vate wealth alone.[11] But more typically, especially after 1756, the titular General Farmer functioned as the chief of a coterie of financial backers. From at least the mideighteenth century most titular General Farmers obtained part, and in many cases the major part, of their capital contribution from creditors who, under a variety of techniques, had legal claim to the enjoyment of portions of the emoluments and profits of the titulary.

The most informal method of raising money for capital was for the General Farmer to borrow on his personal note. After 1756 many General Farmers, in order to maintain their places, resorted to money lenders who usually charged 6 to 7 percent interest and sometimes as high as 10 and 12 percent.[12] Normally these lenders had no legal claims upon the place in the Company. But frequently they would lend only upon the basis of contracts entitling them to attach portions of the income from the place. In such cases the lenders were called *participés*.[13]

Occasionally the *participé*, the better to protect his interests, became an *adjoint* or legally recognized associate of the titular General Farmer, sharing in his administrative duties in the General Farms as well as dividing the emoluments and profits of the place. Thus, when Lavoisier first entered the Company in 1768, he did so as the *adjoint* of the General Farmer Baudon. Lavoisier provided one half of Baudon's capital contribution, or 780,-000 livres, and, since Baudon was an elderly man in poor health, assumed nearly all of the administrative duties of the aged tax-farmer. Although Lavoisier was a well-to-do man, he could obtain the necessary 780,000 livres only by borrowing on personal note. When Baudon died

[11] De Janzé, *Les Financiers d'autrefois*, pp. 187, 268. De Laborde had an independent income of 600,000 livres a year from West Indian sugar plantations. Bouret had made a huge fortune in grain speculation before he became a General Farmer.

[12] D'Argenson, *Journal et mémoires*, IX, 110. In 1755 the marquis noted that the General Farmers already were having difficulty borrowing money on their places even at 10 percent interest.

[13] Lavoisier, *Oeuvres*, VI, 158; *Encyclopédie méthodique: Finances*, III, 298.

and Lavoisier succeeded to his place, he went into debt to the extent of a million livres to raise the required 1,560,-000 livres.[14] The Company and the government disliked the practice of placing the personal creditors of the General Farmers within the administrative circles of the General Farms. Most were not of Lavoisier's industrious turn of mind; they were interested only in keeping watch upon their debtors.

The most common method of raising capital avoided this danger of admitting strangers to the councils of the Company of General Farmers. If a General Farmer did not have sufficient funds to subscribe the capital of his place, he could divide his place into parts, called *croupes*. He then offered an investor a half, quarter, sixth, or eighth *croupe* of his place. The investor thus became a *croupier*, a "sleeping partner" who shared the capital investment with the titular General Farmer and shared in all emoluments, interests, and profits to the extent of his part.[15] However, the *croupier* had no legal voice in Company affairs; he did not sign the *acte de société*, nor did he share the administrative duties of his titulary. By the mid-eighteenth century nearly every place in the Company was divided into *croupes*. The case of General Farmer Jacques Delahante may be taken as not atypical.

In 1763 Jacques Delahante, son of a financial director in the service of the duc d'Orléans and grandson of an obscure surgeon from Soissonais, was a director in the *Hôtel des Fermes*. He was the fast friend of General Farmer Desfourniels. Industrious, well educated, and with many powerful friends at court, he was designated to take the place of Desfourniels when that tax-farmer should choose to retire. But Delahante was not a rich man; he had only a moderate legacy in real estate, inherited from his father. In 1763 General Farmer Desfourniels fell ill, and his wife and daughter urged him to

[14] Grimaux, *Lavoisier*, pp. 32, 40.
[15] *Encyclopédie méthodique: Finances*, I, 448.

resign in favor of Delahante. He was agreeable and sent the young director to court to seek the *brevet du roi*. After much maneuvering, Delahante finally got the ear of the confessor of the queen, who spoke in his favor to her majesty, who in turn presumably advanced his case before the king. Eventually the *brevet* was obtained. Desfourniels in the meantime died. The question of financial arrangements now arose. The capital contribution in 1763 was 1,250,000 livres. Delahante was able to raise half of that sum himself, principally by mortgaging real estate and from personal loans advanced to him by General Farmer Borda. The Desfourniels family then came forward as *croupiers* in the other half of the investment. By formal contract, the widow, the daughter, and her husband were declared interested in the place as well for capital as for emoluments and profits (or loss) each for a sixth *croupe*, to be divided between the surviving two in the case of the death of one. The remaining three-sixths *croupes* of the place belonged to Delahante.[16] Thus General Farmer Jacques Delahante assumed all the administrative duties of a place in the Company, but he enjoyed only one half of the profits. In financial matters he was only the formal head in the Company of General Farmers of a small family investment group.

Arrangements of this sort seem to have been the most common way of financing places in the Company, especially among the tight family units from which the bulk of the late-eighteenth-century General Farmers were drawn. When Tronchin took the place of General Farmer d'Epinay in 1762, he held but a quarter *croupe* in his own right, the rest of the place being shared between the retired d'Epinay and his wife. In 1768 the General Farmer Roussel held no more than a sixth *croupe* in his place, the remaining parts being in the name of his sisters and cousins. In 1774, of sixty places in the Company, only twenty-two were not divided into *croupes*; of the

16 Delahante, *Une Famille de finance*, I, 300-301.

remainder, most were financed by *croupiers* who were either relatives of the titular General Farmer or who were retired General Farmers and their survivors.[17] The system of *croupes* was a legitimate manner of raising funds for investment in the Company, but it was subject to abuses. For as long as the Company of General Farmers was in existence, court intrigue, patronage, and favoritism forced unwanted, and often undesirable, *croupiers* upon various of the places in the organization. Often an aspirant General Farmer discovered that, in order to obtain his *brevet du roi*, he had to accept a small-share *croupier* whether he needed the extra funds or not. Frequently, the royal *croupier* was able to raise only a portion of his share of the capital contribution, but the titular General Farmer was forced to divide the profits of the place with him nonetheless. Even more serious was the common practice of the court in assigning flat pensions against places in the Company as a means of satisfying clients or of rewarding faithful servants. Periodically the Company complained of these practices to the controller-general, and periodically the government made halfhearted gestures to eliminate the abuses. But each time the monarchy found itself in financial distress, the list of royal *croupiers* and pensioners grew longer. Out of the ten leases between 1726 and 1780, only two, La Rue (1743) and Girandin (1749) were unburdened with these royal *croupes et pensions*.[18] They appear to have reached a climax under the Lease David of 1774.

In 1776 the list of all *croupes et pensions* for the Lease David of 1774 was published, to the chagrin and embarrassment of the government.[19] In this list it was

[17] De Janzé, *Les Financiers d'autrefois*, p. 390; Comparadon, *Les Prodigalités d'un fermier-général*, p. 35.

[18] Turgot, *Oeuvres*, IV, 151-152; Lavoisier, *Oeuvres*, VI, 158-160. Royal *croupes et pensions* were finally eliminated in 1780 by Necker.

[19] The list was first published in the spurious *Mémoires de l'abbé Terrai, contrôleur-général des finances*, pp. 220-230. The actual author was one Coquereau, a clerk, who stole the list of *croupes et pensions* for the Lease David from the *contrôle-générale*. A corrected

revealed that of sixty places in the Company, fifty-five were burdened with the payment of pensions which in total reached the sum of 400,000 livres a year. Among the pensioners were members of the family of the royal controller-general Terray, several courtesans, and other *protégées* of the court. It was further disclosed that the family of Mme de Pompadour had a quarter *croupe* of the place of General Farmer Ancourt in addition to a 12,000 livre pension assigned against the place of General Farmer St. Hilaire. Mme du Barry benefited by 200,000 livres in *croupes* on the place of General Farmer Bouret d'Erigny. But the greatest scandal, in the eyes of contemporaries, was that the king himself was a *croupier* in the Company of General Farmers. He was *croupier* for a quarter of the place of General Farmer De La Haye, for a quarter of the place of General Farmer Saleur, and for a half of the place of General Farmer Poujaud. In other words, the monarch drew profits from the General Farms equivalent to those of a full place in the Company of General Farmers. In terms of financial interest, Louis XV was in the curious position of being one of his own tax-farmers.

The imposition of the royal *croupes*, and especially of the pensions, was expensive and annoying to the titular General Farmers whose places were encumbered. But the pensions seem to have been generally accepted as but another of the several informal taxes which each tax-farmer must pay the monarchy for the privilege of a place in the Company, while the royal *croupes* normally were individually small and distributed lightly among the places. They did not represent a serious invasion of the Company of General Farmers by the powers of the court but rather a raid which could be contained with relative ease. The royal *croupiers* never threatened the characteristic pattern of Company financing which, after about the mid-eighteenth century, was one of investment by closely inter-

---

version of the list, the work of the editor G. Schelle, may be found in Turgot, *Oeuvres,* IV, 155-156.

married or interconnected groups in what was increasingly regarded as a kind of closed, almost family, corporation.[20] Thus, the Company of General Farmers was more than a simple partnership of large but legally limited scope. It was rather a consortium of forty to sixty small investment groups rallied around the titular General Farmers, many of whom regarded themselves not so much as enterprisers or administrators but as trustees of family estates. To some degree, therefore, the rigid form of the partnership was bent to provide some of the functional if not juridical flexibility of a joint-stock company. The Company reached beyond the restricted core of formal partners into a surrounding circle of investors whose names never appeared on the *actes de société* but whose influence on Company policy was probably important. Yet in the last analysis the body of "sleeping partners," or *croupiers*, was never large and never anonymous. It was a known and intimate part of the world of the active partners, of the General Farmers.

THE GENERAL FARMERS AND THE
FINANCIAL ARISTOCRACY

The General Farmers occupied a conspicuous place in the state and society of old-regime France. As a group

[20] The publication of the list of *croupes et pensions* in 1776 created a considerable public uproar and the whole system of *croupes* was condemned outright. But careful study of the list reveals that most *croupes* were legitimate arrangements of the Delahante type, arrangements usually among members, former members, and their relatives, of the Company. Aside from the king's own *croupes*, those which can be identified as imposed by sheer favoritism were usually small ones of an eighth or even less. Furthermore, it must be realized that many, such as those belonging to the families of Mme de Pompadour or the royal controller-general Terray, did not actually violate the dictum that Company financing was overwhelmingly restricted to an intermarried circle of tax-farming financiers. Mme de Pompadour was, after all, a close relative by blood and marriage to many General Farmers; so also was the Terray family. Given the highly personal nature of old-regime politics and administration, the situation was not unusual. Finally, it should be recognized that the system of royal *croupes et pensions* was a devious way for the monarchy to attach part of the profits of tax-farming to its own benefit.

they were a junior but maturing branch of the new "state nobility"[21] which, upon the failure of the great families of "feudal" origin to seize control of the monarchy just after the death of Louis XIV, increasingly dominated and supplied the leadership of the governments of Louis XV and Louis XVI. By the late eighteenth century the General Farmers emerged as chiefs of a royal financial corps which displayed the primary characteristics of an aristocracy:[22] wealth, high status in society,[23] inherited position in the state, and an intense degree of *esprit de corps*.[24] This financial aristocracy seems to have been traveling at the end of the Bourbon monarchy the same road to formal nobility which the *noblesse de la robe* had journeyed upon a century or more in the past.

When in 1726 the Company of General Farmers was legally reconstituted after twenty years of inactivity, its membership was a motley of financial speculators, stock jobbers, court favorites, and newly rich bureaucrats drawn from the upper echelons of the General Farms. Of the forty, only twelve had any experience in previous tax-farming companies. This group had been drawn largely from the ranks of the predatory commissioners of the *régie* Cordier. They had been selected principally on the basis of patronage. During the negotiation of the Lease Carlier, all the powers and factions of the court had competed to seek preferment for clients, friends, and creditors. Each newly appointed General Farmer seemed shel-

---

[21] Ardascheff, *Les Intendants de province sous Louis XVI,* pp. 17-21.

[22] Du Bled, "Manieurs d'argent et fermiers-généraux dans l'ancien régime," *Révue économique internationale,* III (1905), 526-527.

[23] Roustan, *The Pioneers of the French Revolution,* pp. 144-176. Roustan brilliantly shows that in the middle and late eighteenth century the financiers, especially the General Farmers, had outgrown the evil reputation of their institutional ancestors, the *partisans* and *traitants* of the sixteenth and seventeenth centuries. Fair-minded contemporaries recognized that most General Farmers were men of sound education, skill in a difficult profession, and honorable instincts. Some were regarded as men of great culture and cultivation. Save among some hide-bound representatives of the old nobility, they were accepted in the highest social circles.

[24] Sénac de Meilhan, *Considérations sur les richesses,* pp. 75-87.

tered under the wing of a great noble, a learned judge, or a well-situated woman.[25] Yet this seemingly incoherent body of men of diverse social, often humble, backgrounds, bound together in a common interest to exploit the General Farms, formed the nucleus of the Company of General Farmers which perpetuated itself from 1726 to the end of the old regime.

Once in possession of the Lease Carlier, the General Farmers closed ranks. It was impossible profitably to administer the great mechanism of the General Farms so long as places in the Company were endangered by every shift in court clique and influence. The tax-farmers sought to insulate themselves from the presence of totally unacceptable men forced on the Company by favoritism at Versailles. They sought to entrench themselves and their families in the Company by reducing changes in membership to the minimum required for an orderly procession of new men entering to take the places of those retiring. The success of this program, during a vulnerable period following immediately upon signature of the Lease Carlier, was due largely to the conservative complacency of Cardinal Fleury, whose long tenure as Louis XV's chief minister lasted from 1726 to 1742.[26] Under the Cardinal's protection the Company stabilized as it enriched its membership. Once achieved, continuity of membership was perpetuated under the influence of the royal controller-general Orry, who valued "above all else the friendship which the financiers bore him." [27]

By the time Orry departed from office (1745), consolidation of the position of the General Farmers was completed. The second generation of the tax-farming dynasties was already entering the Company, and the General Farmers were no longer on the defensive against the court. They seized the offensive and with their influ-

[25] Thirion, *La Vie privée*, pp. 26-27.
[26] Carré, "Louis XV, 1715-1774," *Histoire de France illustrée*, VIII, Part two, 93-95.
[27] D'Argenson, *Journal et mémoires*, II, 27.

ence penetrated to the center of government, to the king himself.   Mme de Châteauroux, the first *maîtresse en titre* of Louis XV, was connected and related, through her benefactor the court banker Pâris de Montmartel, to many influential General Farmers.[28]   Her successor, the marquise de Pompadour, was the daughter of a *commis de ferme* the godchild of the financiers Pâris la Montagne and Pâris de Montmartel, the protégée of one General Farmer, Le Normand de Tournehem, and the wife of another, Le Normand d'Etoile.[29]   Moreover, by the mideighteenth century the influence of the General Farmers, now usually men not only of wealth but of assured and cultivated manner, stretched beyond the immediate entourage of the king.   The tax-farming families interlaced at every level with the high nobility, the magistracy, and the clans which supplied the state with its chief administrators, such as the intendants in the provincial generalities and in the central offices of the ministries in Paris.[30]

[28] Dubois-Croneau, *Pâris de Montmartel: Banquier de la cour,* p. 137; Luynes, *Mémoires,* VI, 175.
[29] E. and J. de Goncourt, *Madame de Pompadour,* p. 15; Luynes, *Mémoires,* VII, 67; Mouffle d'Angerville, *La Vie privée de Louis XV,* I, 308-309, Mme de Pompadour secured the appointment of at least five General Farmers, all closely related to men already in the Company.   See also Thirion, *La Vie privée,* pp. 157-179.
[30] To take but a few examples, the royal controller-general Machault often growled at the Company of General Farmers, but he married his brother to the niece of General Farmer de Chévéry.   This alliance distressed the doughty Marquis d'Argenson, no friend of the financiers, yet Grimod du Fort, credited with being one of the most unregenerated of tax-farmers, married into the d'Argenson-Béthune family to enter the highest brackets of the nobility.   The niece of the royal controller-general Terray was the wife of one General Farmer and the mother of another.   Grimod de la Reynière married one daughter to Moreau de Beaumont, *intendant des finances,* and another to Lamoignon de Malesherbes, first president of the Paris *Cour des Aides,* later chancellor of France and chief author of many remonstrances subjecting the General Farmers to the severest criticism.   Malesherbes' sister married the son of the General Farmer Senozan.   Caze de la Bove, intendant of Brittany, was the nephew of one General Farmer and the grandson of another.   Thiroux de Crosne, intendant of Rouen, was the son, grandson, and great-grandson of General Farmers as was Dupleix de Bacquencourt of Burgundy.   Du Cluzel of Tours was the son of a General Farmer, and the brother of Sénac de Meilhan, in-

While the state nobility was thus being suffused with the progeny of *la finance,* the financiers themselves, within their own base of operations, the Company of General Farmers, were achieving to a remarkable degree the goal of an exclusive, continuous membership. Throughout the period from 1726 to the end of the old regime the Company was dominated by an interlocking group of professional tax-farming families. The surnames of Lallémont, La Live, Le Riche, Belfort, Goddard, Grimod, Bouret, De la Borde, Parseval, Dupin, De la Garde, Poujaud, Paulze, Tessier, Douet, Delahante, Bouilhac, and Daugny appeared on *acte de société* after *acte de société* as grandfathers, fathers, sons, brothers, and nephews. Fathers and sons [31] frequently sat side by side in the *assemblées* and a web of family relationships bound the dominant clans together.[32]

Between 1726 and 1789 there were twelve leases, each involving forty to sixty General Farmers. During this span of sixty-three years, save for the year 1756, when twenty new places were created upon the elimination of the subfarming companies,[33] new family names did not

---

tendant of Provence, was a General Farmer. See Sénac de Meilhan, *Considérations sur les richesses,* pp. 347-348; D'Argenson, *Journal et mémoires,* VI, 246-257; Ardascheff, *Les Intendants de province,* pp. 43-45.

[31] D'Argenson, *Journal et mémoires,* VI, 82.

[32] Janzé, *Les Financiers d'autrefois,* pp. 100-163, 177-189; Mouffle d'Angerville, *Vie privée de Louis XV,* I, 261-317; Delahante, *Une Famille de finance,* I, 219. For example, the Grimod family produced five General Farmers, the La Lives four, the Lallémonts three; three Bourets were General Farmers simultaneously in the mid-eighteenth century. Among the later General Farmers, Delville was Châlut de Verin's son-in-law; Delville's son succeeded to his father's place. Paulze's daughter married Lavoisier. De la Haye married Mlle. Pignon, daughter of one of the foremost General Farmers and sister to another. De Parseval married all his children within the circle of the Company.

[33] The abolition of the subfarmers completed the monopoly of the Company of General Farmers over the General Farms. In exchange for an additional twenty places, the Company rid itself of the nuisance of supervising more than two hundred subfarmers in whose appointment it had very little control. Competition for places in the subfarming companies was cut-throat. In 1738 some seven thousand per-

begin appearing in any quantity, nor were old names dropped until the years 1763 to 1765. During that brief period, a time when the financial strain of increasing partnership capital contributions was at its peak, twenty of the older General Farmers resigned their places in favor of younger men. But the shift did not mean a break in continuity despite the one-third loss in membership. On the contrary, as in the case of Delahante, the new partners were mostly hand-picked if not related to the retiring financiers while these latter retained contact with the Company by becoming *croupiers* to their successors. The next great shift in membership occurred in 1780, when the places in the Company were reduced to forty. Thirty-six General Farmers resigned. The sixteen vacant places were filled with executives drawn from the upper echelons of administration. But again the break was more apparent than real. The newly elevated General Farmers were mostly directors already connected by blood, marriage, or friendship with the high chiefs of the Company of General Farmers.[34]

Despite its financial and social solidarity the Company could not entirely escape, of course, the erratic pressures of the court. When places fell vacant, there was always a crowd anxious to push into the golden circle of the tax-

---

sons contested for one hundred vacant places. In 1749 the rush of supplicants was so great that the park at Compiègne (the court then being at that chateau) was covered with tents for them to sleep in. In 1755, just prior to the abolition of the subfarms, the solid bourgeois *avocat* Barbier heard that the controller-general had received three thousand petitions for places in the subfarming companies. When in the next year the subfarming companies were abandoned, the consternation in Paris was great. Barbier gloomily estimated that the abolition of the subfarms deprived some four hundred Parisian families of their accustomed sources of income. However, most of the twenty new General Farmers came from the subfarms, many with their relatives as *croupiers*. See Barbier, *Journal historique*, III, 73-74, 105, IV, 98-99.

[34] Material for this paragraph has been drawn from the *départements des messieurs,* published annually in the *Almanachs Royals* from 1725 to 1789. Compare Thirion, *La Vie privée,* pp. 517-523. There are some discrepancies between the two.

farmers. The king was often besieged by importunate courtiers seeking to nominate a General Farmer, and Louis XV occasionally granted his favor on the basis of sheer patronage.[35] But in the whole continuous body of the Company, after about 1750, these were important only because their often scandalous behavior reflected adversely upon the reputations of their more sober-minded colleagues.[36] They were always in the minority, a minority that dwindled toward the end of the reign of Louis XV and all but vanished in the reign of his successor.[37] The second and third generation of General Farmers shed the vulgarity that characterized many of their ancestors in the original company of 1726. By the end of the old regime the General Farmers were men of newer spirit; enlightened men hardly less wealthy than their forefathers had been in the days of Cardinal Fleury but softened in their manners and attitude toward the state and the taxpayers; skillful men trained in the General Farms; on the

[35] Louis XV sometimes sold options (*bons de place*) good for the first, second, or third place to fall vacant. Such options were not guarantees of placement; they merely gave the option-holder a prior claim for appointment. Properly used the options established a certain order among the claimants. But under a monarch such as Louis XV, abuses were inevitable. The options fell into wrong hands; the Company then bought them up to prevent undesirables from gaining a place. Louis at times created options as a kind of blackmail to force the Company to make gifts. Several scandals involving the highest circles of the court occurred in the 1740s and 1750s concerning bogus options hawked to innocents by swindlers. See Barbier, *Journal historique*, II, 341-342, III, 37-38; D'Argenson, *Journal et mémoires*, II, 256, 436; Luynes, *Mémoires*, VI, 113-114; Boislisle (ed.), *Lettres de M. de Marville*, I, 127, 130-131.

[36] It is pertinent to observe that once placed a General Farmer seems to have been practically unremovable so long as he maintained his share of the capital fund of the Company. During the entire reign of Louis XV, only two General Farmers, La Live d'Epinay and La Riche de la Popelinière, were ever cashiered by order of the king. Both were fantastic libertines (although the latter was famous in the history of French music) whose extravagances were damaging to the reputation of the Company. See Comparadon, *Les Prodigalités d'un fermier-général*, p. 35.

[37] Capéfique, *Histoire des grandes opérations financières*, I, 146-168.

whole conscientious men within the limits imposed upon them by the tax-farming system.[38]

The chief device used to consolidate the Company around the dominant families and to provide for continuity in membership was the system of adjuncts. Upon the signature of each lease certain persons were designated as *adjoints sur les places* by royal decree. The adjunct was not a partner in the Company of General Farmers but was rather an associate in the place of his titular General Farmer. Although occasionally a creditor or even a *croupier* (as in the case of Lavoisier) might obtain such a position, normally the adjunct was the son or nephew of the titular General Farmer with no legal financial interest in the Company. These young men served an apprenticeship in the General Farms; often they worked as supernumerary controllers in the Provincial Directions or as clerks in the *Hôtel des Fermes*. Frequently the adjunct stood in the place of the titular in the event of his absence from his administrative obligations. For these labors the adjunct received no remuneration other than that given him informally by the General Farmer to whom he was attached. But he was the heir apparent to the place of his titular.[39]

In law the adjunct was a *survivancier*, a person with an imprescriptible right to succeed to an office;[40] he had a legal claim upon the place of his titular. Should that place fall vacant, it could not be preempted by any other claimant. In this manner, any General Farmer could designate his own successor and in effect turn his appointive office into an inheritable property. All that was needed was the consent of the king; for the monarch created the survivorship. Royal cooperation was never too difficult to obtain, although it might be expensive.

[38] Sénac de Meilhan, *Considérations sur les richesses*, pp. 338, 345-348; *Encyclopédie méthodique: Finances*, II, 203-205.

[39] Delahante, *Une Famille de finance*, I, 197-199.

[40] *Répertoire universel de jurisprudence*, XVI, 614.

The system of adjuncts was, however, often abused by individual General Farmers. Incompetents were frequently guaranteed a place in the Company by being designated to survive an aged General Farmer about to retire. Immature boys often stood as adjuncts while experienced individuals trained through years of work in the bureaucracy could not hope to gain admittance. Especially after 1763, crass money lenders attempted to buy survivorships in the Company. Periodically the government attempted to set standards of quality, the king refusing to grant the necessary survivorship in cases of manifest incapacity.[41] But it was not until 1780 that the system was regularized to the maximum advantage of the Company. Under authority of a writ issued in 1780, Necker ordered that in the future only the sons of General Farmers would be admitted to the status of adjunct. According to the enabling act, his majesty wished to reward his faithful Farmers by gratifying their natural hope "of passing their places to their children" and trusted that, with such assurance of the prosperity of their sons, the fathers would be content with the lessened rate of profits imposed upon them by the terms of the Lease Salzard of 1780.[42] This decision to limit the adjuncts in the Company to the sons of General Farmers was maintained with but few exceptions. In 1780 eight of the forty General Farmers had their sons listed as adjuncts, and in the cases of three others exceptions for the extraordinary abilities of nephews had been granted.[43] By these devices the Company of General Farmers obviated the need of venal proprietorship of its places; practically, it possessed the major part of them as surely as the financiers of the General Receipts owned their offices.

Thus through *de facto* inheritance of place, through alliances that connected the high officials of the General Farms

[41] Turgot, *Oeuvres*, IV, 151.

[42] *Encyclopédie méthodique: Finances*, I, 12-13.

[43] Clément and Lemoine, *M. de Silhouette, Bouret et les derniers fermiers-généraux*, pp. 324-325.

bureaucracy with the intermarried clans of the General Farmers, and through the system of *croupes* which enabled even the families of retired or deceased tax-farmers to remain associated with the enterprise, the Company of General Farmers became a closed corporation. In this context many of the organizational ambiguities of the Company and its administration of the General Farms become intelligible. The distinction between the passive and active General Farmers, between those few financiers who actually ran the enterprise and those who played only a nominal role in the administrative assemblies reflected a reasonable division of labor between a "board of trustees" preoccupied with protecting family investments and an administration of younger members concerned primarily with the management of the business. Moreover, the increasingly sharp line drawn between the higher and lower brackets of General Farms employees was itself a function of the late eighteenth-century practice of introducing into the old tax-farming dynasties new talent drawn from among the professionally trained bureaucrats. Thus the tax-farming suzerains of the General Farms, themselves already nearing formal inclusion in the new state nobility, were assured of an orderly system of recruitment into their ranks.

The writ of 1780 concerning the adjuncts ratified a tendency which had long been in evidence: the General Farmers, leaders of the antique financial corps, were, in the late eighteenth century, being transformed into an aristocracy.[44] Yet it was a curious aristocracy; for although its economic foundations were not in the land, neither did they rest solidly upon the commercial and industrial enterprises of capitalism.[45] The assets of the

[44] Sagnac, *Le Formation de la société française moderne*, II, 169-170.
[45] The capital of the early (c. 1726) General Farmers seems to have come from three main sources: wealth already accumulated by families long engaged in the royal financial service; fortunes made in speculation either during the chaotic days of the late reign of Louis XIV or during the time of John Law's "System"; family savings of

General Farmers consisted almost exclusively of capital frozen in the permanent royal debt; [46] their incomes derived from an archaic financial enterprise which lived only because the monarchy could not afford to let it die.

THE COMPANY AND THE GROWTH OF THE ROYAL DEBT:
THE FINANCIAL ROLE

The Company of General Farmers owed its existence to its financial role in the service of the late Bourbon monarchy. In the mid-eighteenth century all of the ways in which tax-farming could be used as a source of credit were not only exploited but distorted in such a fashion as to make the elimination of tax-farming an impossibility short of a total reformation of the entire fiscal and financial system of the old regime. Tax-farming had always been a method of tax-anticipation based upon the advance of short-term credits from the tax-farmer to the royal treasury. But between 1749 and 1774, years of war and chronic budgetary deficits, this short-term function of the tax-farmer was subordinated to the relatively new role of the Company as a prime investor in long-term government debt, a debt that was carried from lease to lease and never paid back. In the process the General Farmers

---

middle-class professional groups. Throughout the remainder of the old regime, predominantly the General Farmer's capital seems to have come from the first with the third fairly important. The second source seems to have diminished. Except in the case of De Laborde, there is little evidence of commercial or industrial capital seeking investment in the Company; conversely, there is little evidence to indicate that the General Farmers invested their profits in industrial or commercial enterprises. The whole question, however, is of considerable importance and one which requires further intensive research, perhaps through examination of the biographies of the General Farmers.

[46] Mollien, *Mémoires d'un ministre,* I, 161. Mollien observes that, although the General Farmers were credited with being among the most wealthy men of France, actually they possessed very little beyond capital sunk in the royal debt. So long as return on that investment was maintained, they were rich in terms of income. When that capital was wiped out during the Revolution, they were, in terms of land, houses, and negotiable securities, comparatively poor.

acquired a mortgage on the General Farms that could not be canceled; in fact, by 1774 it was apparent that it could only be increased and extended indefinitely into the future. Thus, as the obsolete and costly system of tax-farming became irrevocably fastened on the fiscal system, its character changed. The risk-taking aspects of the enterprise diminished, and the General Farmers emerged, in economic and financial terms, as a peculiar class of rentiers which, in return for a guaranteed annual income, invested its entire wealth in the permanent government debt.

The financial history of the Company of General Farmers between the years 1726 and 1789 may be divided into three fairly clear-cut periods. The first extended from 1726 to 1750; the second, from 1750 to 1776; and the third, from 1776 to the end of the old regime. The first period was for France as a whole one of the relative internal calm and well-being. Cardinal Fleury, whose influence over the king was in ascendency from 1726 to 1743, dominated the government and committed it to a policy of conservative stability at home and peace abroad. No fiscal or financial reforms were undertaken; by like token, no excessive burdens were placed upon the existing system of taxes and sources of credit. The economy entered a phase of mild prosperity marked by a gentle upward sloping of the general long-term price level. Until 1740 large-scale military adventures were avoided and the king's taste for extravagance was restrained.[47] However, in 1740 the great War of the Austrian Succession (1740-1748) began, generating the first serious financial crisis since the collapse of John Law's System. [48]

During this period from 1726 to 1750 the credit rela-

---

[47] Carré, "Louis XV, 1715-1774," *Histoire de France illustrée,* VIII, Part Two, 117-123. The minor War of the Polish Sucession (1733-1735) was purely peripheral and one which Fleury easily financed by means of a special but temporary *dixième* on income and the moderate flotation of new *rentes* and *tontines.*

[48] Marion, *Histoire financière,* I, 177; Clamageran, *Histoire de l'impôt,* III, 292-296.

tionship of the Company of General Farmers and the royal treasury was unstrained and normal within the framework of the customary tax-farming system.[49] Four leases were negotiated without difficulty, the annual lease price rising only gradually from 80,000,000 livres to 92,-000,000 livres with additional taxation added to take care of each increase.[50] Throughout this time the only large-scale advance to the treasury required of the Company was the bondsmoney which remained fixed at 8,000,000 livres at 4 percent per annum despite the gentle rise in annual lease prices. The bondsmoney retained its primitive character as a guarantee of good faith, and its size was determined solely by the value of the permanent royal investment in the General Farms plus the value of salt and tobacco inventories on hand at the time of the lease

[49] The one exception to this statement requires some explanation. In 1729 Fleury began a refunding operation concerning certain *rentes*. He ordered the Company to reimburse some 5,250,000 livres of these *rentes* at the rate of 500,000 livres a month by means of a lottery the cost of which was to be borne entirely by the Company. In effect this was a forced loan of a little over 5,000,000 livres a year. The General Farmers accepted, for they knew that at bottom the cardinal was their chief ally and they did not wish to antagonize him. In 1730, however, Fleury proposed a similar operation involving the liquidation of certain Indies Company stock at a cost of 400,000 livres a month. The Company, anxious to be rid of this sort of unpredictable levy upon its resources, now offered the cardinal a proposition. In return for relief from the burden of liquidating *rentes* and shares, the tax-farmers offered to anticipate the renewal of the lease on the General Farms by two years (Carlier was not due to expire until 1732), promising to pay 84,000,000 livres a year for the last two years yet to run on Carlier and for the next six years thereafter. The Company proposed a new lease of an eight year term to cover this deal. The government hastened to comply and negotiated the Lease Desboves in secret two years before the expiration of Carlier. Thus the government gained by a devious route an advance without interest of some 8,000,000 livres. The whole affair was exceptional, however. See Duclos, *Mémoires sécrètes,* II, 372; Marion, *Histoire financière,* II, 149-151; Clamageran, *Histoire de l'impôt,* III, 244-246.

[50] The leases were: Carlier, 1726; Desboves, 1732. Forceville, 1738; La Rue, 1744. (The dates represent the beginning of the lease rather than the date of signature.) By additional taxation is meant the attachment of such valuable revenues as the *domaines d'Occident* and the *tabacs* to the receipts of the General Farms. See Appendix p. 285.

signature.[51]   At the close of each lease it was duly liquidated by deduction from the last annual lease price.   The
Company, of course, promptly advanced it again to secure the next contract.   Thus, while the bondsmoney was
actually in the nature of a long-term debt carried forward
from lease to lease, it was a moderate one that could
easily have been paid had Fleury chosen to abandon tax-
farming.

In terms of its own internal financial affairs, the Company maintained its total capital fund at about 33,800,000
livres for each lease.   The sum was ample to provide for
the posting of the bondsmoney and to finance current
General Farms operations.[52]   It was not until the War of
the Austrian Succession that the debt-service and nonfiscal
charges assigned for payment against the General Farms
increased in sufficient volume to create serious treasury
overdrafts on the annual lease price installments.   Even
then the Company's capital was large enough to enable
the tax-farmers to carry the government without recourse
to excessive flotation of short-term *billets des fermes* in
the money market.   Such *billets des fermes* as were negotiated were easily liquidated within the course of the

[51] *Bail fait à Forceville,* Arts. 551 and 602.   In 1738 the capital investment and inventory value of the General Farms was placed at
7,979,317 livres.

[52] The capital fund for each lease was regarded as a distinct entity.
So also the income of the Company from tax yield of a preceding
lease could never legally be used to pay for expenses of the current
lease.   Ordinarily it was a matter of four to six months after the beginning of a lease before the Company received income from taxes
which could be used to finance current operations.   In the meantime,
it was under certain heavy obligations.   First, a large part of its capital was immediately tied up in the bondsmoney credited to the treasury's account.   Second, it must pay annual lease installments out of
capital until tax returns reached Paris.   Third, it must disburse heavy
debt service charge without interruption and accept other charges as
presented.   Fourth, it must pay wages, buy salt and tobacco and so on.
The Company needed a large amount of capital so as to maintain a
safe proportion among these factors.   Should any or all of the first
three factors increase at a rate disproportionate to the fourth, the
Company must either raise its capital fund or negotiate *billets des
fermes* at short-term to pay current expenses.   See Lavoisier,
Oeuvres, VI, 136.

current lease by deduction as fiscal charges from annual lease price.

In most respects the second period (1750-1776) in the financial history of the General Farms was the converse of the first. Already in 1740 peace had been disrupted by the Austrian war. The financial wreckage left in the wake of that conflict had scarcely been cleared away when the rumblings of the Seven Years War (1756-1763) were heard. That mighty imperial collision completely un-hinged the finances of the state. As early as April, 1756, the deficit stood at 67,000,000 livres; by 1759 it had risen to 118,000,000 livres. Declaration of partial bankruptcy in that year temporarily eased the strain. But during the closing years of the war deficits were still running in the vicinity of 200,000,000 livres with 203,000,000 livres of debt falling due each year. The conclusion of peace only brought to the surface the permanently distressed condi-tion of the royal treasury. For several years after the war there was a normal deficit of a least 50,000,000 livres a year. Aa late as 1770 the current deficit was 63,000,000 livres; debts falling due totaled 110,000,000 livres, and 153,000,000 livres of revenue of the year 1770 had al-ready been spent in 1769.[53]

Bankruptcy proceedings in 1770 momentarily relieved the pressure, but the rupture in the financial system was permanent. In 1776 French arsenals were already pre-paring munitions for a new struggle with Great Britain; in 1778 France intervened in the War of American In-dependence, and the monarchy tilted into its final and fatal bankruptcy.[54]

Paradoxically, throughout most of this time of troubles France as a whole was prosperous. But the monarchy could tap the wealth of the country only partially and in-

[53] Gomel, *Les Causes financières de la révolution française,* I, 9-12, 30-31; Marion, *Histoire financière,* I, 170-171, 191; Clamageran, *His-toire de l'impôt,* III, 323-325; Guillamat-Vallet, *Le Contrôleur-générale Silhouette,* pp. 135-146.

[54] Marion, *Histoire financière,* I, 254-255, 277, 290-291; Clamageran, *Histoire de l'impôt,* III, 430-435.

adequately. Class and provincial privilege exempted the wealthiest elements of society from payment of direct taxation. Sporadically the government attempted to bring the first and second estates more directly under its fiscal heel. But every concession was purchased at the price of open warfare between the "absolute" monarchy and the powers of the clergy and nobility. Every effort to distribute the burden of direct taxation equitably among all classes was sabotaged and vitiated by the privileged orders.[55] In consequence, the monarchy turned increasingly to indirect taxation for relief. Between 1760 and 1780, by means of surtaxes, the rates of all receipts of the General Farms (except *tabacs*) increased 30 percent, and annual lease prices were augmented by increases of from eight to nineteen millions every six years.[56] But even with increased revenues, the deficits remained. The only alternative was to borrow. As the distraught and often impotent finance ministers flitted in and out of office, loans of every description and type were piled on loans. Credit was snatched from every possible source, from the municipalities, from the church, from venal offices, from the *pays d'état*, from the financial corps, from the Company of General Farmers.

After 1749 the Company of General Farmers was under incessant pressure to lend its capital and credit to the state. Its holdings in long-term debt rose with great rapidity, and the bondsmoney lost its simple character as a security for good behavior equal to the investment and inventory value of the General Farms. The bondsmoney was transformed into a genuine advance remittance of lease price in the form of a permanent loan.[57]

In 1749 the Lease Girandin was negotiated for a lease price of 102,000,000 livres, about 11,000,000 livres higher

[55] Marion, *Histoire financière*, I, 172-176, 205-223, 267-272.
[56] See Appendix p. 285.
[57] The phrase *cautionnement du prix de bail* (bondsmoney) became old fashioned; in the later leases the phrase *avances à titre de prêt* was used, although such advances always included a figure for bondsmoney.

than that of the preceding Lease La Rue. But the bondsmoney required jumped from the traditional 8,000,000
livres to 20,000,000 livres.[58] The Lease Henriet of 1756
was signed for an annual lease price only about 8,000,000
livres higher than that of Girandin, but the advance soared
to 60,000,000 livres.[59] In the Lease Prévost of 1762 the
advance was pushed upward to 72,000,000 livres, 60,000,-
000 livres of which was the old debt of Henriet resubscribed by the Company and carried forward under Prévost. The remainder represented a further loan of 12,-
000,000 livres. Yet the annual lease price of Prévost was
augmented by only 8,000,000 livres over that of Henriet.[60]
Despite an elaborate schedule of deductions from annual
lease prices intended to liquidate this debt in the six-year
term of the lease, the desperate government refused to allow the Company to reimburse itself even a sou. Thus
negotiations on the next lease, Alaterre of 1768, opened
with the government firmly in the debt of the company.
The advance required to secure Alaterre was set at 72,000,-
000 livres of old debt resubscribed and carried over from
Prévost plus 20,000,000 livres in a new loan, making a
total of 92,000,000 livres advance on a lease price of 132,-
000,000 livres.[61] The figure of 92,000,000 livres represented the maximum long-term credit drawn from the
Company at one time. In 1774, although the annual lease
price of the Lease David was increased to 152,000,000
livres,[62] the advance remained at 92,000,000 livres. The

[58] Lavoisier, *Oeuvres*, VI, 136.

[59] *Collection des comptes rendus*, pp. 19-20; Lavoisier, *Oeuvres*, VI,
137-138; Marion, *Histoire financière*, I, 178-180. 20,000,000 livres of
the 60,000,000 livres was used to liquidate the advance made on
Girandin (or technically, Bocquillon, to whom the lease subrogated
upon the former's death).

[60] Bosquet, *Dictionnaire raisonné des domaines*, I, 348-349; Lavoisier, *Oeuvres*, VI, 139. A large part of the increase in the annual
lease price of Prévost was due to the incorporation of the receipt of
Bar et Lorraine into the lease.

[61] Lavoisier, *Oeuvres*, VI, 139-140, 161-162.

[62] From the traditional body of the General Farms were detached, at
this time, various minor taxes to an annual value of 8,442,000 livres;
but new taxes (the *sous pour livre* of 1770) were added to a value of

sum contained no new loans but was simply a resubscription of the advance of Alaterre carried over to David.[63] The 92,000,000 livres advance was a permanent long-term loan, the original heart of which (60,000,000 livres) had been carried forward from lease to lease for eighteen years and which was never reimbursed.

This enormous expansion in long-term debt held by the Company was paralleled by an intensive exploitation of the traditional short-term role of the tax-farmer. The Company augmented its capital funds by adding to its membership in 1756 and by raising the capital contributions of each place. But by 1767 the capital fund almost exactly equalled the advances to government; [64] in other words, almost the entire capital fund of the Company of General Farmers was frozen, immediately upon signature of a lease, in the government debt. When this occurred, nothing was left to finance the current operations of the General Farms. As the government assigned debt-service and nonfiscal charges against lease price, the treasury's account was soon overdrawn. In these circumstances the Company had no alternative but to negotiate *billets des fermes* in the money market.

The volume of *billets des fermes* fluctuated from lease to lease, year to year, but after 1756 masses of them were always in circulation. Immediately upon signature of the Lease Henriet of 1756, the Company began negotiating *billets* at the rate of some 23,000,000 livres a year; payment in principal and interest on these notes was deducted from annual lease prices as charges.[65] In 1759 the hemorrhage of current receipts into the constant financing of *billets* was so great that the government

---

25,155,295 livres. See Lavoisier, *Oeuvres,* VI, 165-185, for the complete details of this lease.

[63] *Ibid.,* VI, 141-143; Clamageran, *Histoire de l'impôt,* III, 442-443; Delahante, *Une Famille de finance,* I, 231-232, See Appendix p. 285.

[64] Lavoisier, *Oeuvres,* VI, 139-142.

[65] *Collection des comptes rendus,* pp. 34-35.

ordered a temporary suspension of payment, a step equivalent to admission of partial bankruptcy.[66]

Payment was resumed on a limited scale in 1761. Soon after the opening of the Lease Prévost of 1762, Lavoisier estimated that at least 60,000,000 livres in unredeemed and newly issued *billets des fermes* were in circulation. By 1767 abatement of charges against lease price following the end of the Seven Years War enabled the Company to reduce this figure to 48,500,000 livres. But three years later the amount of the *billets des fermes* in circulation was back to 60,000,000 livres. Once again the government declared partial bankruptcy and suspended payment.[67]

In order to provide for an orderly retirement of this mass of floating debt, the government authorized the Company to conduct a lottery. The first winners were paid in full; the rest were to be paid at reduced rates according to a complicated priority system stretching to 1782.[68] The Company financed the lottery privately but was to be reimbursed by an annual deduction from lease price. By 1774 the volume of *billets* had been reduced to 37,735,000 livres, but the Company had been allowed to deduct only a fraction of the costs of the lottery.

Thus by the time Turgot entered upon his brief term as controller-general in 1774, the government was inextricably caught in the net of debt that bound it to the Company of General Farmers. The new finance minister did not disguise his distaste for tax-farming and would have liked to rid the fiscal-financial service of the tax-farmers. But suppression of the Company and conversion

[66] Marion, *Histoire financière*, I, 196-197. In the same year 72,000,000 livres of *rescriptions* on the General Financial Receivers of the *taille* were also suspended as were interest payments of numerous sorts of permanent debts.

[67] Lavoisier, *Oeuvres*, VI, 139; Marion, *Histoire financière*, I, 212, 213, 254-255.

[68] Harbulot, "Etudes sur les finances de l'ancienne France," *Révue des sciences politiques*, LVIII (1935), 207.

of the General Farms into a *régie* could be accomplished only by liquidation of a long-term debt of 92,000,000 livres and of a short-term debt of some 37,700,000 livres. Louis XVI's treasury was in no condition either to retire this debt quickly or to repudiate it. The first alternative the monarchy simply could not afford; the second would have collapsed the entire structure of *rentes* which rested as a charge upon the annual lease prices.[69]

The best that Turgot could afford to do was to permit, for the first time in nearly twenty years, a modest annual repayment of 20,000,000 livres on the long-term advance and a gradual liquidation of the *billets des fermes*. But fundamental reform of the General Farms obviously had to wait upon basic renovations in the entire fiscal and financial structure. Turgot was not given the time; he fell in 1776 before the combined force of the court, the Parlements, the guilds, perhaps the Company, certainly the queen.[70] Necker became his successor after an interval of six months.

With the advent of Necker, whose first tenure as finance minister was from 1776 to 1781, the financial history of the Company of General Farmers entered its final phase in a period that witnessed the collapse of the old monarchy. Once again war destroyed all semblance of order in state finances. Despite an appearance of prosperity, engendered by a short-term inflation, large segments of the economy were in a depressed condition. Taxes were surcharged for the last time in 1780 and 1781; within the terms of the existing system of privilege-corroded fiscality, the economy could bear no more. Inflation pushed the receipts to unprecedented levels, but also made the burden appear more intolerable. In any case, receipts from taxation were incapable of closing the gap between income and outgo. Hence a frantic, final burst of bor-

---

[69] Véri, *Journal*, I, 371-373, 378-380; Mollien, *Mémoires d'un ministre*, I, 68.

[70] Dakin, *Turgot*, pp. 252-256.

rowing marked the closing years of the old regime. Necker proceeded to borrow 530,000,000 livres in four years, most of it entirely unfunded. His successors, Joly, D'Oremesson, and Calonne dropped all restraint. Calonne borrowed 652,000,000 livres in the three years between 1783 and 1786. Yet in 1788 the current deficit was at least 126,000,000 livres, with debt service charges alone consuming over 50 percent of annual expenditures.[71]

The period 1776 to the end of the old regime was a paradoxical one for the Company of General Farmers. As has been shown earlier, the General Farms itself was dismembered, and the tax-collecting function of the Company was severely limited. Its administration of the General Farms was subjected to increasingly strict government supervision. Moreover, in the orgy of borrowing, the ancient financial corps was in part circumvented in favor of newer and richer sources of credit. Necker, D'Oremesson, and Calonne made no secret of their lack of sympathy with the antique Company.[72] Yet throughout this period of stress and change the Company, although reduced in size and influence, remained a solidly entrenched and lucrative enterprise. This was because Necker, like Turgot, could not liquidate the long-term debt. Indeed, despite a much-publicized show of reform, he found a way to suck still more credit from the financial corps he professed to mistrust.

In 1780 the Lease David expired and the Lease Salzard was negotiated. At that time the long-term debt stood at an irreducible 72,000,000 livres,[73] there were still 16,135,000 livres of 1774 *billet des fermes* outstanding, and the annual overdraft of the treasury averaged 10,000,000 livres. Necker could afford to liquidate none

---

[71] Gomel, *Les Causes financières de la révolution française*, I, 251-258; Marion, *Histoire financière*, I, 320-303, 341-342, 356-357, 365-366, 381; Braesch, *Finances et monnaie révolutionnaires*, II, 200-210.

[72] Mollien, *Mémoires d'un ministre*, I, 197.

[73] Reduced from the 92,000,000 livres in 1774 by virtue of a 20,000,000 livre deduction from annual lease price permitted by Turgot and Necker.

of these debts, yet he wished to win acclaim by appearing to attack the tax-farming system. His solution to the problem was deft.[74]

Necker first split the old General Farms into three parts. The Company of General Farmers, reduced from sixty to forty members, continued at the head of the attenuated General Farms. At the head of each of the new administrations for *aides* and *domaines,* Necker placed a company of twenty-five commissioners. To reduce the Company of General Farmers to forty members meant the retirement of twenty partners. It was necessary to liquidate their portion of 72,000,000 livres debt in shares of 1,560,000 livres each. The government could not afford to do this out of general funds. Therefore, each of the fifty new commissioners was required to post a surety bond of 1,000,000 livres. This gave Necker 50,000,000 livres. Then each of the remaining General Farmers resubscribed his share of the capital fund of the Company, a matter of 1,560,000 livres each. This gave Necker 62,400,000 livres, or a total advance from ninety financiers (for the commissioners were drawn or supported by money from the old financial corps) of 112,400,000 livres. This was an advance greater by 20,000,000 livres than had ever previously been drawn from the tax-collecting financiers. The Swiss banker could now easily reimburse the retiring twenty General Farmers their full 31,200,000 livres and still have 81,200,000 livres in long-term loans, 9,200,000 livres more than when the transaction had started. The state was now 81,000,000 livres in debt to ninety financiers, whereas before it had been 72,000,000 livres in debt to sixty.[75]

In terms of the position of the Company as long-term creditor of the state, the forty General Farmers simply had resubscribed 62,400,000 livres of the old debt which

74 Gomel, *Les Causes financières de la révolution française,* I, 330-331.

75 Marion, *Histoire financière,* I, 319-320; Véri, *Journal,* II, 392-393; Lavaquéry, *Necker,* pp. 170-171.

had been carried forward on every lease since 1756. Thus, while limited in size by the Lease Salzard of 1780, the Company remained a significant investor in long-term debt. In the matter of short-term debt, the Lease Salzard provided for an orderly method of repayment of the outstanding 16,135,000 livres of old 1770 *billets des fermes;* these were finally retired in 1784. But already before that date the process of royal borrowing on the basis of *billets des fermes* had begun anew.

Necker had hardly finished his reform of the General Farms when he resigned his position as finance minister under attack from all factions whose interests he had seemed to threaten. His successors, bearing now the full financial consequences of the American war, faced with mounting deficits and an empty treasury, turned frantically to borrowing to pay back loans so as to maintain credit on which to borrow again. Joly de Fleury followed Necker, imposed the final *sous pour livre* in surtaxes on all *perceptions,* recreated venal offices which Necker had suppressed (such as the duplicate General Financial Receivers), and grasped at every possible source of credit. Thirty million livres were drawn from the Company of General Farmers, and new *billets des fermes* to that amount were negotiated in the Paris money market.[76] Joly fell from office, and D'Oremesson followed in his place.

D'Oremesson was an avowed enemy of the General Farmers. Strongly influenced by the American Committee which was agitating for suppression of the tobacco monopoly, anxious to negotiate trade treaties with England and Holland and to reform the *gabelles* and *traites,* D'Oremesson regarded the Company as an anachronism of which he was determined to be rid.[77] On October 24, 1783, he issued a writ suppressing the Lease Salzard and offering the current membership of the Company a limited

[76] Marion, *Histoire financière,* I, 341-344.
[77] Clément and Lemoine, *Silhouette, Bouret et les derniers fermiers-généraux,* pp. 231-233.

régie contract for the continuance of its administration of the *gabelles, tabacs, traites,* and *entrées* until such time as those receipts could be reformed or eliminated.[78] D'Oremesson had acted without sufficient financial preparation. Immediately upon arrival of this news in the money market, the holders of the 30,000,000 livres worth of *billets des fermes* rushed to demand payment. The General Farmers refused to honor them on their own credit, thus facing the treasury with the prospect of declaring itself bankrupt. For there was no money with which the government could redeem these short-term notes. On November 8, 1783, thirty General Farmers, joined by the court banker, Michault d'Harvely, sought and obtained audience with the king. For his majesty's instruction they depicted the abyss which would open at his feet should D'Oremesson's plans be carried out; short-term credit would be ruined and any repudiation of the long-term debt could mean nothing but bankruptcy. The king was thoroughly frightened.[79] He retracted the writ on the spot and dismissed the controller-general. The next day a new writ returned to the Company its rights under the Lease Salzard.[80] The holders of the *billets des fermes,* gratified to discover that the Company was still a power in the realm, ceased demanding payment on their notes. The credit of the tax-farmers still served to defend their place in the fiscal service.

Calonne succeeded D'Oremesson and immediately plunged deeper into debt. Preferring to deal with the new capitalist lenders who drew upon the resources of the international money market, Calonne nevertheless did not overlook the Company of General Farmers. When the Lease Mager of 1786 was negotiated, the Company resubscribed the 62,400,000 livres advance and carried it over into Mager. Calonne demanded more credit; the

---

[78] *Encyclopédie méthodique: Finances,* II, 125.

[79] Mollien, *Mémoires d'un ministre,* I, 89-92.

[80] Marion, *Histoire financière,* I, 350. The *traites* were continued in *régie* pending reform of the tariff system. The General Farmers served as the commissioners.

Company agreed to accept two additional members, which added 3,120,000 livres in new debt. A year later two more places were added to increase the total long-term debt still held by the Company to 68,840,000 livres just prior to the Revolution.[81]

Thus to the end the king, buried under debts, still had need of his tax-farmers. He was still under the necessity of paying a high price, in terms of their profits, for the financial aid the General Farmers could render the royal treasury.

THE PROFITS OF TAX-FARMING

In the folklore of eighteenth-century France no more common stereotype existed than the figure of Turcaret,[82] the immensely rich, gross, and low-born *traitant* whose wealth derived from the profits of tax-farming. Turcaret was the invention of the playwright Le Sage, yet much of contemporary speculation concerning the profits of the Company of General Farmers was equally imaginative.[83] While there can be no doubt that the profession of tax-farming in post-1726 France was extremely lucrative, any attempt to reconstruct the total pecuniary rewards of that profession was then, and is now, impossible.

The total earnings of a General Farmer from participation in the Company were divided into three sorts of income: managerial salary, paid to him annually for administrative duties; interest, paid annually on his invest-

---

[81] Mollien, *Mémoires d'un ministre,* I, 106-110; *Encyclopédie méthodique: Finances,* I, 74.

[82] Le Sage, *Turcaret* (first played in 1708; first published in 1737). See Tzaneff, *L'Homme d'argent au théâtre français,* pp. 145-162. The rapacious and vulgar behavior of many tax-farmers in the later reign of Louis XIV was justly summed up in the figure of Turcaret. But by the mid-eighteenth century, Turcaret bore little resemblance to the actual financiers then in the Company of General Farmers. However, it was always a literary convention to ridicule the *traitant* and as a cliché, no matter how inaccurate, Turcaret survived to the end of the old regime.

[83] For examples of common, fantastic "calculations" of the General Farmers' profits, see Mirabeau, *Théorie de l'impôt,* p. 203; Darigrand, *L'Anti-financier,* p. 60; Le Trosne, *De l'administration provinciale et de la réforme de l'impôt,* p. 168.

ment of capital in the enterprise; entrepreneurial profits, the difference between annual lease price and net yield. Informed contemporaries knew that, in 1774, for example, the salary of each General Farmer amounted to 24,000 livres plus 4,200 livres as an expense account. They knew also that the rate of interest on invested capital of 1,560,000 livres per place in the same year, was 10 percent on the first 1,000,000 livres and 6 percent on the remainder, or a return of 133,000 livres a year. This, combined with salary, represented the General Farmer's fixed, guaranteed annual income (161,200 livres), which, of course, he shared to a greater or lesser degree with his *croupiers* and personal creditors.[84] But, on the question of entrepreneurial profits, even close associates of the Company could do no more than express a reasoned opinion.

No exact figures on entrepreneurial profits were available to the general public in the eighteenth century; it is possible that even the government did not possess them until about 1749. There are no such figures in existence today. No two authorities agreed even on the profits of a single lease, let alone the whole series from 1726 to 1786. Yet all agreed that the Company suffered no loss on any post-1726 lease; on the contrary, all agreed that profits continually mounted, at an unspecified rate, especially from 1756 to the Revolution. This phenomenon may be accounted for only in terms of a peculiar coincidence of factors (economic, fiscal, financial, and political) which created, for the tax-farmers, an ideal, even classical situation. Basic to the situation was the economic development of France in the years between 1726 and 1786.

After a short period of readjustment following the

[84] Salary and interest which varied from 6 to 7 percent up to 1774 was paid by the Company initially. However, by a devious system of accounts, in the ultimate the king assumed them both as cost borne by him. In 1780, for the first time, the king openly assumed the payment of salary and interest, the first being increased to 30,000 livres and the second being reduced to 5 percent. The accounting technique mentioned was of considerable importance; it is presented in Lavoisier, *Oeuvres,* VI, 158, 622, 631-632. See also *Encyclopédie méthodique: Finances,* I, 74.

collapse of John Law's System, the French economy in general entered a period of growth basically unaffected by the recurrent financial crises of the state and by the several wars engaged in by the monarchy. Commercial, industrial, and agricultural expansion was buoyed up by a gradual increase in population and was accompanied by a sustained rise in general prices which curved upward slowly from about 1733 to 1758, rose swiftly to a peak in the early 1770s, then entered a period of consolidation until just prior to the Revolution when the ascent was resumed. This long-term economic development was, of course, not without its discontinuities, nor did it affect all localities or all segments of the population equally favorably. Overseas trade almost quadrupled; the seaports and their hinterlands prospered. But in the interior, save for Paris, the rate of urban growth was slower, and overland trade remained sluggish. For agriculture, and especially vinaculture, the period after about 1778 was one of recession, despite short-term price increases, due largely to crop failures in certain areas. Some parts of the trading and industrial community also were in distress just prior to 1789. Nonetheless, it can be said that for France as a whole the period 1726 to 1789 was one of general economic quickening and of growing material well being.[85]

In fiscal terms this economic development meant multiplication of exchanges taxed by the *aides, traites,* and *entrées,* increased purchasing power reflected, perhaps, in the insatiable demand for tobacco and increased use of salt *de vente volontaire* (as well as in increased smuggling activity). It affected the registry taxes of the *domaines* through enlargement of the volume of legal business attendant upon property conveyances. Gross yields constantly increased, being forced upward by the general movement of prices and, especially during the period of

[85] Labrousse, *La Crise de l'économie,* xxii-xli; Sée, *Histoire économique,* I, 316-401.

consolidation after 1770, by the imposition of a 30 percent increase in rates between 1760 and 1781. Even as reflected in the net receipts of government represented by annual lease prices, approximately the same range of taxation produced, in 1788, two and one half times the revenue of 1726.

In the demographic, economic, and fiscal context just described, the basic mechanics of tax-farming automatically operated in the favor of the tax-farmer. Leases were negotiated once every six years, at which time the annual lease prices were fixed for the duration of the contract. Moreover, due to the extreme slowness of the accounting systems employed by both the General Farms and the government, the only verified statistics upon which to estimate future yields and hence upon which to base a new lease price were already at least four years out of date at the time of lease negotiation. In these circumstances, it was impossible for the net receipt of government ever to rise proportionately to increases in gross yield. In a time of general economic acceleration, the gap between gross yields and annual lease price inevitably widened at an increasing rate in the course of a lease's term. In other words, the rate of profit tended always to increase.[86]

Given the existence of tax-farming in the first place, only a flexible pricing system providing for progressive yearly increases in annual lease price during the course of the lease, could have equitably rectified the situation. Such a system was never employed. The mechanics of tax-farming were not inappropriate when applied in a context of relative economic stability in which gross yields

---

[86] Mollien, *Mémoires d'un ministre,* I, 102: "One inevitably abandoned to the General Farmer, at the expense of the public treasury, profits which he had not even the merit of earning through his own efforts." This was even more the case since costs of collection do not seem to have been excessive on the functional tax-collecting levels of administration nor to have risen at as fast a rate as annual lease prices, as witnessed by the Company's low wage policy.

did not vary appreciably from year to year; such a context had existed during Colbert's time. But applied in the dynamic economic world of the late eighteenth century, tax-farming was obsolete. Without risk, even without great effort so far as most financiers were concerned, the tax-farmers automatically profited. In this perspective the distinction between entrepreneurial profit and interest on investment lost some of its validity. The profits were only rich supplements to rentier income from wealth invested in the royal debt. They were more nearly akin to dividends on preferred stock than to increment earned from risk capital.

The automatic profitability of tax-farming in a period of inflation was bolstered by the political influence and financial power of the Company as it operated within the orbit of a corrupt court and a bankrupt government. Thus, up to 1749 there can be little question that lease prices were held at abnormally low levels by virtue of the ignorance, indifference, or connivance of interested high government officials. The Lease Carlier of 1726 was signed at a lease price of 80,000,000 livres, a figure openly known to be at least 10,000,000 livres less than the *net* yield of the *régie* Cordier for the year 1725. Estimates of the profits made during the six years of the Lease Carlier vary widely, but even Lavoisier admitted that the General Farmers cleared at least 25,000,000 livres between 1726 and 1732, a figure which he seems to regard as in excess of some normal, legitimate sum which he left unspecified. Other estimates placed the profits of the Lease Carlier in the vicinity of 60,000,000 livres.[87] In any case, there was general agreement that the Carlier profits were scandalous; it is certain that combined with

[87] Lavoisier, *Oeuvres*, VI, 133-135; Marion, *Histoire financière*, I, 144-145. In addition to the Lease Carlier, the Company signed a special *bail des restes* with the government designed to enable it to collect certain taxations retroactively to the year 1721. Lavoisier admitted that profits on this lease came to 6,000,000 livres; other estimates placed them as high as 38,500,000 livres.

the profits reaped from the notorious *régie* Cordier, they formed the foundation of the fortunes of the General Farmers for the rest of the century.[88]

The abnormally low lease price established for Carlier affected all leases from 1732 to 1749.[89] It was not until that year that the controller-general Machault (1745-1754), was able to correct the basic 10,000,000 livres error of Carlier. The Lease Girandin of 1749 was signed at a price about 9,000,000 livres a year more than that of its predecessor without the addition of new taxation. To this Machault added about 1,500,000 livres in annual profits sequestered from the subfarmers.[90] Consequently, between 1750 and 1756 the treasury received as annual lease price approximately what it should have received during 1726 and 1732.

With Machault, the blind indifference or corruption of government officials seems to have diminished. But at the same time the increasing financial dependence of the treasury upon the Company made it vulnerable to suggestions that only high profits could induce the financiers to continue to increase their investment in the royal debt. In the midst of the crisis of the Seven Years War and immediately thereafter, the debtor government was in no position to haggle too strenuously with the creditor tax-farmers. On at least two occasions (the Leases Prévost and Alaterre), the lease prices were permitted to rise only moderately, so as to allow the Company a high net yield out of which to finance *billets des fermes*. Lease prices rose from 102,000,000 livres in 1749 to 152,000,000 livres in 1774, but the successive augmentations were

[88] Capéfique, *Histoire des grandes opérations financières,* I, 149-152.

[89] Between 1726 and 1742 the lease prices were raised to 92,000,000 livres. But each successive lease contained new elements, such as the *domaines d'Occident* or the *tabacs,* which compensated for the increase. As to the profits on those leases, there are no firm figures. It might be assumed that they were high.

[90] Marion, *Machault d'Arnouville,* pp. 371-374. Instead of allowing the Company to negotiate the subfarming leases, as was customary, Machault did it himself, thereby saving the state the 1,500,000 livres.

never proportionate to the gross yields swelling on a wave of economic expansion and fattened by additional taxation, especially the *sous pour livres* surtaxes. Thus for thirty-one years prior to 1780, years of war and state bankruptcy, the profits of tax-farming continued to mount from lease to lease, both in absolute quantity and in rate.[91] During the Lease David of 1774 a climax was reached. According to all accounts, the profits on this contract were the greatest of any lease except the flagrantly abusive Lease Carlier. The figures of General Farmer Delahante bear testimony to this conclusion. He estimated that during the six years of David (1774-1780), each of the sixty places in the Company of General Farmers cleared a profit of at least 940,000 livres, or 156,000 livres a year.[92] When this sum is added to the 161,200 livres already received for salary and interest on capital invested, in 1774, in the royal debt, the resultant 313,000 livres gives an indication of the value before taxes of a place in the Company of General Farmers.[93] It also indicates the cost of tax-farming to the government and to the taxpayer. On this basis, the annual "profit" on David came to

[91] Lavoisier, *Oeuvres,* VI, 138-141; Delahante, *Une Famille de finance,* I, 419. Delahante prints a list of profits received by his ancestor General Farmer Jacques Delahante as recorded by his nephew, E. M. Delahante; the list covers the Leases Prévost, Alaterre, David, Salzard, and Mager and includes Jacques' profit after one half of his place's profits had been deducted and paid to his *croupiers.* Besides Lavoisier's statements concerning the Lease Carlier, the chemist-financier presented figures on profits covering the Leases Henriet, Prévost, and Alaterre. The two sets of data do not agree in detail, yet both confirm the steady upward movement of profits from 1756 onward.

[92] Delahante, *Une Famille de finance,* I, 419; Mollien, *Mémoires d'un ministre,* I, 67-68, gives 200,000 livres total income of a place (salaries, interest, and profits) totaling a 20 percent return on invested capital all told.

[93] It is interesting to compare this income per place with the annual net income of a great noble such as Lafayette; in 1777 the marquis enjoyed, after taxes, 146,000 livres. In contrast, in 1788 the Archbishop Lémoinie de Brienne had a total income in excess of 924,000 livres. See Sagnac, *La Formation de la société française moderne,* II, 325-326.

18,780,000 livres. This was the total price per year of a loan of 92,000,000 livres. It was the price of a wasteful, obsolete system, borne in the last analysis by the taxpayer.

The government was not entirely indifferent to this state of affairs. It could not, because of its need for the tax-farmers' long- and short-term credits, directly attack the system. But it could compensate itself for some of the loss. From 1749 on, the period of the growth of the royal debt held by the Company, the king directly attached part of the profits per place of every lease. The government recognized that the cumbersome mechanism of tax-farming operating in the late eighteenth century automatically produced an unearned increment. By means of special taxation on "surplus profits" it attempted deviously to modify this condition to its own benefit.

In 1748 a 10 percent tax was levied upon the profits of the Lease Girandin and all succeeding contracts. In 1759 the controller-general Silhouette made a feeble and futile attempt to commandeer 50 percent of the profits of the Lease Henriet.[94] But in 1763 the controller-general, Bertin, imposed an additional 20 percent tax on the profits of places, bringing the total of such taxation to 30 per-

[94] In 1759 Silhouette announced that one half of the profits of the Company were attached by the king. All royal *croupes et pensions* were suspended. Silhouette then created a fictitious joint-stock company with assets founded upon the anticipated total of the king's half of the profits and sold 72,000 "shares" of 1,000 livres, each bearing 5 percent interest and entitling the bearer to an unspecified dividend. The "shares" sold among the bourgeoisie of Paris were at first greeted with enthusiasm, but it soon became apparent that the biggest buyer was the Company of General Farmers itself. Silhouette was soon dismissed from office and gradually the affair was liquidated. In 1761 the rate of the dividend was fixed at 1½ percent per annum, retroactive to 1759. The Company then paid the king 1,080,000 livres a year retroactive to 1759 as an addition to the stated lease price of the Lease Henriet of 1756. The sum was the exact equivalent of the total 1½ percent of the face value of the "share." The king dropped his claim in one half of the profits and in effect the "shares" had been converted into 6½ percent bonds, owned mostly by the Company. Thus the maneuver, at first advertised as a conversion of the Company to a joint-stock basis, was nothing more than a forced loan on

cent,[95] at which level it remained to 1780. In that year the king, under the terms of the Lease Salzard, announced that henceforth he would share one half of the profits with the Company of General Farmers.

The Lease Salzard of 1780, creation of Necker, provided for two lease prices, one a *prix rigeureux* of 122,900,000 livres for *gabelles, tabacs, traites,* and *entrées* only, the other a *prix espéré* of 126,000,000 livres for the same range of taxation. The Company could take no profit if the receipts of the treasury were less than 122,900,000 livres; it could take 2 percent of the profits on any receipt between that figure and 126,000,000 livres; it could take 50 percent of the profits on any receipt above the last figure.[96] Since receipts were always above 126,000,000 livres, this meant that the king had placed a limitation on the Company's rate of profit to his own benefit. In actuality, the gain to the king was less than it seemed. The arrangement added another 20 percent to the 30 percent of the profits which he had already been enjoying since 1763, but the action was accompanied by revocation of the royal *croupes et pensions,* the sum total of which was only slightly less than the amount to be anticipated from the additional 20 percent. Similar arrangements were incorporated into the last Lease Mager of 1786, with the *prix rigereux* set at 144,000,000 livres and the *prix espéré* at 150,000,000 livres.

The Lease Salzard of 1780 clearly and overtly spelled the end of untrammeled tax-farming, although it was but the culmination of a tendency which had been evident since at least 1763. Under its terms (and those of its successor, the Lease Mager of 1786), the General Farms

---

which the Company in the end lost nothing and gained a good investment. See Guillamat-Vallet, *Le Contrôleur-général Silhouette,* pp. 78-79; Marion, *Histoire financière,* I, 92; Bosquet, *Dictionnaire raisonné des domaines,* II, 345-349.

[95] Lavoisier, *Oeuvres,* VI, 140-141.

[96] *Encyclopédie méthodique: Finances,* I, 74-81. The full text of the Lease Salzard is printed here. See also *Répertoire universel de jurisprudence,* VII, 341-345.

was a bastard cross between a tax-farm and a *régie intéressé*.[97] It did not thereby become conspicuously less profitable. The total profits on Salzard may have been as much as 45,960,000 livres; split fifty percent with the king and the Company, this yielded 574,000 livres per place. Anticipated profits on the Lease Mager for 1788 came to 24,600,000 livres for the single year.[98] Had the profits on this last lease ever been calculated, it might have been the most profitable, for king and tax-farmer, of the long series of leases that began in 1726.

But the profits of the Lease Mager were never calcuated much less distributed. Already in 1786, when the lease was signed, it was apparent that only a basic social and fiscal reform, involving the direct taxation of the clergy, the nobility, and the privileged places could save the royal treasury. When this was proposed to the spokesmen of the privileged orders meeting as an Assembly of Notables in 1787, the nobles and the clerics served notice that they would accept reform only on their own terms—the control

[97] The arrangement for a new General Commission of the *aides* provided for a company of commissioners which received a bonus of two sous per livre on the first 6,000,000 livres surplus receipt above 42,000,000 livres which it guaranteed to deliver under pain of forfeiture of surety bonds. If the receipt rose above 48,000,000 livres a year, the commissioners received a supplemental bonus of three sous per livre on all surplus above 42,000,000 livres. Since yield was always well above the former figure, the company of commissioners consistently gained 25 percent, plus a salary for each member and interest on his surety bond. The king, however, bore the entire cost of collection. For the new General Administration of the *domaines,* a similar company of commissioners was formed which guaranteed a minimum of 42,000,000 livres in receipts to the treasury. On anything above that figure the king shared the profits on the basis of 75 percent to himself and 25 percent to the company. The commissioners also received salaries and interest on their surety bonds. The basic similarity of these two arrangements to tax-farming is obvious. See Marion, *Histoire financière,* I, 319-320; Necker, *De l'administration,* I, 76.

[98] In the Lease Salzard provision was also made for a fictitious forty-first place which was assigned a full share of the profits to be split among the leading bureaucratic officials of the General Farms. See Delahante, *Une Famille de finance,* I, 419; Braesch, *Finances et monnaie révolutionnaires,* II, 78, 206.

of the state by the old aristocracy. These terms the monarchy rejected, but in rejecting them soon found it had no alternative but to call upon all estates, upon the nation, for counsel and guidance in its travail. On August 8, 1788, a royal edict summoned a meeting of the traditional Estates-General to take place May 1, 1789. By June of 1789, the Estates-General had been transformed into a revolutionary National Constituent Assembly. The end of the old regime and with it the Company of General Farmers was at hand.

9. The End of the Company of General Farmers

In 1789 the parish of Allainville-en-Beauce expressed, in its *cahier de doléance*, a widely held sentiment:

When the thinking man reflects on the immense treasures of the General Farmers who, in abusing the confidence of the king, are the bloodsuckers of the nation and drink in golden cups the tears of the unfortunates, is he not seized with holy indignation? Can he prevent himself from voting, with a speed equal to its enormous expense, the abolition of this whole corps whose continued existence will ruin France . . . ? Yes, the Frenchman, the citizen, so zealous, so transported with love for his kings, can hope to be happy only when, enlightened as to the taxes, he will be able to compare his obligations and expenses with the fruit of his labor and balance the one with the other, which can not be accomplished without the total suppression of the General Farms.[1]

At the end of the old regime the General Farms and the Company of General Farmers were among the most detested institutions of the Bourbon monarchy. This was in part due to a deep-seated aversion to tax collectors characteristic of the French in all ages.[2] The tax-farmers

---

[1] "Cahiers de doléance du bailliage d'Orléans pour les états généraux de 1789," *Collection des documents inédits sur l'histoire économique de la révolution française,* I, 515-516.

[2] The present writer places on record the following coincidence of language and intent in two similar incidents occurring over three hundred years apart. According to Dupont-Ferrier, *Les Institutions*

of the Middle Ages were cursed as *maltôtiers* and hated
as exploiters of the poor. The *partisans* and *traitants* of
the sixteenth and seventeenth centuries were vilified in
popular broadsides,[3] scourged by moralists,[4] and berated
by reformers who deplored their presence in the realm.[5]
The *financiers* were held up to ridicule by the wits of the
eighteenth century.[6] In times of economic distress and
financial crisis, the tax-farmers were always singled out
for abuse. They were convenient objects upon which popular discontent could be vented.

In the period during and following the Seven Years
War, when a maturing public interest in economic and
financial affairs created an insatiable market for works
on taxation, the General Farmers were the target of an

financières, II, 94, at Angers in 1451 the wife of an innkeeper resisted
with violence the attempts of an employee of the local tax-farmer to
search her husband's establishment for contraband. Her chaplain,
rushing to her aid, encouraged her with the words, "Tuez! Tuez! Ces
ribaux fermiers! Il ne leur fault à chascun qu'un coup de daque!"
According to Marion, *Histoire financière,* II, 91, in 1790 in the district of Pérone, the *curé* of Longueville urged his flock to attack the
local *commis des fermes* with the words, "Tuez! Massacrez ces
commis . . . ne laissez jamais subsister pareils êtres . . . je marcherai
à votre tête."

[3] For example, see Moreau (ed.), *Choix de Mazarinades,* I, 113-
138, 277-293. Among the more moderate expressions used to castigate
the tax-farmers were, "Sangsues populaires," "Hommes . . . de luxure
et d'avarice" who delight in the "vols et aux violences qu'ils faites à
et d'avarice" who delight in the "vols et aux violences qu'ils ont faites
à tout le monde."

[4] For example, see La Bruyère, "Sur les biens de fortune," *Oeuvres
de la Bruyère,* II, 176. "Ces gens ne sont ni parents, ni amis, ni
citoyens, ni chrétiens, ni peut-être des hommes: ils ont de l'argent."

[5] For example, see Boisguilbert, "Factum de la France," *Les Économistes financières au XVIIIe siècle,* pp. 296, 319, and Vauban,
"Projet d'une dime royale," *loc. cit.,* p. 150.

[6] For example, see Montesquieu, *Les Lettres persanes,* I, 99 (Letter XLVIII), "Qui est cet homme . . . il faut bien que ce soit un
homme de qualité; mais il a la physiongomie si basse qu'il ne fait
quères honneur aux gens de qualité, et, d'ailleurs, je ne lui trouve
point d'education . . . Cet homme . . . est un fermier. Il est autant
au-dessus des autres par ses richesses, qu'il est au-dessous de tout le
monde par sa naissance."

unprecedented barrage of criticism. Despite censorship,[7] books, broadsides, pamphlets, and songs, some inspired by intrigue against the Company, some written from honest indignation, poured from the presses to castigate the tax-farmers and their hirelings.[8] Works such as Mirabeau's *Théorie de l'impôt* (1760), a savage attack on financial malpractices, the target of which was the General Farmers, were received with avid enthusiasm. In it Mirabeau announced that the salvation of France depended upon only one condition, "to purge our language . . . of the odious word Financier".[9] Gross, malicious exaggerations, such as Darigand's *Anti-financier* (1763)[10] in which the crimes and malversations of the tax-farmers were depicted in lurid prose, were widely read and discussed. Proponents of single-tax systems[11] blamed the troubles of France upon the diversity of its taxes and laid responsibility for the diversity upon the tax-farmers. Among the physiocrats, it was the fashion to insist that financiers were among the principal banes of civilized states[12] and that all the evils of indirect taxation were aggravated by the system of tax-farming.[13] According to them, aboli-

---

[7] The attack in the public press upon the Company and upon the *commis des fermes* was so serious that the Company obtained a royal edict forbidding public discussion of finances. In 1776 the edict was recapitulated in a new royal declaration. See *Recueil général des anciennes lois*, XXII, 400; *Répertoire universel de jurisprudence*, IV, 85.

[8] René Stroum, *Bibliographie historique des finances de la France au XVIIIe siècle, passim*.

[9] Mirabeau, *Théorie de l'impôt*, p. 442.

[10] Darigrand, *L'Anti-financier*, pp. 40-68.

[11] Roussel de la Tour, *Richesses de l'état, passim*. This pamphlet advocating a single tax had an extraordinary reception among the reading public. It ran into several editions.

[12] Quesnay, "Maximes générales du gouvernement économique d'un royaume agricole," *Principaux économistes: Physiocrates*, I, 104 (Maxims xxviii and xxix).

[13] Saint-Péravy, *Mémoire sur les effects de l'impôt indirect*, pp. 101-109. See also Le Trosne, *De l'administration provinciale*, pp. 2-11, 130-265. Saint-Péravy's was a work of popularization; Le Trosne's was perhaps the most lucid and sophisticated statement of physio-

tion of the General Farms was prerequisite to any reform of the state.

To this chorus of denunciation of tax-farming were added the magisterial voices of the Parlements and *Cours des Aides*. In 1778 was published a collection of remonstrances of the Paris *Cour des Aides* on the subject of taxation. Among them was the *Grandes Remonstrances* of 1775 in which the court declared the fiscal codes to be an odious jumble which "no one, except the financiers, has studied or could study." It accused the General Farmers of obtaining laws "which would excite internecine war if applied literally. Their *commis* are authorized to conduct the most severe searches . . . without respect for rank, birth, or dignities." They have demanded and obtained arbitrary powers; it is necessary that the court come to the defense of "a people oppressed by this monstrous administration." The taxes are inherently vicious, but the root of evil lies in the method of their collection, "for these taxes are less onerous by reason of the sums the royal treasury receives than by the costs of administration and the gains of the Farmers." The court called upon the king to ameliorate the lot of the people "groaning under a tyranny which gets worse each day" ; he must defend his realm from the "avidity of the Farmer and the caprices of th Administration." [14]

The *Grandes Remonstrances* created a public sensation.[15] It confirmed, with the authority of the highest fiscal court of the realm, all that the publicists had been saying for a generation. It seemed to lend sanction to the belief that tax evasion, smuggling, hostility toward the General Farms was not a crime but a legitimate de-

---

cratic theory; both agree that the economic damage wrought by indirect taxation was aggravated by the General Farms.

[14] *Recueil de la Cour des Aides,* pp. 628-693.

[15] Marion, "Turgot et les grandes remonstrances de la Cour des Aides (1775)," *Vierteljahrschrift für Social-und-Wirtschaftsgeschichte,* I (1903), 303-313.

fense of property and public order against a predatory band of plunderers who through corruption had usurped the royal power.

Thus the Company entered its last decade with public opinion actively aroused against it. It was attacked and condemned for every policy, every action taken to secure the revenues of the General Farms. The Company's attempt to curb salt smuggling by monopolizing the salt trade of the *pays rédimés* was regarded as evidence of its unquenchable thirst for profits. Despite the rulings of all Parlements but those of Rouen and Rennes, the battle with the tobacconists over the preparation of snuff was lost by the General Farmers in the arena of public opinion; they stood condemned as frauds and adulterators. Advocates of free trade accused them of deliberately frustrating attempts to reform the *traites*. Wine producers suffering an economic crisis in the wine industry blamed the tax-farmers for the surtaxing of the *aides*.[16] The building of the *entrées* wall of Paris at a time of acute distress among the working class of the capital seemed only to prove the callousness of the General Farmers. Among all classes it was the common assumption that the tax-farmers were responsible not only for harsh means of collection, but for the existence, continuance, and increase of the taxes themselves and for the budgetary deficits that made the levies necessary in the first place.[17]

When, in 1782, Louis Sebastien Mercier declared that he could not pass by the *Hôtel des Fermes* without being consumed by a desire "to reverse this immense and infernal machine, which seizes each citizen by the throat and pumps out his blood," [18] he was voicing a common emo-

[16] Labrousse, *La Crise de l'économie,* xliv, 323-359, 395-402, 480-483, 552-564, 580-600.

[17] "Cahiers de doléances de la sénéchaussé de Marseilles pour les états-généraux de 1789," *Collection de documents inédits sur l'histoire économique de la révolution française,* p. 42.

[18] Mercier, *Tableau de Paris,* III, 119.

tion. Seven years later, in 1789, the General Farmers were almost universally condemned in the *cahiers de doléance*. The general attitude may be summed up in the words of the *cahier* of the parish of Bicxeuil:

Finally the General Farmers must be suppressed, for would it not be better that the immense sums which they gain, or rather which they extort, were sent to the royal treasury than to the hands of these avid *traitants*? At least the people would have the consolation of seeing the money . . . turned to the profit of the state, in place of the chagrin of seeing the price of their sweat enriching the General Farms.[19]

The political revolution wrought in June of 1789 by the assumption of power by the National Constituent Assembly in Versailles was preceded and accompanied by an insurrection against the fisc. Customs houses were destroyed; *greniers à sel* were burned. General Farms employees, hunted from their posts, sought the protection of the army. "The supplies which maintain the salt and tobacco monopolies were pillaged . . . collection was troubled everywhere it was not suspended, the smugglers themselves accomplished with arms the overthrow of the interior customs lines." [20]

As collection of taxes ceased in the provinces, the Assembly began liquidating the General Farms. In August, 1789, the Company was ordered to close its books and to continue only on the account of the king. The *gabelles*, at first only renovated and ameliorated, were finally abrogated on March 14, 1790. The *traites* were converted in a uniform tariff by decree of October 20, 1790. On December 5, 1790, the *contrôle* and *insinuation* were reshaped into the modern *enregistrement*. The *entrées* were abandoned on February 19, 1791, and the *aides* went on March 2, 1791. On March 20, 1791, the tobacco monopoly was canceled. On the same day, the Lease Mager of 1786

[19] "Cahiers de doléances du bailliage de Blois," *Collection de documents inédits sur l'histoire économique de la révolution française*, II, 329.

[20] Mollien, *Mémoires d'un ministre*, I, 144.

was declared null and void; the General Farms had ceased to be.[21]

Among the delegates to the Constituent Assembly, the suppression of the General Farms was greeted with satisfaction but little enthusiasm.[22] The Assembly was near the end of its labors. It had already made far more radical excisions from the body of the old regime. But outside the Assembly popular passions in Paris were being stirred by inflamatory propaganda against the General Farmers. In his news letter *Ami du peuple,* Marat denounced Lavoisier and called for vengeance against the General Farmers [23] in the most vituperative language. Disgruntled former employees of the General Farms accused the General Farmers of having cheated them of wages and pensions. When still other former employees defended their old chiefs, the malcontents replied in public print: "Where could more cruel masters be found? . . . Tremble, you who have sucked out the blood of unhappy wretches." [24] It was suggested that the millions of livres stolen by the tax-farmers might be reclaimed by the nation.

In this atmosphere, on July 22, 1791,[25] the Assembly created a Commission of Liquidation composed of six former General Farmers. The commission was directed to evaluate all expropriated rights and goods to establish a just compensation for the former tax-farmers and to settle accounts between the Company and the royal treasury by January, 1793. In addition, the former General Farmers were instructed to continue the sale of the remaining stocks of salt and tobacco and to collect the new customs duties until the state could find other officials.

[21] *Collection complète des lois,* II, 81-88, 241, 281-285, 324, 503-505.
[22] *Archives parlémentaires,* first series, XXIII, 670-672, XXIV, 222-223.
[23] McKie, *Antoine Lavoisier,* pp. 318-320; Joubert, "Les fermiers-généraux sous la terreur," *Le correspondant,* LXXIX (1869), 660-661.
[24] Quoted in Grimaux, "La mort de Lavoisier," *Révue des deux mondes,* LXXIX (1887), 888.
[25] *Collection complète des lois,* III, 150-153.

The commission set to work. But the task confronting it was next to impossible to accomplish. The insurrection against the fisc had burned or scattered nearly all General Farms accounts and records. Popular resentment frus-strated any attempt to sell salt or tobacco. Moreover, as the commission struggled to complete its assignment, the Assembly yielded to the Convention and the monarchy gave way to the republic. The Revolution moved into the orbit of civil and foreign war. The economy was, in 1793, again in depression; the treasury of the republic was empty of hard cash. In these circumstances the old rumor that three to four hundred million livres lay in the estates and strong boxes of the General Farmers gained cur-rency.[26]

The commission could not finish its work by January, 1793, and petitioned for an extension of time. The request was granted, but not without protest from the floor of the Convention. On February 26, 1793, Citizen Carra arose to demand, "Why the nation can not take back its fortune from the hands of those who have despoiled it?" He pro-posed the creation of an investigating commission to examine all leases back to 1740, to judge the legitimacy of profits taken, and to order the restitution of embezzled funds. Carra urged haste, crying, "No, you will not leave these stupid bloodsuckers in the shadow of repose without making them disgorge all the blood they have sweated from the body of the people." [27] But momentarily the issue was side-tracked while the Committee of Public Safety was established and the Jacobins seized control of the Revolution from the Girondins.

On June 5, 1793,[28] the Commission of Liquidation, ac-cused of deliberately stalling the audit in hopes of a mon-archical restoration, was suppressed. The goods and

---

[26] Mollien, *Mémoires d'un ministre,* I, 160-161; Grimaux, "La mort de Lavoisier," *Révue des deux mondes,* LXXIX, 889; Delahante, *Une Famille de finance,* II, 217-224.

[27] *Réimpression de l'ancien Moniteur,* XV, 577-578, 579.

[28] *Collection complète des lois,* V, 391.

papers of the General Farmers were placed under the seal of the law. There followed a summer of indecision while the political terror was mounted in the midst of military defeat, internal insurrection, and economic stagnation. Finally, on September 24, 1793, the seals were lifted and the General Farmers were ordered to complete the liquidation by August 1, 1795.[29] But at the same time a special Commission of Surveillance was appointed by the Convention to examine independently all accounts of the Company from 1774 to 1789. It was directed to find evidence of the abuses and proof of the malversations of which the Convention was already convinced the tax-farmers were guilty. The commission was headed by one Dupin, a former controller-general in the General Farms service; it was staffed exclusively by former employees, one of whom had been convicted and jailed of a 200,000 livres peculation.[30]

Under these conditions the General Farmers resumed the process of liquidation, while Dupin and his associates searched for proof that the Company had for years been defrauding the state. The Jacobin phase of the Revolution moved to its climax; the outcome for the General Farmers, execrated, target of envious private interest, for years the focus of popular resentment, for decades depicted as rich and iniquitous, was inevitable.

On November 3, 1793, Citizen Bourdon, impatient at a report presented to the Convention by a member of the finance committee concerning the progress of the liquidation, exclaimed: "That is the hundredth time the General Farmers have been spoken of. I demand that these public bloodsuckers be arrested and that if their accounts are not tendered in a month, they be delivered to the blade of the law." Within twenty-four hours nineteen General Farmers were locked up in the Port Royal; in the next

29 *Ibid.,* VI, 229-230.
30 Joubert, "Les Fermiers-généraux sous la terreur," *Le Correspondant,* LXXVII, 663. Dupin had owed his promotion to Paulze, father-in-law of Lavoisier.

few days their number grew to twenty-eight. Dupin led
the Convention in wild denunciations; from all sides cries
arose to force the tax-farmers to repay the three to four
hundred million livres which (it was believed) they had
stolen from the state. Removed from Port Royal in late
December and imprisoned in the *Hôtel des Fermes*, the
General Farmers struggled to complete the balancing of
accounts.[31]

The Commission of Surveillance published its report,
which was read by Dupin in the Convention, on May 5,
1794. The General Farmers were formally declared to
be in the debt of the state by 130,345,262 livres, 12 sols,
1 denier. They were officially accused of bribery and malversation, of having taken illegal interest on advances to
the treasury, of having retarded remittance of lease price
to the treasury, and of having adulterated their snuff.
Apprised of these charges before they had been formally
drawn up, Lavoisier published, in his "Réponses aux in-
culpations faites contre les ci-devant fermiers-généraux,"[32]
a complete refutation. His work was ignored by the revolutionary authorities. On May 6, twenty-eight General Farmers were confined in the Conciergerie. The
state impounded their goods and chattels against payment
of 130,000,000 livres.

Trial before the Revolutionary Tribunal followed almost
immediately. The last of the General Farmers were
charged with counterrevolutionary activity. Nothing was
said of the indictments brought against them by Dupin
and the Commission of Surveillance. They were tried and
guillotined as a group on May 8, 1794.[33]

The goods and chattels of the dead General Farmers re-

[31] Grimaux, "La Mort de Lavoisier," *Révue des deux mondes,*
LXXIX, 892-904.

[32] Lavoisier, *Oeuvres,* VI, 569-570.

[33] Grimaux, "La Mort de Lavoisier," *Révue des deux mondes,*
LXXIX, 916-921; Joubert, "Les Fermiers-généraux sous la terreur,"
Le Correspondant, LXXVII, 668-678. Twenty-eight General Farmers
died on May 8, 1794. Six more joined their colleagues within a few
weeks.

mained impounded by the state pending settlement of the alleged 130,000,000 livres debt. But the Thermidorian reaction gave their widows and heirs the opportunity to press for posthumous exoneration and release of the property. The case was fought within the legislative halls, councils, and courts of the Directory and the Empire. A new commission was appointed to liquidate the accounts of the Company of General Farmers. On May 1, 1806, the Council of State declared the affair closed. The heirs of the last General Farmers were permitted to repossess their property. The results of the final audit disclosed that instead of the Company of General Farmers being in the debt of the treasury for 130,000,000 livres, the treasury had overdrawn its account with the General Farms by 8,000,000 livres.[34] But nothing was said of the 68,400,-000 livres in long-term government debt held by the Company in 1789.

Thus ended one of the most characteristic institutions of the old regime; thus was finished the career of one of the most famous groups of men produced by the society of eighteenth-century France.

[34] Delahante, *Une Famille de finance,* II, 481-489.

Appendix

LEASES ON THE GENERAL FARMS, 1726-1786

Lease	Date[a]	Lease Price (in Livres)		Advances (Bonds-money and loans)
Carlier	1726	80,000,000		8,000,000
Desboves	1732	84,000,000		8,000,000
Forceville	1738	91,830,000		8,000,000
La Rue	1744	92,000,000	(peace)	8,000,000
		91,153,000	(war)[b]	
Girandin[c]	1750	104,265,000[d]		20,000,000
Henriet	1756	110,000,000		60,000,000[h]
Prévost	1762	124,000,000	(peace)	72,000,000
		118,000,000	(war)[e]	
Alaterre	1768	132,000,000		92,000,000
David	1774	152,000,000		92,000,000
Salzard[f]	1780	122,900,000	(*prix rigereux*)	62,400,000[i]
		126,000,000	(*prix espéré*)	
Mager[g]	1786	144,000,000	(*prix rigereux*)	65,520,000[j]
		150,000,000	(*prix espéré*)	68,840,000[k] (in 1788)

a. The date is the year in which the lease went into effect. Negotiation and signature of the lease generally was accomplished six months previously.
b. In effect to 1748.
c. The *adjudicataire-général* Girandin having died, in 1751 a new Lease Bocquillon was in effect for the unexpired term.
d. Effective lease price, that is, 101,149,000 livres actual price plus

SIMPLIFIED ADMINISTRATIVE ORGANIZATION OF THE
GENERAL FARMS

Company of General Farmers
|
General Direction (*Hôtel des Fermes*)
|
Provincial Direction

THE COMPANY OF GENERAL FARMERS: ASSEMBLÉES (c. 1763)

1. Assemblées de la ferme générale:
   Caisses (10 General Farmers)
   Administrative (19 General Farmers)
   Personnel (9 General Farmers)
   Cautionnements (6 General Farmers)
   Retraites (not known)
   Contentieux (not known)
   Archives (4 General Farmers)
2. Assemblées des régies des fermes:
   Grandes gabelles (21 General Farmers)
   Petites gabelles (11 General Farmers)
   Tabacs (25 General Farmers)
   Traites (26 General Farmers)
   Entrées de Paris (12 General Farmers)
   Aides (10 General Farmers)
   Aides (10 General Farmers)
   Aides (10 General Farmers)
   Aides (9 General Farmers)
   Domaines (20 General Farmers)

1,500,000 livres sequestered profits of subfarms added to General Farms lease price.
e. In effect to 1764.
f. Containing only *gabelles, tabacs, traites,* and *entrées de Paris.*
g. Containing only *gabelles, tabacs,* and *entrées de Paris.*
h. Places in the Company increased to sixty and subfarming eliminated.
i. Places in the Company reduced to forty.
j. Places in the Company increased to forty-two.
k. Places in the Company increased to forty-four in 1788.

THE COMPANY OF GENERAL FARMERS: ASSEMBLÉE
ADMINISTRATIVE (c. 1763)

1. Assemblée Administrative
   |
   Department of General Receipts (Treasury)
   In charge of a Receiver General
   |
   Caisse de Paris
   |

   Bureau de Dépense   Bureau de Recettes
                           181 General Provincial
                              Receivers

2. Assemblée Administrative
   |
   Department of General Accounts
   |
   Bureau Général _____ Bureau des Etats au vrai
   In charge of a Controller-General
   |
   Bureaux des comptes (11)
   Each in charge of a Controller
   Grandes gabelles
   Petites gabelles
   Tabacs
   Traites
   Domaines d'Occident
   True aides
   Droits y jointes
   Droits y jointes
   Entrées de Paris
   Sous pour livre

THE COMPANY OF GENERAL FARMERS: ASSEMBLÉES FOR
PERSONNEL (c. 1763)

		Retraites (added 1768) Number of
Personnel 9 General Farmers	Cautionnements 6 General Farmers	General Farmers not known

Department of Personnel
(no department head)

Bureau des Cautionnements et Commissions In charge of a Director-General	Bureau des Retraites In charge of a Director-General (added 1768)

THE COMPANY OF GENERAL FARMERS: ASSEMBLÉE DES
CONTENTIEUX (c. 1763)

Contentieux
Number of General Farmers not known

Department of Legal Affairs
(No department head)

Conseil de ferme

Contentieux de Lorraine	Contentieux des aides

THE COMPANY OF GENERAL FARMERS: ASSEMBLÉE DES
ARCHIVES (c. 1763)

Archives
4 General Farmers

General Secretariat
In charge of a Secretary-General

ADMINISTRATION OF GABELLES ET TABACS (c. 1763)

3 Assemblées
Grandes gabelles, Petites gabelles, tabacs
57 General Farmers [a]
|
10 Bureaux de Correspondance [b]
Each serving as a communication center
Each in charge of a Director supervised by a
Correspondent General Farmer
|
Provincial Directions for gabelles and tabacs
35 with gabelles and tabacs combined and 11 for tabacs alone
Each in charge of a Provincial Director [c]
|
District
2 or 3 to each Direction
Each in charge of a Controller-General [c]
|

(Gabelles)	(Tabacs)
Grenier à sel	Bureau Général
244 in grandes gabelles	1 or 2 to each Direction
135 in petites gabelles	Each in charge of an
Each in charge of a Receiver	Entrepôseur Général
|	|
Retailers	Entrepôt
	453 in 1774
	Each in charge of an
	entrepôseur
	|
	Tobacconists
	c. 10,000 in 1783

a. Correspondent General Farmers appointed from this group.
b. In addition to the *Bureau de Correspondance* there was a *Bureau Général* for *gabelles* directing the procuring of salt, and handling the *pays de saline* and *quart boullion*. Also a *Bureau Général* for *tabacs* directing purchases, manufacture, distribution, and cultivation.
c. Often in charge of both *tabacs* and *gabelles*.

ADMINISTRATION OF THE TRAITES (c. 1763)

Assemblées des Traites
26 General Farmers
|
Bureaux de Correspondance (5) [a]
Each serving as a communication center
Each in charge of a Director supervised by a
Correspondent General Farmer
|
Provincial Directions (c. 41)
Each in charge of a Provincial Director
|
District (2 or 3 to each Direction)
Each in charge of a Controller-General
|
Bureau principal (number unknown) [b]
Each in charge of a Receiver
|
Bureau de recette (number unknown) [b]
Each in charge of a Receiver
|
Bureau de conserve (number unknown) [b]
Each in charge of a Customs Inspector

a. In addition, one Bureau Général directing the sale of confiscated goods and handling international tariffs.
b. Total of all *bureaux* c. 1,400.

ADMINISTRATION OF THE TRUE AIDES (c. 1763)

4 Assemblées des Aides
(39 General Farmers)
|
4 Bureaux de Correspondance
Each in charge of a Director supervised by a
Correspondent General Farmer
|
Provincial Directions [a] (c. 16)
Each in charge of a Provincial Director
|
Bureau des aides [a] (c. 191)
Each in charge of a Receiver
|
Bureau des aides [a] (2,000-3,000)
Each in charge of a Buraliste

a. On each level, two organizations functioned in parallel: one for inventory and one for the collection of the tax. The title of the inventory official was *contrôleur-ambulant*.

ADMINISTRATION OF THE DOMAINES (c. 1763)

Assemblée des Domaines
(20 General Farmers)
|
Bureaux de Correspondance (5) [a]
Each in charge of a Director supervised by a
Correspondent General Farmer
|
Provincial Directions (c. 32)
Each in charge of a Provincial Director
|
Districts (c. 94)
Each in charge of a Vérificateur or an Inspecteur
|
Bureau de contrôle (c. 152)
Each in charge of a Contrôleur Ambulant
|
Major Bureau de contrôle (c. 680) [b]
Each in charge of a Contrôleur des actes
|
Minor Bureau de contrôle (c. 3,000-4,000) [b]
Each in charge of a Buraliste

a. Plus one special bureau for *domaines* proper.
b. Grades according to volume of business.

Bibliography

Almanachs royals. Paris: L'Harry, 1703-1785.

Anonymous. Sur les finances: Oeuvres posthumes de Pierre André. London: n.p., 1775.

Archives parlementaires. First series, Vols. XXIII-XXIV.

Ardascheff, Pavel N. Les Intendants de province sous Louis XVI. Paris: Alcan, 1909.

Argenson, Réné de Voyer de Paulmy, Marquis d'. Journal et mémoires. 9 Vols. Paris: Jules Rénouard, 1859-1867.

Arnould, Charles M. De la balance du commerce et des rélations commerciales extérieurs de la France. 2 Vols. Paris: Busson, 1794.

Aucoc, Léon. Le Conseil d'état avant et depuis 1789. Paris: Imprimérie Nationale, 1876.

Avenal, Georges d'. Histoire de la fortune française. Paris: Payot, 1927.

——— Richelieu et la monarchie absolue. 4 Vols. Paris: Plon et Nourrit, 1884-1890.

Bail des Fermes-Royales-Unies fait à M. Jacques Forceville le 16 Septembre, 1738. Registré en la chambre des comptes le 31 Decembre, 1738, et en la Cour des Aydes le 22 des mesmes mois et an. Paris: De l'Imprimérie Royale, 1739.

Barbier, E. J. Journal historique et anecdotique du règne de Louis XV. 6 Vols. Paris: Jules Rénouard, 1847-1856.

Beaulieu, Eugène-Pierre. Les Gabelles sous Louis XIV. Paris: Berger-Lavrault, 1903.

Besson, Emmanuel. Un Chapitre de notre histoire financière: L'Enregistrement et la ferme-générale. Paris: Guillaumin, 1893.

Bigo, Robert. Bases historiques de la finance moderne. Paris: Colin, 1933.

Bled, Victor du. "Manieurs d'argent et fermiers-généraux dans l'ancien régime," Révue économique internationale, III, 1905.

Boisguilbert, Pierre Le Pesant de. "Factum de la France." Les Économistes financiers au XVIIIe siècle. Edited by Eugène Daire. Paris: Guillaumin, 1843.

Boislisle, A. de (editor). Lettres de M. de Marville, Lieutenant-général de police au ministre Maurepas, 1724-1747. 3 Vols. Paris: Champion, 1896-1905.

Bonneau, Jacques. Les Législations françaises sur les tabacs sous l'ancien régime. Paris: Libraire de la Société du Recueil Sirey, 1910.

Bosquet, ———. Dictionnaire raisonné des domaines et droits domaniaux. 3 Vols. Rouen: J.-J. le Boullenger, Imprimeur du Roi, 1762.

Bouchard, Léon. Système financière de l'ancienne monarchie. Paris: Guillaumin, 1891.

Bouchary, Jean. Les Maniers d'argent à la fin du XVIIIe siècle. 3 Vols. Paris: n.p., 1939-1942.

Braesch, Frédéric. Finances et monnaie révolutionnaires. 3 Vols. Nancy and Paris: La Maison du Livre Français, 1934-1936.

Brunet de Grandmaison, Pierre. Dictionnaire des aydes, ou les dispositions de toutes des ordonnances de 1680 et 1681 . . . distribuées dans un ordre alphabétique. 2 Vols. Paris: Prault, Imprimeur des Fermes du Roy, 1750.

Brunot, Ferdinand. Histoire de la langue française des origines à 1900. 10 Vols. Paris: Colin, 1905-1948.

"Cahiers de doléances du bailliage de Blois . . . pour les états généraux de 1789." Edited by F. Lesueur and A. Cauchie in Collection des documents inédits sur l'histoire économique de la révolution française. 2 Vols. Blois: Emmanuel Rivière. 1907-1908.

"Cahiers de doléances du bailliage de Contentin pour les états généraux de 1789." Edited by Emile Bridrey in Collection de documents inédits sur l'histoire économique de la révolution française. 3 Vols. Paris: Imprimérie Nationale, 1907-1912.

"Cahiers de doléances de la sénéchaussée de Marseilles pour les états-généraux de 1789." Edited by Joseph Fourrier in Collection de documents inédits sur l'histoire économique de la révolution française. Marseilles: Imprimérie Nouvelle, 1908.

"Cahiers de doléances du bailliage d'Orléans pour les états-généraux de 1789." Edited by Camille Bloch in Collection de documents inédits sur l'histoire économique de la révolution française. 2 Vols. Orléans: Imprimérie Orléanaise, 1906-1907.

Calléry, Alphonse. "La Fraude des gabelles sous l'ancien régime: D'après les mémoires de M. de Châteaubrun, 1730-1786." France judicataire. Part One, 1881-1882.

Capéfique, J.-B. H. Raymond. Histoire des grandes opérations financières. 4 Vols. Paris: Amyot, 1855-1860.

Carré, Henri. "Louis XV, 1715-1774." Histoire de France illustrée depuis les origines jusqu'à la révolution. Edited by Ernest Lavisse. 9 Vols. Paris: Hachette, 1900-1911.

Choix de Mazarinades. Edited by Clélestin Moreau. 2 Vols. Paris: Société de l'histoire de France, 1853.

Clamageran, Jean-Jules. Histoire de l'impôt en France. 3 Vols. Paris: Guillaumin, 1867-1876.

Cole, Charles W. French Mercantilism, 1663-1700. New York: Columbia University Press, 1943.

Collection complète des lois, décrèts, ordonnances, règlemens et avis du conseil d'état. Edited by J. B. Duvergier. 24 Vols. Paris: Guyot et Scribe, 1824-1828.

Collection de comptes-rendus, pièces authentiques, états et tableaux concernant les finances en France depuis 1758 jusqu'en 1787. Edited by Charles Joseph Mathon de la Cour. Lausanne: n.p., 1788.

Comparadon Emile. Les Prodigalités d'un fermier-général: Complément au mémoires de Mme. d'Epinay. Paris: Charavey, 1882.

Coquereau, ———. Mémoires de l'abbé Terrai, contrôleur-général des finances. London: n.p., 1776.

Daire, Eugène (editor). Principaux économistes: Physiocrates. 2 Vols. Paris: Guillaumin, 1846.

Dakin, Douglas. Turgot and the Ancien Régime in France. London: Methuen, 1939.

Darigrand, ———. L'Anti-financier, ou relève de quelques unes des malversations dont se rendant journellement coupables les fermiers-généraux . . . etc. Amsterdam: n.p., 1763.

Delahante, Adrien. Une Famille de finance au XVIIIe siècle. 2 Vols. Paris: J. Hertzel, 1880.

Dictionnaire géographique, historique, et politique des Gaules et de la France. Edited by Jean-Joseph d'Expilly. 6 Vols. Paris: Bauchéand Durand, 1762-1770.

Douçet, Roger. Les Institutions de la France au XVIe siècle. 2 Vols. Paris: Picard, 1948.

Dubois-Croneau, Robert. Pâris de Montmartel: Banquier de la Cour. Paris: n.p., 1917.

Duclos, Charles. Mémoires sécrètes sur les règnes de Louis XIV et de Louis XV. 2 Vols. Paris: n.p., 1791.

Du Hautchamp, ————. Histoire du système des finances sous la minorité de Louis XV pendant les années 1719 et 1720. 6 Vols. The Hague: Pierre de Hondt, 1739.

Dupont-Ferrier, Gustave. Etudes sur les institutions financières de la France à la fin du moyen âge. 2 Vols. Paris: Firmin-Didot, 1930-1932.

————. Les Officiers royaux des bailliages et sénéchaussées et les institutions monarchiques locales en France à la fin du moyen âge. Paris: E. Bouollon, 1902.

Duval, Sieur. Elémens de finances contenant des instructions nécessaires pour les personnes qui sont dans les emplois . . . etc. Paris: Mesnier, 1736.

Elzinger, S. "Le Tarif de Colbert de 1664 et celui de 1667 et leur signification," Economisch-Historisch-Jaarboek, Vol. XV, 1929.

Encyclopédie méthodique: Finances. Edited by J. P. Rousselot de Surgy. 3 Vols. Paris: Panckoucke, 1784-1787.

Encyclopedia of the social sciences. Edited by E. R. A. Seligman. 15 Vols. New York: Macmillan, 1930-1934. Vol. XIII ("Revenue Farming," by W. Lotz).

Encyclopédie, ou dictionnaire raisonné des sciences, des arts, et des métiers. Edited by Diderot and d'Alembert. 17 Vols. Paris: Neufchâtel, etc.; Braisons, etc.; 1751-1765.

Esmein, Ahdémar. Cours élémentaire d'histoire du droit français. 9th ed. Paris: Larue et Forçel, 1908.

Forbonnais, François Véron de. Recherches et considérations sur les finances de France depuis l'année 1559 jusqu'à l'année 1721. 2 Vols. Basle: Frères Cramer, 1758.

Frémy, Elphège. "Premières tentative de centralisation des impôts indirects, 1584-1614," Bibliothèque de l'Ecole des Chartres, Vol. LXXII (1911).

Funck-Brentano, Frantz. Mandrin: Capitaine-Général des contrebandiers. Paris: Hachette, 1908.

Göhring, Martin. Die Ämterkäuflichkeit im ancien régime. Berlin: Verlag Dr. Emil Ebering, 1928.

Gomel, Charles. Les Causes financières de la révolution française. 2 Vols. Paris: Guillaumin, 1892.

Goncourt, Edmond and Jules de. Madame de Pompadour. Paris: n.p., 1891.

Gottschalk, Louis. Lafayette between the American and French Revolutions, 1783-1789. Chicago: The University of Chicago Press, 1950.

Goudar, André de. Les Intérêts de la France malentendus. 3 Vols. Amsterdam: Jacques Cour, 1756.

Grimaux, Edouard. "La Mort de Lavoisier," *Révue des deux mondes,* Vol. LXXIX (1887).

—— Lavoisier, 1743-1794. Paris, 1899.

Guillamat-Vallet, Maurice. Le Contrôleur-général Silhouette et ses réformes en matière financière. Paris: n.p., 1914.

Harbulot, Maurice. "Etudes sur les finances de l'ancienne France," *Révue des sciences politiques,* LVII (1934), LVIII (1935).

Harsin, Paul. Les Doctrines monétaires et financières en France du XVIe au XVIIe siècles. Paris: Alcan, 1928.

Hauser, Henri. "Les Caractères généraux de l'histoire économique de la France du milieu du XVIe siècle à la fin du XVIIIe," *Révue Historique,* LXXIII, 1934.

Hennet, A. J. Ulpien. Théorie du crédit public. Paris: n.p., 1816.

Heuman, P. "Un traitant sous Louis XIII: Antoine Feydeau," Etudes sur l'histoire administrative et sociale de l'ancien régime. Edited by George Pagès. Paris: Alcan, 1938.

Janzé, Alix de. Les Financiers d'autrefois: Fermiers-généraux. Paris: Ollendorf, 1886.

Joubert, André. "Les Fermiers-généraux sous la terreur," *Le Correspondant,* Vol. LXXIX (1869).

Labrousse, C.-E. La Crise de l'économie française à la fin de l'ancien régime et au début de la révolution. Paris: Presses Universitaires de France, 1944.

La Bruyère, Jean de. Oeuvres de La Bruyère. Edited by G. Servois. 6 Vols. Paris: Hachette, 3rd edition, 1922.

Law, John. Le Denier royal. Edited by Paul Harsin. Annales de la Société scientifique de Bruxelles, 1927.

Lavaquéry, Emile. Necker: Fourrier de la révolution. Paris: Plon, 1933.

Lavisse, Ernest. "Louis XIV de 1643 à 1689," Histoire de France illustrée depuis les origines jusqu'à la révolution. Edited by Ernest Lavisse. 9 Vols. Paris: Hachette, 1900-1911.

Lavoisier, Antoine. Oeuvres de Lavoisier. Edited by Edouard Grimaux. 6 Vols. Paris: Imprimérie Nationale, 1862-1893.

Lefebvre de la Bellande. Traité général des droits d'aides. Paris: n.p., 1760.

Lemoine, Alfred and Clément, Pierre. M. de Silhouette, Bouret et les derniers fermiers-généraux. Paris: Didier, 1872.

Levasseur, Emile. Histoire du commerce de la France. 2 Vols. Paris: Rousseau, 1911.

—— Recherches historiques sur le système de Law. Paris: n.p., 1854.

Lévy-Bruhl, Henry. "Les Différentes espèces de sociétés de commerce en France au XVIIe et XVIIIe siècles," *Révue historique de droit français et étranger*, Fourth Series (1937).

Luynes, Charles Philippe d'Albert, duc de. Mémoires sur la cour de Louis XV, 1735-1758. 17 Vols. Paris: Dussieux and Soulié, 1860-1865.

Marion, Marcel. Dictionnaire des institutions de la France au XVIIe et XVIIIe siècles. Paris: Picard, 1923.

—— Histoire financière de la France depuis 1715. 6 Vols. Paris: Rousseau, 1914-1931.

—— Les Impôts directs sous l'ancien régime principalement au XVIIIe siècle. Paris: Edouard Cornely, 1910.

—— Machault d'Arnouville: Etude sur l'histoire du contrôle-général des finances de 1749-1754. Paris: Hachette, 1891.

—— "Turgot et les grandes rémonstrances de la Cour des Aides (1775)," *Vierteljahrschrift für Social-und-Wirtschaftsgeschichte*, Vol. I (1903).

Martin, Germaine. L'Histoire du crédit en France sous le règne de Louis XIV. Paris: Libraire de la Société du Recueil Sirey, 1913.

Mathiez, Albert. "Lafayette et le commerce franco-américaine à la veille de la révolution," *Annales historique de la révolution française*, Nouvelle Série, Vol. III (1926).

McKie, Douglas. Antoine Lavoisier: Scientist, Economist, Social Reformer. New York: Henry Schuman, 1952.

Mercier, Louis Sebastien. Tableau de Paris. 8 Vols. Amsterdam: n.p., 1782-1783.

Milne, Pierre. L'Impôt des aides sous l'ancien régime. Paris: Rousseau, 1908.

Mirabeau, Victor Riquetti, marquis de. Théorie de l'impôt. 2d ed. Paris: n.p., 1761.

Mollien, François-Nicolas. Mémoires d'un ministre du trésor public, 1780-1815. 2 Vols. Paris: Guillaumin, 1898.

Monin, Hippolyte. Etat de Paris en 1789: Etudes et documents sur l'ancien régime à Paris. Paris: n.p., 1889.

Montesquieu, Charles de Secondat, baron de. Les lettres persanes. Edited by Elie Carcassone. 2 Vols. Paris: Roches, 1929.

—— The Spirit of the Laws. Translated by Thomas Nugent. New York: Hafner, 1949.

Moreau de Beaumont. Mémoires concernant les impositions et droits. 5 Vols. Paris: Imprimérie Royale, 1768-1769, 1789.

Mouffle d'Angerville. Vie privée de Louis XV ou principaux évenémens, particularités et anecdotes de son règne. 4 Vols. London: John Peter Lyton, 1781.

Narbonne, Pierre. Journal des règnes de Louis XIV et Louis XV. Paris: n.p., 1886.

Necker, Jacques. De l'administration des finances de France. 3 Vols. Paris: n.p., 1784.

—— Le Compte rendu au roi. Paris: Imprimérie Royale, 1781.

Noël, Octave. Etude historique sur l'organization financière de la France. Paris: Carpentier, 1881.

Nussbaum, Frederick T. "American Tobacco and French Politics," *Political Science Quarterly,* Vol. XL (1925).

—— "Lafayette's Attack upon the Tobacco Farm in the American Committee of 1786," *The Journal of Modern History,* Vol. III (1931).

—— "The Revolutionary Vergennes and Lafayette versus the Farmers-General," *The Journal of Modern History,* Vol. III (1931).

Ordonnances de Louis XIV, Roy de France et de Navarre, sur le fait des gabelles et des aydes, donnés à S. Germain en Laye aux mois de mai et juin 1680. Paris: De l'imprimérie du Roy choisi par ordre de Sa Majesté pour l'impression de ses nouvelles ordonnances, 1681.

Orfeuil, A. Rouillé d'. L'Ami de français. Constantinople (?), 1771.

Pagès, Georges. La Monarchie d'ancien régime en France. Paris: Colin, 1928.

Perrot, Ernest. Les Institutions publiques et privées de l'ancienne France jusqu'en 1789. Paris: Recueil Sirey, 1935.

———. Inventoire des arrêts du conseil du roi, Janvier-Février, 1730. Paris: Les Presses Modernes, 1937.

Pessard, Gustave. Nouveau dictionnaire historique de Paris. Paris: Eugène Rey, 1904.

Pion, J.-F.-J. La Ferme générale des droits et domaines du roi, depuis sa création jusqu'à la fin de l'ancien régime. Paris: Giard et Briere, 1902.

Piétre, François. La Réforme de l'état au XVIIIe siècle. Paris: Les Editions de France, 1935.

Pitre, Georges. La Ferme-générale en Bourgogne et l'inspection de M. de Caze, 1745-1746. Dijon: Barbier, 1908.

Poujaud, ———. Plan général de régie, ferme des domaines et droits y jointes. Paris: De l'imprimérie de G. Lumesle, imprimeur des Fermes du Roy, 1751.

Quesnay, François. "Maximes générales du gouvernement économique d'un royaume agricole." Principaux économistes: Physiocrates. Edited by Eugène Daire. 2 Vols. Paris: Guillaumin, 1846.

Rambaud, Benoit. La Question des fermiers généraux en France et à l'étranger: Etude d'économie rurale. Paris: A. Pédone, 1913.

Recueil alphabétique des droits des traites uniformes de ceux d'entrée et de sortie des cinq grosses fermes, de douane de Lyons et de Valence, précédé d'observations sur ces droits et des cas ou ils sont exigibles. Edited by N. Maquien-Grandpré. 4 Vols. Paris: n.p., 1786.

Recueil de qui s'est passé de plus intéressant à la Cour des Aides depuis 1756 jusqu'au mois de Juin 1775. Edited by Lamoignon de Malesherbes. Brussels: n.p., 1779.

Recueil générale des anciennes lois françaises, depuis l'an 450 jusqu'à la révolution de 1789. Edited by Jourdon, Decreusy, Isambert. 29 Vols. Paris: Berlin-Le-Prieur, 1821-1833.

Réimpression de l'ancien Moniteur. 32 Vols. Paris: n.p., 1863-1870.

Répertoire universel et raisonné de jurisprudence civile, criminelle, canonique et bénéfisciale. Edited by Pierre J.-J. G. Guyot. 17 Vols. Paris: Visse, 1784-1785.

Rousset, August. Histoire des impôts indirects. Paris: Rousseau, 1883.

Roustan, M. The Pioneers of the French Revolution. English translation. Boston: Little, Brown and Company, 1926.

Roux, Pierre. Les Fermes d'impôts sous l'ancien régime. Paris: Rousseau, 1916.

Sagnac, Philippe. La Formation de la société française moderne. 2 Vols., Presses Universitaires de France, 1945-1946.

—— "Le Crédit de l'état et les banquiers," *Révue d'histoire moderne et contemporaine,* Vol. X (March-July), 1908.

Saint-Julien, A. de and Bienaymé, G. Histoire des droits d'entrée et d'octroi à Paris. Paris: Société d'imprimérie et libraire administrative, 1887.

Saint-Péravy, M. de. Mémoire sur les éffects de l'impôt indirect sur les révenus des propriétaires des bien fonds. London: n.p., 1768.

Sée, Henri. Histoire économique de la France. 2 Vols. Paris: Colin, 1939-1942.

—— La Vie économique et les classes sociales en France au XVIIIe siècle. Paris: Alcan, 1924.

Seligman Collection. Uncatalogued déliberations, ordres, lettres-circulaires, mémoires. Special Collections, Columbia University Libraries, New York.

Sénac de Meilhan, Gabriel. Considérations sur les richesses et de luxe. Amsterdam: n. p., 1787.

—— Le Gouvernement, les moeurs et les conditions en France avant la révolution. Hamburg: n. p., 1795.

Smith, Adam. An Inquiry into the Nature and Causes of the Wealth of Nations. Modern Library edition. New York: Random House, 1937.

Soudois, Henri. "Difficultés monétaires au début du XVIIIe siècle," *Journal des Economistes,* Vol. III (1924).

Stroum, René. Bibliographie historique des finances de la France au XVIIIe siècle. Paris: Guillaumin, 1895.

—— Les Finances de l'ancien régime et de la révolution. 2 Vols. Paris: Guillaumin, 1885.

Thirion, Henri. La Vie privée des financiers au XVIIIe siècle. Paris: Plon, Norrit, 1895.

Tour, Roussel de la. Richesses de l'etat. Paris: n.p., 1763.

Trosne, Guillaume-François le. De l'administration provinciale et de la réforme de l'impôt. Basle: n.p., 1779.

Turgot, A. R. J. Oeuvres de Turgot et documents le concernant. Edited by G. Schelle. 5 Vols. Paris: Alcan, 1922-1923.

Tzaneff, Stoyan. L'Homme d'argent au théâtre français jusqu'à la révolution. Gap: Imprimérie Louis Jean, 1934.

Vauban, Le maréchal de. "Projet d'un dîme royale." Les économistes Financières au XVIIIe siècle. Edited by Eugène Daire. Paris: Guillaumin, 1843.

Véri, Abbé. Journal de l'abbé Véri. 2 Vols. Paris: Jules Tallandier, 1929-1931.

Villain, Jean. Le Recouvrement des impôts directs sous l'ancien régime. Paris: Librairie Marcel Rivière, 1952.

Viollet, Paul. Le Roi et ses ministres. Paris: Libraire de la Société du Recueil Sirey, 1912.

Vührer, Adolphe. Histoire de la dette publique en France. 2 Vols. Paris: Berger-Levrault et Cie., 1886.

Vuitry, Adolphe. Le Disordre des finances et les excès du speculation à la fin du règne de Louis XIV et au commencement du règne de Louis XV. Paris: Calman-Lévy, 1883.

Weber, Henry. La Compagnie française des Indes. Paris: Rousseau, 1904.

Wybo, Bernard. Le Conseil de commerce et le commerce intérieur de la France au XVIIIe siècle. Paris: F. Laviton, 1936.

Index